LANCHESTER LIBRARY

3 8001 00771 2668

KU-144-308

Lanchester Library

WITHDRAWN

CONTEMPORARY PERSPECTIVES ON PROPERTY, EQUITY AND TRUSTS LAW

CONTEMPORARY PERSPECTIVES ON PROPERTY, EQUITY AND TRUSTS LAW

Edited by

MARTIN DIXON

GERWYN LL H GRIFFITHS

OXFORD
UNIVERSITY PRESS

OXFORD
UNIVERSITY PRESS

Great Clarendon Street, Oxford OX2 6DP
Oxford University Press is a department of the University of Oxford.
It furthers the University's objective of excellence in research, scholarship,
and education by publishing worldwide in

Oxford New York

Auckland Cape Town Dar es Salaam Hong Kong Karachi
Kuala Lumpur Madrid Melbourne Mexico City Nairobi
New Delhi Shanghai Taipei Toronto

With offices in

Argentina Austria Brazil Chile Czech Republic France Greece
Guatemala Hungary Italy Japan Poland Portugal Singapore
South Korea Switzerland Thailand Turkey Ukraine Vietnam

Oxford is a registered trade mark of Oxford University Press
in the UK and in certain other countries

Published in the United States
by Oxford University Press Inc., New York

© The Editors and Contributors 2007

The moral rights of the authors have been asserted
Database right Oxford University Press (maker)

First published 2007

All rights reserved. No part of this publication may be reproduced,
stored in a retrieval system, or transmitted, in any form or by any means,
without the prior permission in writing of Oxford University Press,
or as expressly permitted by law, or under terms agreed with the appropriate
reprographics rights organization. Enquiries concerning reproduction
outside the scope of the above should be sent to the Rights Department,
Oxford University Press, at the address above

You must not circulate this book in any other binding or cover
and you must impose the same condition on any acquirer

British Library Cataloguing in Publication Data
Data available

Library of Congress Cataloging in Publication Data
Contemporary perspectives on property, equity, and trusts law / edited by
Martin Dixon.
p. cm.
ISBN-13: 978-0-19-921984-1 (alk. paper) 1. Trusts and trustees–United States.
2. Property–United States. 3. Equity–United States. I. Dixon, Martin.

KF730.C66 2007
346. 7305'9—dc22

2007034294

Typeset by Cepha Imaging Private Ltd, Bangalore, India
Printed in Great Britain
on acid-free paper by
the MPG Books Group

ISBN 978-0-19-921984-1

3 5 7 9 10 8 6 4 2

Coventry University Library

FOREWORD

It is timely to have these *Contemporary Perspectives on Property, Equity and Trusts Law*. There is plenty of life left in these old areas of the law, as becomes obvious on reading this perceptive collection of essays by leading scholars.

Scope or, indeed, a need for developing the law further arises for a variety of reasons, exemplified in these essays. A quiet corner of the law may become of much practical utility and lead to a need for case law, whether elucidating some novel points or clarifying the underlying philosophy of the law. A busy mainstream area of the law involving an increasingly wide range of people may become increasingly fuzzy in order to try to achieve social justice: high-level case law or legislation or both may be needed to produce more justifiable, clearer justice.

Legislation designed to improve the law may itself create further difficult problems of interpretation; it may even have broader or lesser consequences than intended.

More scope for legislation to develop the law, eg as to the trust, exists in offshore common law jurisdictions, while civil law jurisdictions have been finding it worthwhile to introduce their own new laws, eg as to the trust concept, taking account of other jurisdictions' successful laws. At the same time, with increasing fears over money laundering, terrorist funding and tax evasion via the use of trust funds, OECD and EU pressures have led to extensive and onerous regulation of the trust industry, not just in the interests of higher standards but in the interests of greater transparency and less confidentiality. Loss of much privacy is the price paid for the 'eternal vigilance' said to be the 'price of liberty'.

Are we becoming over-legislated and over-regulated? When is legislation appropriate? How far can the courts satisfactorily develop the law in accordance with the needs of society in the areas under consideration – and how do we judge those needs? Read on.

The Honourable Mr Justice David Hayton
LLB, LLD, (Newcastle University), MA, LLD (Cantab)
Caribbean Court of Justice, 8th May, 2007

PREFACE

This collection of essays from leading scholars in the field of property law and equity attempts to shed new light on some old, but central, concepts. We have divided the chapters into two broad sections for ease of reference, although as with everything in the law, this is almost as much a matter of convenience as it is of principle. Part One concentrates on the law of real property, with essays on topics of importance to both the scholar and the practitioner. Part Two on trusts and equity concentrates on matters of principle – an issue which is to the fore-front of the debate about what trusts are and how they can be used in the modern world.

Each author has chosen a topic close to their own heart, but a common theme was to consider issues that have relevance in the modern law, be they historic in origin or products of our modern age. Some of the pieces have been prompted by new or impending legislative developments that have not yet been tested in the courts or which still cause problems for judges, practitioners and students alike. The Charities Act 2006 (Luxton) remains a dark horse – will it be thoroughbred or beach donkey? – and there is much legislative and administrative law about the regulation of trustees (Hudson) that is unexplored. The Land Registration Act 2002 (Dixon) is little litigated to date despite its overarching importance and the impact of the Disability Discrimination Act 1995 (Lawson) on landlords is causing much angst in both the residential and commercial sectors. In the commercial world, so little is written about developers' options (Castle) that we might think they are hardly ever used, instead of being the staple of so many property transactions. The Law Commission has proposed changes to the regime of co-ownership of the family home (Cooke) and this may well require a sharper understanding of the Trusts of Land and Appointment of Trustees Act 1996 (Probert). In the law of trusts, the changing nature of equitable rights (Watkin) is all the more significant as traditional trusts concepts are moulded to the new world of international finance and investment (Ganado and Griffiths). Finally, if we do not understand what property rights are, and how they impact on us (Hopkins and Watt), it is difficult to develop the law at all rationally.

Without doubt, and hopefully, not everyone will agree with what is written here – the essays are offered both for their analysis and for the thoughts they may provoke.

Martin Dixon
Gerwyn LL H Griffiths

CONTENTS

Contents

EDITORS

Dr Martin Dixon
Reader in the Law of Real Property, Queens College, University of Cambridge
Visting Professor of Law, City University, London

Prof. Gerwyn LL H Griffiths
Professor of Equity and the Law of Property, University of Glamorgan
Visiting Senior Fellow, University of Cambridge

LIST OF CONTRIBUTORS

Richard Castle
Former Associate, Department of Land Economy, University of Cambridge

Prof. Elizabeth Cooke
Professor of Law, University of Reading

Martin Dixon
Reader in the Law of Real Property, Queens' College, University of Cambridge
Visting Professor of Law, City University, London

Dr Max Ganado
Senior Partner, Ganado & Associates – Advocates, Malta

Prof. Gerwyn LL H Griffiths
Professor of Equity and the Law of Property, University of Glamorgan
Visiting Senior Fellow, University of Cambridge

Nicholas Hopkins
Senior Lecturer, Law, University of Southampton

Prof. Alastair Hudson
Professor of Equity and Law, Queen Mary, University of London

Anna Lawson
Senior Lecturer, School of Law, University of Leeds

Prof. Peter Luxton
Professor of Law, The Cardiff Law School

Rebecca Probert
Senior Lecturer, Law, University of Warwick

Prof. Thomas Glyn Watkin
First Welsh Legislative Counsel, Honorary Professor of Law, University of Wales, Bangor

Gary Watt
Reader in Law, University of Warwick

ABBREVIATIONS

DDA	Disability Discrimination Act
DRC	Disability Rights Commission
EU	European Union
FATF	Financial Action Task Force
FSA	Financial Services Authority
ISC	Independent Schools Council
LRA	Land Registration Act 2002
NCVO	National Council for Voluntary Organisations
OECD	Organisation for Economic Cooperation and Development
OUP	Oxford University Press
TTA	Trusts and Trustees Act
UCITS	Undertakings for Collective Investment in Transferable Securities

TABLE OF CASES

TABLE OF LEGISLATION

UNITED KINGDOM STATUTES

PART I

THE LAW OF REAL PROPERTY

1

HOW SHOULD WE RESPOND TO UNCONSCIONABILITY? UNPACKING THE RELATIONSHIP BETWEEN CONSCIENCE AND THE CONSTRUCTIVE TRUST[1]

Nicholas Hopkins

A. Introduction

The use of unconscionability as a rationale for intervention has enjoyed an apparent revival not only in English law but throughout the common law world.[2] This is a development that has attracted a degree of academic support,[3] but also some powerful criticism.[4] This chapter takes as its starting point the fact that courts *do* rationalize intervention in a number of circumstances as responding to unconscionability. It leaves to one side the normative question of whether courts *ought* to do so. Its purpose is to consider the form that the response should take. In particular, it is concerned with the extent to which that response should involve the imposition of a constructive trust. This matter is closely connected to the normative question as, in some contexts, concern at the use of the constructive

---

[1] This chapter is based on part of a paper delivered to the Property and Trusts Section of the Society of Legal Scholars' Annual Conference, University of Strathclyde, September 2005. The full version of that paper is published as N Hopkins, 'Conscience, Discretion and the Creation of Property Rights' (2006) 26 LS 275.

[2] See, for example, P Parkinson, 'The Conscience of Equity' in P Parkinson (ed), *The Principles of Equity* (2nd edn, 2003) Sydney: Lawbook Co, 29–54, 29.

[3] M Halliwell, *Equity and Good Conscience in a Contemporary Context* (London: Old Bailey Press 1997); A Mason, 'The Place of Equity and Equitable Remedies in the Contemporary Common Law World' (1994) 110 LQR 238.

[4] See, for example, R Meagher, D Heydon and M Leeming, *Meagher, Gummow and Lehane's Equity Doctrines and Remedies* (4th edn, Australia: Butterworths, 2002) xii. The authors decry what they consider to be the 'indiscriminate and excessive reliance on unconscionable conduct as a test for intervention'.

trust has been integral to criticism of the use of unconscionability as the rationale for intervention.[5] The argument presented in this chapter is that there is a need to separate the finding of unconscionability from the imposition of a constructive trust.[6] Where intervention is rationalized on the basis of unconscionability, that concept should also govern our response. The courts' response should go no further than is appropriate and proportionate to counter the unconscionable conduct. In many cases this will still lead to the imposition of a constructive trust. However, in limited circumstances, where the trust is not appropriate, the courts should have discretion as regards the remedy.

This chapter focuses on responding to unconscionability within the principle enunciated in *Rochefoucauld v Boustead* and in transfers 'subject to' rights in favour of the claimant. There are three reasons for this focus. First, unconscionability does not exist as a concept at large. As Parkinson notes, 'the conscience of equity must not be given a life of its own, independent of the specific doctrines through which it finds expression'.[7] Hence, it is preferable to analyze how we respond to unconscionability in the context of specific doctrines. Second, *Rochefoucauld v Boustead* and 'subject to' transfers involve unconscionable conduct of the same type. In both instances, the constructive trust is imposed on the acquisition of land and the unconscionability that provides the foundation of the trust relates specifically to the conduct of the defendant in reneging on a positive stipulation pursuant to which land has been transferred. Third, doubts as to the appropriateness of imposing a constructive trust have underpinned recent criticism of the use of unconscionability as the rationale for intervention in these doctrines.[8]

This chapter is structured as follows. The development of intervention in *Rochefoucauld v Boustead* and in 'subject to' transfers is first explained. The relationship between constructive trusts and unconscionability is then considered before suggesting how courts should respond to unconscionability within these principles. The model of remedial discretion advocated is then explained by reference to its development in proprietary estoppel before an analysis of its

---

[5] See, for example, S Bright, 'The Third Party's Conscience in Land Law' [2000] Conv 399, 403–7; B McFarlane, 'Constructive Trusts Arising on a Receipt of Property *Sub Conditione*' (2004) 120 LQR 667, 682–93.

[6] Cf: P O'Connor, 'Happy Partners or Strange Bedfellows: The Blending of Remedial and Institutional Features in the Evolving Constructive Trust' (1996) 20 Melb ULR 735, 738–9. She discusses the separation of the remedial constructive trust from the underlying principle of liability (unjust enrichment) in the US and Canada. In those jurisdictions, liability is dependent upon a finding of unjust enrichment, but the imposition of a constructive trust does not follow automatically from that finding.

[7] Above n 2, p 53.

[8] Above n 5.

possible use in cases within *Rochefoucauld v Boustead* and those involving a 'subject to' transfer.

B. Intervention through *Rochefoucauld v Boustead* and in 'Subject To' Transfers

The paradigm case within *Rochefoucauld v Boustead* arises where land is transferred from the claimant to the defendant on an undertaking that the defendant will hold the land on trust for the claimant. The trust is not evidenced in writing, as required by section 53(1)(b) Law of Property Act 1925. However, the defendant is precluded from relying on non-compliance with section 53 as to do so would enable the statute to be used as an instrument of fraud. The basis of intervention was seen by Lindley LJ as being the unconscionability or fraud of the transferee in seeking to deny the trust. He explained, ' . . . it is fraud on the part of a person to whom land is conveyed as a trustee, and who knows it was so conveyed, to deny the trust and claim the land himself'.[9] It should be noted that nothing turns on any distinction between the concept of (equitable) fraud referred to by Lindley LJ and unconscionability, terms which have been defined by reference to each other.[10] In that case, the existence of fraud enabled parol evidence to be admitted to establish the trust. The court classified the trust as an express trust on the basis that it was one the parties intended to create.[11] However, the classification of the trust as express was necessary to prevent the claim failing under the prevailing provisions of the Statute of Limitations and is addressed specifically in that context. Subsequently, the basis of intervention has been explained as lying in the defendant's attempt to renege on an agreement to hold on trust. This interpretation is consistent with (and arguably implicit in) Lindley LJ's reference to the defendant's attempt to deny the trust and claim the land for him or herself. It is explicitly adopted as the basis of the principle in *Bannister v Bannister*.[12] There, Scott LJ explained intervention as arising where the absolute character of a conveyance is set up to defeat 'the true bargain' under which a beneficial interest is to belong to another. The trust was classified (without discussion) as constructive and this classification is now favoured. Oakley, for example, explains the basis of this constructive trust in the following terms: '[What] brings about the intervention of equity is the acquisition of property on

---

9 [1897] 1 Ch 196, p 206.
10 See, for example, *Nocton v Lord Ashburton* [1914] AC 932, p 954; *Kitchen v Royal Airforce Association* [1958] 2 All ER 241, p 249.
11 [1897] 1 Ch 196, p 208.
12 [1948] 2 All ER 133.

the strength of an oral undertaking or agreement followed by an attempt to renege on the undertaking or agreement because of the lack of the necessary statutory formalities.'[13]

Lindley LJ's concept of unconscionability in *Rochefoucauld v Boustead* is sufficiently broad to incorporate an extension to the paradigm case, where the intended beneficiary of the trust is not the transferor him or herself but a third party to the agreement. The existence of this extension is generally accepted, though it is difficult to find clear authority for the application of the case to such facts. In *Rochefoucauld v Boustead* itself there were three parties involved in the transaction, though the case is (correctly) seen as being in substance an agreement for the benefit of the transferor. There, land was transferred from a mortgagee to the defendant who had agreed with the mortgagor to hold on trust for her. Hence the beneficiary had an existing proprietary right in the land (an equity of redemption) and the effect of the agreement was to give up that right and for a new right (the trust) to be created in her favour. *Bannister v Bannister* was applied in *Neale v Willis*,[14] though it is doubtful that the case in fact falls within the *Rochefoucauld v Boustead* principle. In *Neale v Willis* the Court of Appeal intervened to prevent the defendant reneging on an undertaking that property would be jointly owned by his wife pursuant to which his wife's mother had provided a loan in connection with the purchase. Hence the defendant had entered into an agreement that his wife, a third party, would have an interest in the house. However, this agreement was not made with the transferor and the transfer was not made pursuant to the agreement. The agreement was instead part of a separate transaction connected with obtaining finance for the purchase. In the absence of stronger authority it may at least be noted that there is no serious doubt (judicial or academic) as regards the application of *Rochefoucauld v Boustead* in a three-party case. Further, the principle in *Rochefoucauld v Boustead* has been influential in the development of intervention where land is transferred expressly 'subject to' rights in favour of a third party. Reference to *Rochefoucauld v Boustead* in the development of that principle may therefore be seen as implicit acceptance of its own application by extension in a three-party case.

Hence *Rochefoucauld v Boustead* establishes that a constructive trust is imposed in response to a transferee reneging on an oral trust pursuant to which land is transferred. The trust is a response to the transferee's unconscionable conduct in seeking to renege on the agreement to hold on trust. The nature of the transferee's conduct is the same regardless of whether the intended beneficiary of the trust is

---

[13] A Oakley, *Constructive Trusts* (3rd edn, London: Sweet and Maxwell, 1997) 53–4.
[14] [1968] 19 P&CR 836.

6

the transferor or a third party and, equally, the court responds to both situations by the imposition of the trust. In a three-party case, however, an additional question arises: in whose favour should the constructive trust be imposed, the transferor or the intended beneficiary? To date this point remains unresolved, with no clear authority and conflicting academic opinion.[15]

By reference to the principle in *Rochefoucauld v Boustead*, courts have developed a further principle enabling intervention where land is transferred 'subject to' rights in favour of the claimant, a third party to the transfer, and the transferee seeks to renege on the 'subject to' agreement. As in *Rochefoucauld v Boustead*, intervention has been rationalized on the basis that it is unconscionable for the transferee to renege on the agreement. In response to this conduct, the transferee has been held to be a constructive trustee for the claimant, with his or her anticipated rights taking effect under the trust.

Intervention on the basis of a 'subject to' provision was first considered in *Binions v Evans*.[16] There, the transferee (the claimant in the action) purchased land 'subject to' rights in favour of the defendant. The defendant was the widow of an employee of the transferor to whom the transferor had agreed (in a written document) to allow rent-free occupation for life. The transferee obtained a discount on the purchase in return for the 'subject to' agreement but, notwithstanding, sought possession against the defendant. By reference to *Bannister v Bannister*, Lord Denning MR considered the court should impose a constructive trust on the transferee 'for the simple reason that it would be utterly inequitable for the plaintiffs to turn the defendant out contrary to the stipulation subject to which they took the premises'.[17] Lord Denning MR's judgment is weak authority: it is an alternative ground for decision given in a minority judgment.[18] However, the principle he advocated was applied in *Lyus v Prowsa Developments Ltd*[19] where land was sold in exercise of a mortgagee's power of sale 'subject to'

---

[15] T Youdan, 'Formalities for Trusts of Land, and the Doctrine in *Rochefoucauld v Boustead*' (1984) 43 CLJ 306, p 334 considers the authorities to support intervention in favour of the intended beneficiary. Oakley above n 13, p 56 notes that no doubt has been cast on the ability of the third party to enforce the agreement. In contrast, J Feltham, 'Informal Trusts and Third Parties' [1987] Conv 246, p 249 finds 'no strong line of authority' in favour of the third party and argues against intervention in their favour.

[16] [1972] 1 Ch 359.

[17] [1972] 1 Ch 359, p 368.

[18] The majority considered the defendant to have a beneficial interest under a settlement within the Settled Land Act 1925 which bound the transferee as a purchaser with notice (the 'subject to' clause evidencing notice). Lord Denning MR's preferred solution was that the defendant had a contractual licence at the time of the transfer which was itself a property right binding the transferees through notice. The personal status of contractual licences was subsequently established in *Ashburn Anstalt v Arnold* [1989] Ch 1.

[19] [1982] 1 WLR 1044.

a third party's (the claimant in the action) estate contract. Dillon J identified the fraud (or unconscionability) in issue, by reference to *Rochefoucauld v Boustead*, as consisting in 'the first defendant reneging on a positive stipulation in favour of the [claimants] in the bargain under which the first defendant acquired the land'.[20]

Intervention pursuant to a 'subject to' provision was subsequently considered (though not applied) in *Ashburn Anstalt v Arnold*,[21] which is generally accepted as providing the most authoritative exposition of the principle.[22] There, Fox LJ emphasized that the mere inclusion of a 'subject to' clause is not a sufficient basis for intervention, noting that 'the court will not impose a constructive trust unless it is satisfied that the conscience of the estate owner is affected'.[23] The inclusion of the clause is not conclusive as to the existence of an agreement as it may have been inserted to protect the vendor from liability to the transferee for non-disclosure of existing interests. As regards the agreement itself, it is established that this must relate to the creation of new rights in favour of the third party.[24] This requirement is linked to determining the purposes of the 'subject to' clause: evidence of an agreement to recognize 'fresh rights' demonstrates that its inclusion is not merely to protect the vendor from liability for non-disclosure of existing rights.[25] It also, perhaps, deflects attention from the highly contentious issue of enforcing rights outside the priority rules that form the bedrock of land law. The existing (non-enforceable) right is not directly binding on the purchaser, though essentially the same result is achieved indirectly through the creation of fresh rights.[26]

In Lord Denning MR's initial discussion of intervention in *Binions v Evans* it is apparent that the unconscionable conduct in issue is the same in substance as that in *Rochefoucauld v Boustead*. Intervention arises because the transferee reneges on a positive stipulation pursuant to which the land is transferred. This origin of the principle is further reflected in Dillon J's definition of the requisite unconscionability in *Lyus v Prowsa Developments Ltd*. The factual context of the cases does, however, differ. In 'subject to' transfers the claimant of

---

[20] [1982] 1 WLR 1044, p 1054.

[21] [1989] Ch 1.

[22] See, for example, *Lloyd v Dugdale* [2002] 2 P&CR 13, para 52.

[23] [1989] Ch 1, pp 25–6.

[24] This is evident in the discussions of the principle in *Lyus v Prowsa Developments Ltd* [1982] 1 WLR 1044 and *Ashburn Anstalt v Arnold* [1989] Ch 1. See further the summary of the principle in *Lloyd v Dugdale* [2002] 2 P&CR 13, para 52(3).

[25] Cf: *Ashburn Anstalt v Arnold* [1989] Ch 1, p 26.

[26] N Hopkins, *The Informal Acquisition of Rights in Land* (London: Sweet and Maxwell, 2000) pp 49–51. The difference between constructive trusts imposed to enforce existing rights and those imposed to recognize new rights is discussed by McFarlane, above n 5, pp 669–74.

rights has invariably been a third party to the transfer, whereas, as has been seen, *Rochefoucauld v Boustead* initially developed where the claimant was the transferor. Further, the cases differ as regards the nature of the interest to be enjoyed by the third party. As has been seen, *Rochefoucauld v Boustead* developed where the interest conferred is a beneficial interest under a trust. The agreement reneged upon is an oral agreement for a trust, with the only bar to enforcement being the absence of written evidence within section 53(1)(b) Law of Property Act 1925. In 'subject to' cases the nature of the third party's interest is not so confined but has included property rights that do not involve the creation of a trust (for example, the estate contract in *Lyus v Prowsa Developments Ltd*) and interests that are merely personal (in particular, contractual licences). This difference does not appear significant as regards the classification of the transferee's conduct as unconscionable. The transferee's conduct, consisting of reneging on the agreement, is exactly the same, regardless of the type of interest that was to be conferred on the claimant. However, this difference does beg the question as to whether the courts' response to the unconscionable conduct, the imposition of a constructive trust, should also be the same. To answer this question, it is first helpful to consider the relationship between unconscionability and constructive trusts.

C. Constructive Trusts and Unconscionability

In *Carl-Zeiss Stiftung v Herbert Smith (No 2)* Edmund Davies LJ commented that 'English law provides no clear and all-embracing definition of a constructive trust. Its boundaries have been left perhaps deliberately vague, so as not to restrict the court by technicalities in deciding what the justice of a particular case may demand'.[27] The imposition of a trust in response to unconscionability has been seen as the common denominator in the different circumstances in which the constructive trust is imposed. Hence in *Paragon Finance plc v DB Thakerar & Co*, Millet LJ explained: 'A constructive trust arises by operation of law whenever the circumstances are such that it would be unconscionable for the owner of property . . . to assert his own beneficial interest in the property and deny the beneficial interest of another.'[28] The 'vague boundaries' of constructive trust doctrine thus appear dependent on our understanding of what constitutes unconscionable conduct. A constructive trust cannot be imposed unless the defendant's conduct is considered unconscionable and so, in this respect, unconscionability appears to be a pre-condition to the imposition of the trust.

---

[27] [1969] 2 Ch 276, p 300.
[28] [1999] 1 All ER 400, p 409.

As Millet LJ had previously observed in *Lonrho plc v Fayed (No 2)*,[29] the jurisdiction of equity to grant relief 'for every species of fraud and other unconscionable conduct' is one that cannot be exhaustively defined as it must retain 'an inherent flexibility and capacity to adjust to new situations by reference to mainsprings of the equitable jurisdiction'.[30] Hence new circumstances giving rise to a constructive trust in response to different types of unconscionable conduct continue to be recognized.[31]

Given the close relationship between constructive trusts and unconscionability there is a danger that the scope of constructive trust doctrine is seen as synonymous with the scope of unconscionability: that is, that unconscionability is seen not merely as *a pre-condition* to the constructive trust but as *necessarily leading to* the imposition of the trust. It is notable, for example, that in developing intervention within *Rochefoucauld v Boustead* and 'subject to' cases, the courts have not explicitly distinguished between establishing unconscionability and determining how to respond to unconscionability. These principles have developed by reference to the scope of constructive trust doctrine. A finding of unconscionability by the defendant reneging on a positive stipulation pursuant to which land was transferred necessarily led to the imposition of a constructive trust.

To understand the relationship between unconscionability and constructive trusts it is useful to consider the place of constructive trusts in the general body of trust law. In *Westdeutsche Landesbank Girozentrale v Islington London Borough Council*,[32] Lord Browne-Wilkinson considered unconscionability to be the foundation of the whole of the law of trusts. He forwarded four propositions: (first) that equity (and trusts) operate on the conscience of the owner of the legal interest; (second) therefore, that a person cannot be trustee unless his or her conscience is affected by knowledge of the trust or the factors giving rise to the trust; (third) that there must be identifiable trust property; (fourth) that from the date a trust is established the beneficiary has a proprietary interest in the trust property.[33] Lord Browne-Wilkinson considered these to be 'fundamental' and 'uncontroversial'.[34]

---

[29] [1992] 1 WLR 1.

[30] [1992] 1 WLR 1, p 9.

[31] The most recent significant development appears to be the recognition of the '*Pallant v Morgan* [1953] 1 ch 53 equity' in *Banner Homes Group plc v Luff Developments Ltd* [2000] Ch 372 in the context of a failed commercial joint venture for the acquisition of land.

[32] [1996] AC 669.

[33] [1996] AC 669, p 705.

[34] [1996] AC 669, p 705.

While Lord Browne-Wilkinson's judgment has attracted widespread criticism, this has been focused on his first two propositions.[35] For constructive trusts, in the present context, it is the third and fourth propositions that appear of most interest.[36] These propositions suggest that the nature of the interest enjoyed by a beneficiary under a constructive trust is the same as under any other trust: that is, the beneficiary must have a proprietary right in identifiable trust property. Lord Browne-Wilkinson acknowledged one exception to the need for identifiable trust property, in relation to the constructive trust imposed on a person who dishonestly assists in a breach of trust but 'who may come under fiduciary duties even if he does not receive identifiable trust property'.[37] However, the use of the constructive trust both in claims based on dishonest assistance and those (now) based on unconscionable receipt has been criticized as a misnomer.[38] While, in the latter case, identifiable trust property is received, in neither case is property held on trust. Instead, the 'trustee' is made personally accountable in equity.[39]

In a case within *Rochefoucauld v Boustead*, or involving a transfer 'subject to' (unlike claims to dishonest assistance and unconscionable receipt), the trustee does hold identifiable trust property. In *Rochefoucauld v Boustead*, where the unconscionability relates to reneging on an agreement for an express (but unenforceable oral) trust, the beneficiary receives an orthodox beneficial interest: that is, a proprietary interest in the land which, created expressly, would generally be given effect under a trust. The express trust fails only for non-compliance with statutory formalities. This is not the case in a 'subject to' transfer where, as has been noted, the trust has been imposed to protect property rights which, created

---

35 P Birks, 'Trusts Raised to Reverse Unjust Enrichment: the *Westdeutsche* Case' [1996] RLR 3; R Chambers, *Resulting Trusts* (Oxford: Clarendon Press 1997) pp 203–9; W Swadling, 'Property' in P Birks, and F Rose (eds), *Lessons of the Swaps Litigation*, (London: Mansfield Press, 2000) pp 242–72; S Worthington, *Proprietary Interests in Commercial Transactions* (Oxford: Clarendon Press, 1996) Addendum.

36 Constructive trusts are clearly founded on conscience since, as has been seen, unconscionable conduct is a pre-condition of the trust. Lord Browne-Wilkinson's link between conscience and knowledge is contentious for some constructive trusts and is considered by N Hopkins, 'Unconscionability, Constructive Trusts and Proprietary Estoppel', in M Bryan (ed), *Private Law in Theory and Practice* (Abingdon: Routledge-Cavendish, 2007) 199–234. However it is not an issue in the constructive trusts under discussion where the trustees' knowledge is inherent in the parties' agreement or the imposition of a 'subject to' clause.

37 [1996] AC 669, p 705.

38 See, for example, P Birks, 'Trusts in the Recovery of Misapplied Assets: Tracing, Trusts and Restitution' in E McKendrick (ed), *Commercial Aspects of Trusts and Fiduciary Obligations* (Oxford: Clarendon Press, 1992) 149–66, pp 153–6 and P Millett, 'Restitution and Constructive Trusts' (1998) 114 LQR 399, pp 399–400.

39 In *Dubai Aluminium Co Ltd v Salaam* [2003] 2 AC 366, p 404 Lord Millett said, 'I think that we should now discard the words "accountable as constructive trustee" . . . and substitute the words "accountable in equity"'.

expressly, would not be given effect under a trust, and also purely personal interests. In such cases, while there is identifiable trust property (and hence the imposition of a constructive trust is consistent with Lord Browne-Wilkinson's third proposition), the nature of the beneficial interest acquired distinguishes the constructive trust from *Rochefoucauld v Boustead* and from all other situations where a constructive trust is imposed on the acquisition of land. Further, it is not necessarily the case that the beneficiary has a proprietary interest in the trust property, within Lord Browne-Wilkinson's fourth proposition. Where the constructive trust is imposed on a transfer 'subject to' a licence, a personal interest, it appears unresolved whether the effect of the trust is to confer a proprietary right on the licensee.[40]

Constructive trust doctrine may be sufficiently broad to encompass beneficial interests of this nature. However, two reasons may be advanced against the desirability of this use of the constructive trust. First, the novelty of such trusts in the context of trusts imposed on the acquisition of land may result from accident rather than design. In responding to unconscionability in 'subject to' transfers, courts do not appear to have considered the appropriateness of imposing the trust in response. Intervention has developed by reference to the scope of the constructive trust in the *Rochefoucauld v Boustead* principle. Both the nature of the unconscionability and the response (the constructive trust) have been carried over from that principle. It seems evident that the consequences of this have not been properly considered. This is reflected, for example, in the uncertain status of beneficial interests under a constructive trust imposed on a transfer 'subject to' a personal interest. Additionally, following *Binions v Evans*, concern was expressed that intervention on the basis of a 'subject to' transfer would provide a means of circumventing limitations on the enforcement of covenants affecting freehold land.[41] Second, the exclusion of such constructive trusts would bring a welcome coherence to the operation of constructive trust doctrine in relation to the acquisition of land. It would ensure that where constructive trusts are imposed in this context the trust differs from an express trust only in its method of creation. In all cases, the beneficiaries' interest would be of a type generally given effect under a trust when expressly created. This coherence

---

[40] Compare, for example, the views of Hopkins, above n 26, pp 55–7 (that a proprietary right is obtained) with McFarlane, above n 5, p 679 (that the constructive trust enforces merely a personal right). See further R Smith, *Property Law* (4th edn, London: Longman, 2003) pp 471–3. He objects in principle to the constructive trust being used to give proprietary effect to a personal interest, but acknowledges the difficulty of avoiding this conclusion following 'subject to' cases involving licences.

[41] A Oakley, 'The Licensee's Interest' (1972) 35 MLR 551, p 557. These concerns dissipated once the circumstances in which a 'subject to' clause will have effect were clarified in *Ashburn Anstalt v Arnold* [1989] 1 Ch 1. On this point, see Meagher, Gummow and Leeming above n 4, para 43–165.

may be particularly helpful in the context of land law where the designation of an interest as subsisting under a trust may affect the application of priority rules.[42]

It is suggested, therefore, that there is a need to unravel the relationship between unconscionability and constructive trusts. While the constructive trust is one possible response, it should not be seen as the automatic response. Instead, once the ground for intervention (the unconscionability) has been established, the courts should consider the appropriate response to that unconscionability. The consequence of this suggestion and its effect on cases within *Rochefoucauld v Boustead* and 'subject to' transfers will now be considered.

D. Responding to Unconscionable Conduct

The clear consequence of separating the finding of unconscionability from the imposition of a constructive trust is the introduction of remedial discretion. Any suggestion that discretionary remedialism should be introduced requires careful consideration. Birks condemned the separation of liability from remedy to such an extent that he wanted 'remedy' removed from legal vocabulary.[43] In his view, the remedy follows automatically from the event so that the claimant has a right to the remedy and the language of 'rights' is to be preferred. While the argument advanced in this chapter runs counter to that view,[44] it is acknowledged that it remains essential to maintain the 'logical connection' between the event on which the court intervenes and the remedy or response to that event.[45] This connection, it is suggested, informs the boundaries within which discretion may legitimately operate. On this basis, the discretion advocated can be outlined in the following terms.

Where the courts intervene on the basis of unconscionability, a remedy should be provided that is appropriate and proportionate to the unconscionability. A constructive trust should continue to be imposed in all cases where the imposition of a trust is appropriate.[46] As a rule of thumb, a constructive trust is appropriate

---

[42] It may affect, for example, the operation of overreaching and the ability to protect the interest through entry of a notice which, under s 33(a) Land Registration Act 2002, is not permissible in respect of an interest under a trust of land.

[43] P Birks, 'Rights, Wrongs, and Remedies' (2000) 20 OJLS 1.

[44] A direct response to Birks' argument is made by S Evans, 'Defending Discretionary Remedialism' (2001) 23 Syd LR 463.

[45] K Barker, 'Rescuing Remedialism in Unjust Enrichment Law: Why Remedies are Right' (1998) 57 CLJ 301, p 316.

[46] Under this formula there is no discretion for the court to provide an alternative remedy when a trust is appropriate. As such, constructive trusts that do arise remain institutional, not remedial, in nature.

where, but only where, the claimant's interest would be given effect under a trust if created expressly. Where this is not the case, the courts should exercise discretion as to the form the remedy takes. The claimant therefore has a right to a remedy to counter the unconscionability, but the form of that remedy lies within the discretion of the court. Conversely, the defendant has a right that his or her proprietary entitlement is not interfered with by the court more than is necessary to counter his or her unconscionability. In this respect congruence is maintained between the event and the response: the court intervenes on the basis of unconscionable conduct and provides a remedy that goes no further than is necessary to counter that conduct. The court's discretion is therefore limited to determining the form of the remedy. The existence of this limited discretionary remedialism is not unprecedented in English law. As will be seen, it mirrors the remedial discretion exercised in claims to proprietary estoppel.

1. Unconscionability and remedial discretion in proprietary estoppel

Intervention through proprietary estoppel has been accepted as being founded on unconscionability at least since the decision in *Taylors Fashions Ltd v Liverpool Victoria Trustees Ltd*.[47] While the unconscionability in estoppel again relates to reneging on an undertaking (of an assurance the claimant has or will acquire rights), estoppel is distinguished from the other principles under discussion insofar as the unconscionability is also dependent upon a finding of detrimental reliance.[48] The role of unconscionability in establishing an estoppel claim has received renewed interest since the decision in *Gillett v Holt*.[49] This case suggests that unconscionability should be seen as an overriding or umbrella element of an estoppel claim. It feeds into the other elements of the claim (assurance, reliance and detriment) but also provides a general evaluative tool through which the court considers the claim 'in the round'.[50]

Once a claim to estoppel is established the court has discretion to determine the remedy to award.[51] A distinction may be drawn, however, between the *purpose* of the remedy, or the underlying result to be achieved, and the *form* of the remedy.[52]

---

[47] [1982] 1 QB 133.

[48] This distinction between the principles is drawn by S Nield, 'Constructive Trusts and Estoppel' (2003) 23 LS 311, p 321.

[49] [2001] Ch 210.

[50] *Gillett v Holt* [2001] Ch 210, p 225 *per* Robert Walker LJ. For a full analysis of this development see N Hopkins, 'Understanding Unconscionability in Proprietary Estoppel' (2004) 20 JCL 210.

[51] The nature of the discretion is further discussed by E Cooke, 'Estoppel, Discretion and the Nature of the Estoppel Equity', in M Bryan (ed), *Private Law in Theory and Practice* (Abingdon: Routledge-Cavendish, 2007) 181–97.

[52] Cf: S Gardner, 'The Element of Discretion' in P Birks (ed), *The Frontiers of Liability Vol II* (Oxford: OUP, 1994) 186–203, pp 201–3.

While both are within the courts' discretion, the purpose of the remedy is not seen as a matter for decision in each case. Cooke notes that only in a few cases have courts undertaken 'a real exercise of discretion [by asserting] . . . that not merely is the precise order in the courts' hands but also the measure of relief to be effected by the order'.[53] On a case-by-case basis, the courts' discretion appears directed only at determining the form of the order. The purpose of the remedy has previously been thought to lie either in the award of expectations or in the recovery of reliance loss.[54] The form of the order was, however, generally seen as consistent with either view of the purpose of the remedy, as a reliance-based approach in theory was seen as consistent with the award of expectations in practice.[55] The renewed emphasis on unconscionability in establishing the existence of the estoppel claim since *Gillett v Holt* has started to spill over to the determination of the remedy. There is evidence of a shift in the underlying purpose of the remedy from expectations or reliance to a conscience-based approach.[56]

Evidence of a shift to a conscience-based approach to remedies is found both in a revival of the significance of proportionality in determining the remedy and in indications that the 'in the round' evaluation that characterizes the use of unconscionability in establishing the estoppel is being carried over to the exercise of remedial discretion. In *Jennings v Rice*, Aldous LJ suggested that the proportionality of the remedy to the detriment is 'the most essential requirement'.[57] In the context of estoppel remedies, proportionality has been closely linked with unconscionability. In *Waltons Stores v Maher*, Brennan J explained:

> The element which both attracts the jurisdiction of the court of equity and shapes the remedy to be given is unconscionable conduct on the part of the person bound by the equity . . . [In] moulding its decree, the court, as a court of conscience, goes no further than is necessary to prevent unconscionable conduct.[58]

This was cited by Mason CJ in *Commonwealth v Verwayen* in holding that 'a central element of [estoppel] is that there must be proportionality between the remedy and the detriment . . . It would be wholly inequitable and unjust to insist

---

[53] E Cooke, *The Modern Law of Estoppel* (Oxford: OUP, 2000) p 157.

[54] The alternative views are forwarded by E Cooke, 'Estoppel and the Protection of Expectations' (1997) 17 LS 258 and A Robertson, 'Reliance and Expectation in Estoppel Remedies' (1998) 18 LS 360.

[55] A Robertson, 'The Statute of Frauds, Equitable Estoppel and the Need for Something More' (2003) 19 JCL 173, p 187.

[56] This shift may fall within what Gardner describes, above n 52 p 203, as the 'irreducible minimum of discretion as to purpose'. See further S Gardner, 'The Remedial Discretion in Proprietary Estoppel – Again' (2006) 122 LQR 492.

[57] [2003] 1 FCR 501, para 36.

[58] (1988) 164 CLR 387, p 419.

upon a disproportionate making good of the relevant assumption'.[59] The focus on proportionality in that case was a key factor in the court's assertion of a reliance-based approach to remedies. Mason CJ suggested that to do more than prevent the claimant's detriment 'would sit uncomfortably with a general principle whose underlying foundation was the concept of unconscionability'.[60]

Aldous LJ's reference to the primacy of proportionality was made in the context of reasserting the courts' remedial discretion. He explained (immediately prior to his reference to proportionality) that 'the value of [the equity derived from estoppel] will *depend upon all the circumstances* including the expectation and the detriment. The task of the court is to do justice'.[61] There are echoes in this statement of the 'in the round' evaluation conducted to establish an estoppel. Most explicitly, the prevailing view of the courts to the purpose of the estoppel remedy is summarized by Arden LJ in *Ottey v Grundy*. She explained:

> The purpose of proprietary estoppel is not to enforce an obligation which does not amount to a contract [expectations] nor yet to reverse the detriment which the claimant has suffered [reliance] but to *grant an appropriate remedy in respect of the unconscionable conduct*.[62]

The courts' approach to the exercise of remedial discretion in estoppel, in particular the relevance of unconscionability in this context, is far from settled. If confirmed, however, its effect will be to provide congruence between the basis of intervention and the courts' response. The court intervenes in estoppel because it is unconscionable for the representor to renege on the assurance and provides a remedy that is appropriate and proportionate in respect of the unconscionable conduct. The purpose of the remedy having shifted from expectations or reliance to unconscionability, the courts' discretion on a case-by-case basis is focused on determining the form of the order appropriate to give effect to this purpose. The possible use of this model in the principles under discussion will now be assessed.

2. Responding to unconscionability in *Rochefoucauld v Boustead* and on a 'subject to' transfer

In a case within *Rochefoucauld v Boustead*, where the unconscionability relates to reneging on an agreement for an express (but unenforceable oral) trust, the imposition of a constructive trust is entirely appropriate. It is inherent in the nature of the agreement in such cases that the claimant's interest would take effect

---

59 (1990) 170 CLR 394, p 413.
60 (1990) 170 CLR 394, p 411.
61 [2003] 1 FCR 501, para 36 (emphasis added).
62 [2003] EWCA 1176, para 61.

under a trust if created expressly. Therefore, there is no discretion for the court to award an alternative remedy. The outstanding question in that context is whether, in the three-party case, the trust should operate in favour of the transferor or the third party (the intended beneficiary). The criterion of proportionality may be helpful in deciding this issue. It suggests that the trust should go no further than is necessary to respond to the unconscionability. Whether this requires intervention in favour of the transferor or the intended beneficiary may be dependent on the facts. For example, where the transferor is alive and therefore has the opportunity to execute an express trust, there may be no justification in going further than imposing a trust in his or her favour. Where the transferor has died in the belief that the trust is valid, intervention in favour of the third party may be the only effective response to the unconscionability.

Where, however, land is transferred 'subject to' rights in favour of the claimant, and those rights would not be given effect under a trust if created expressly, then the imposition of a constructive trust is not appropriate. In such cases, the courts should exercise a discretion, analogous to that in claims to estoppel, to provide a remedy proportionate to counter the unconscionability. This could include, for example, the grant of the proprietary right envisaged by the 'subject to' agreement (an estate contract in *Lyus v Prowsa Developments Ltd*) or of a purely personal right, such as a licence to occupy (in *Binions v Evans* and *Bannister v Bannister*).[63] This approach would also resolve doubt as to the proprietary or personal status of the claimant's rights.[64] As is the case in claims to estoppel, whether the remedy awarded confers a proprietary right on the claimant would be determined by the classification of such rights as a matter of general property law. A personal right (such as a licence) would not be transformed into a proprietary right (a beneficial interest under a constructive trust) merely through being generated by a 'subject to' agreement.

In 'subject to' transfers, courts have invariably intervened in favour of the intended recipient of rights. There appears to be little, if any, suggestion, analogous to that in three-party cases within *Rochefoucauld v Boustead*, that intervention should instead be made only in favour of the transferor.[65] It is suggested, however, that intervention in favour of the third party is consistent with the criteria of appropriateness and proportionality underlying the award of a remedy founded

---

[63] This is consistent with the outcome advocated by McFarlane above n 5. However, he rejects an analysis based on unconscionability and suggests an alternative rationale for the case law to achieve this result.

[64] Cf: the discussion above n 40 and associated text.

[65] This feature of cases within the principle has, however, generated suggestions that the courts are really concerned with the enforcement of promises and have arisen through previous limitations on privity of contract. See, for example, Bright, above n 5 pp 413–18.

on unconscionability. The effect of factual differences between cases within the scope of that principle and 'subject to' cases is that intervention in favour of the third party is necessary to counter the unconscionable conduct. In *Rochefoucauld v Boustead*, a remedy in favour of the transferor provides him or her with an opportunity to make good the defect that led to the failure of the express trust. A 'subject to' provision generally appears to be used to create new rights in favour of a third party either because that person has existing property rights that will not be enforceable on the transfer,[66] or that person has a personal right (in particular, a contractual licence) that is incapable of binding a transferee. The imposition of a 'subject to' clause to reflect an undertaking by the transferee to recognize new rights in favour of the third party may therefore be the only way the transferor can protect that third party. Hence a remedy in favour of the transferor, unlike in *Rochefoucauld v Boustead*, provides no guarantee that he or she will be able to secure the third party's rights.

E. Conclusion

This chapter has suggested the need to separate the finding of unconscionability from the imposition of a constructive trust. Where the court intervenes on the basis of unconscionability, courts should provide a response that is appropriate and proportionate to counter the unconscionable conduct. Where the imposition of a trust is appropriate (because the claimant's interest, if created expressly, would be a property interest of a type generally given effect under a trust), a constructive trust should continue to be imposed. In other cases, the court should exercise discretion as to the remedy to award. The discretion advocated is modelled on that currently exercised in claims to proprietary estoppel. It is a discretion to determine the form of the remedy that provides an appropriate and proportionate response to the unconscionability.

---

[66] Eg, *Lyus v Prowsa Developments Ltd* [1982] 1 WLR 1044. There, the 'subject to' agreement was contained in a sale pursuant to a mortgagee's power of sale. The claimant's property right (an estate contract) post-dated the mortgage and therefore would itself be unenforceable against the purchaser.

2

PROTECTING THIRD-PARTY INTERESTS UNDER THE LAND REGISTRATION ACT 2002

To worry or not to worry, that is the question

Martin Dixon

The Land Registration Act (LRA) 2002 is designed to change the way we think about land, ownership, and conveyancing. E-conveyancing, broadly defined, is already in operation[1] and the more extensive schemes being tested will bring us a fully electronic conveyancing system within a decade.[2] The Law Commission's Report on which the 2002 Act is based foretells a brave new world where the e-register will govern the vast majority of dealings with land and where 'off-register' transactions and enquiries will be kept to the absolute minimum. Although e-conveyancing does not mean the end to physical inspection of property prior to purchase or mortgage, and will not eradicate pre-contractual enquiries of the seller or borrower, the e-register is meant to be a much more complete 'title mirror' than any version of land registration that has gone before. In this endeavour, HM Land Registry for England and Wales is leading the world, and common law and civil jurisdictions alike, as well as the former centrally planned economies of

---

[1] For example, electronic discharges of mortgages under the e-discharges (EDs) process, the first truly e-conveyancing system that allows direct and automatic changes to be made to the register by non-Registry agencies.

[2] The full pilot will operate from October 2007. It remains to be seen whether e-conveyancing will be compulsory within a decade, or simply (at least initially) an optional system. The original land registration system of the Land Registration Act 1925 was introduced gradually – in fact nationwide compulsion did not arrive until 1 December 1990 – but given that e-conveyancing is to be grafted on to an already working and efficient system, it is arguable that there is no need for 'creeping compulsion' at all.

Eastern Europe and Asia, are already regarding the LRA 2002 with the same interest as a scientist would examine a new species of guinea pig.

In fact, in property law terms, the Land Registration Act 2002 is still in its infancy – barely walking, hardly talking and only just loose from the child restraints of transitional provisions.[3] Some three years after the Act entered into force, both practitioners and academics are reliant on the Law Commission's Report, the Land Registry's Practice Guides and a few specialist texts for guidance about the interpretation and implementation of this monumental legislation. Fortunately, for the most part, the Act is drafted with a clarity that is rarely found in technical legislation, and the everyday experience of the staff of the Land Registry and their commonsense application of the Land Registration Rules have reduced significantly the scope for uncertainty. However, although the Law Commission makes the bold claim that the LRA 2002 heralds a convey-ancing revolution, some commentators have suggested that a more accurate description is that the 2002 Act encompasses 'evolution not revolution'.[4] There is considerable truth in this, for the 2002 Act borrows much from the 1925 Act which it replaced, if not so much in detail then certainly in concepts and methodology. Indeed, although one suspects that the original intention of the Law Commission was to produce legislation that was largely free of the past – and much has been achieved in this regard[5] – the 2002 Act in its final form would be recognizable *as to principles* by a competent registered land practitioner from the 1950s.

One aspect of the Act that has generated a certain amount of noise is the way in which it deals with the priority of third-party property interests on the occasion of a dealing with a registered title, especially when contrasted with the predecessor provisions of the Land Registration Act 1925. Given that much of the 2002 Act is driven by the imperative to establish an effective and efficient system of e-conveyancing, it is axiomatic that an intended transferee of the land – in particular a purchaser or mortgagee[6] – should be able to discover as much as possible about adverse property rights from an inspection of the register.

---

[3] A number of transitional provisions expired on 12th October 2006, three years after entry into force of the 2002 Act. Some remain – for example concerning certain categories of overriding inter-ests – but these are designed to safeguard persons' pre-existing property rights rather than being truly transitional in the sense of easing the transition from the old law to the new.

[4] I cannot lay claim to this pithy and illuminating phrase. I first heard the description used by Professor Edward Burn, still the doyen of property lawyers.

[5] For example, it is true that the 2002 Act offers 'title by registration' rather than 'registration of title' as was the case under the 1925 Act.

[6] The position of a transferee not for value is different and discussed briefly below. Historically, Chancery courts were unwilling to assist a 'volunteer' and the law's preoccupation with 'the purchaser' continues to this day.

Otherwise, e-conveyancing under the LRA 2002 will amount to nothing more than a method of transferring land – like deeds and written contracts – rather than the foundation of a system of title by registration. Thus, the mechanics of registering (and therefore protecting) adverse third-party rights should be simple and effective and should, eventually, be within the orbit of compulsory e-registration. Likewise, or so the story goes, the extent to which unregistered third-party rights are capable of enjoying priority over the interest of a transferee must be subject to the most rigorous scrutiny, for the existence of these unregistered, but binding, interests in any great numbers or magnitude compromises the reflection cast by the e-register.

At first blush, the 2002 Act deals with this issue robustly. It purports to require the registration of very many more third-party rights affecting a registered title than did the LRA 1925, to make the process of their registration simpler and then to punish their non-registration by a loss of priority against a duly registered transferee for value.[7] Similarly, the re-ordering and re-definition of 'unregistered interests which override'[8] is meant to ensure that only those property rights whose substantive registration is impractical or undesirable should be able retain their priority over a transferee for value despite their lack of registration. Even then, for the apparently narrow class of rights that can have this effect, the intent is that they should continue to have priority only if they are, in some sense, *discoverable* by an intended transferee before the transfer. Overriding interests are thus not intended to be a general safety net for a right holder who fails to register but a necessary evil in a system of title by registration whose main concern is transactional certainty. The following analysis will consider whether, taking the LRA 2002 in the round, its provisions are likely to have a significant practical impact on the circumstances in which third-party interests will take priority over a newly registered proprietor of land, or whether despite apparent 'revolution' little has in fact changed.

---

[7] Sections 28, 29, 30 LRA 2002. The grant of a lease for seven years or less, although not generally a registrable disposition, counts as a 'registered disposition' for the purpose of the priority rules, see section 29(4) LRA 2002.

[8] See Schedule 3 to the LRA 2002, considered below.

A. Fundamentals

The basic structure of the LRA 2002 with regard to third-party rights[9] is similar to that of the LRA 1925. Third-party interests can be protected either by a conscious act of registration by the right holder[10] or silently by reason of the interest falling within the ambit of overriding interests. The former occurs either by the use of a Notice, which confers substantive protection on the interest protected, or, in specified circumstances, by the use of a Restriction, which confers protection indirectly by controlling dealings with the title and thus limiting the circumstances in which a transferee may claim priority through registration as the new proprietor.[11] Registration of a third-party interest by means of a Notice is meant to be the default and regular way by which third-party interests are protected, although a Restriction can be equally as effective.[12] 'Unregistered interests which override' the interest of a new registered proprietor[13] are found in Schedule 1 to the Act in reference to first registration of title, and in Schedule 3 in respect of any subsequent disposition of the registered title.[14] In other words, and in very general terms, if the third-party interest is unprotected (that is, not properly registered and not an overriding interest), it is in *danger* of losing its priority and further questions must be asked.

Necessarily, the above picture is simplified, but the point is that the basic structure of the LRA 2002 is similar to that of the 1925 Act and practitioners

---

[9] To be clear, for present purposes, this means rights potentially adverse to the estate owner, held by another person and encompasses, inter alia, proprietary interests such as easements, covenants, options, rights of pre-emption (see section 115 LRA 2002) and proprietary estoppels (see section 116 LRA 2002). Leases not registrable as an estate are also included. Rights of equitable co-ownership, although not necessarily adverse to the registered proprietor, may well become so (or to a successor) and are one of the most common examples of rights in this category. Mortgages are excluded for present purposes, being nearly always substantively registered as a registered charge. Note, however, an equitable mortgage arising from a mere written instrument, or by reason of estoppel, would require protection using the process discussed below.

[10] Or, in certain circumstances, by the registrar, s 37 LRA 2002.

[11] Or making the dealing subject to specified conditions. The Restriction is not *designed* to confer protection – that is the role of the Notice. However, by limiting or preventing dispositions, pre-existing rights are necessarily protected as there may be no registered disposition to take advantage of the priority rule.

[12] For example, a Restriction preventing a disposition without the consent of X, the holder of an option to purchase the land, will be as effective in practice as a Notice protecting the option. Indeed, both may well be used.

[13] Formerly 'overriding interests'. The change of name is not accidental but is meant to emphasize that there is **not** perfect symmetry between the provisions of the LRA 1925 and the LRA 2002.

[14] Schedule 2 concerns the formalities required to complete a registered disposition of a registered title and thus follows logically from Schedule 1 and before Schedule 3, the latter being concerned with the effects of meeting the requirements in Schedule 2.

dealing with registered titles on the 13th October 2003 should have been familiar with the mechanics of the new system, if not with every detail. Of course, the goal of the LRA 2002 is to introduce e-conveyancing and thereby enhance transactional certainty and efficiency, and so there is no surprise that the legislation makes a major effort to ensure that as many third-party rights as possible are brought on to the register and that as few as possible are protected without such registration. A number of strategies are employed to this effect.

(a) The intention is to reduce overriding interests both in number and in extent. The general policy is that interests should override only where it is unreasonable or impractical that they should be entered on the register. Many of the overriding interests defined in the Schedules are comparable to those existing under the 1925 Act, but critically the mere *existence* of a third-party interest falling within the statutory definition may not be enough to ensure its priority. For some overriding interests, their priority over a purchaser depends on their inclusion in the relevant Schedule *and* on the actions of the purchaser and/or the interest holder.

(b) A distinction is made between interests that override a first registration of title and those that override a subsequent disposition of a registered estate. Schedule 1, specifying unregistered interests which override a first registration, appears to be more generous than Schedule 3, which specifies interests which override a dealing with an existing registered title. The intention is that more unregistered interests will have priority at first registration than when an existing registered title is dealt with for value. This reflects the fact that first registration of title does not involve a change in ownership of the land. The existing owner is the person who applies for first registration and the Schedule of overriding interests should accommodate all those unregistered interests which bound that owner prior to registration.[15] If it were otherwise, the mere act of first registration could defeat a third-party interest and not even the 2002 Act goes that far. Conversely, a disposition subject to Schedule 3 always involves a change of registered proprietor or the grant of a significant interest to another person, and the policy of the Act is to confer added protection on such a transferee if they give value. Schedule 3 thus appears to exclude some interests (or some situations) that would have fallen within Schedule 1, primarily by reference to a discoverability criterion. This is, of course, an expression of policy rather than a legal necessity.

---

[15] Of course, that owner may have purchased the land previously and be compelled to register under the compulsory registration provisions, section 4 LRA 2002. However, the owner's status already has been determined by the rules of unregistered conveyancing and first registration is, in this sense, an administrative act rather than a substantive one.

The 2002 Act proceeds on the basis that in a world with e-conveyancing, the purchaser *should* have priority over third-party interests unless those interests are on the register or, as a necessary evil, overriding to the extent that they are discoverable. It is too late to argue about whether this is the best policy choice, but the fact that it stems from policy not necessity may have an impact when Schedule 3 comes before the courts for interpretation.

(c)   There is a duty on 'a person applying for registration' and 'a person applying to register a registrable disposition' to disclose third-party overriding interests affecting the estate to be registered so that they may be entered against the title and so brought on to the register.[16] It is, perhaps, surprising that disclosure should be made by the person whose estate is to be bound, and we might think that this is the last person who would want adverse interests revealed. However, given that, by definition, the third-party right already binds the registered proprietor – it already overrides – the typical applicant for registration has little to lose and possibly something to gain by disclosure,[17] and in any event failure to disclose does not cause the loss of overriding status.[18] To this extent, the duty to disclose will enhance the register as a full record of title. Nevertheless, it is not all plain sailing, and it seems that the existence of this 'duty' is generating some difficulties in practice. First, being cast as a 'duty' suggests that there is a penalty for non-compliance. No penalty is specified in the Act or Rules, but anecdotal evidence suggests that professional advisers are seeking to pass the risk of non-compliance (whatever that is) to the existing proprietor through the contract of sale, or are using pre-contractual enquiries to extract maximum (and often irrelevant) information from the seller. This is not conducive to the smooth operation of e-conveyancing. Second, however, it may well be appropriate to advise applicants for registration *not* to disclose interests about which they are uncertain. Not only would disclosure and registration effectively crystallize a (previously uncertain) adverse right,[19] but simply raising the possibility that an adverse interest might (or might not) exist can generate problems where none existed before. Third-party rights that have been quietly exercised for many years (eg over a shared drain) suddenly assume different proportions

---

16   Section 71 LRA 2002; Land Registration Rules 2003, Rules 28 and 57. Form DI must be used.

17   By ensuring that for the future, the register reflects the true state of his title and that a purchaser can buy or lend with confidence.

18   It would, of course, be absurd if the proprietor by his own failure could cause the adverse right to lose its priority.

19   Although registration by means of a Notice does not guarantee the validity of the right registered – section 32(3) LRA 2002 – it would be difficult for a registered proprietor to later dispute the validity of an interest which he had disclosed.

when revealed on a form for official registration and can generate disputes simply because they have become apparent.

(d) The process by which third-party interests are entered on the register has been simplified, thus encouraging registration. The introduction of a straightforward procedure for the registration of a Notice, which always confers substantive protection,[20] combined with the effective abolition of land and charge certificates, is a welcome simplification of the system that operated under the Land Registration Act 1925. Nevertheless, the 2002 Act is over-ambitious in its goal of encouraging maximum disclosure of the *content* of third-party rights as well as their existence. The two variants of the Notice – the Agreed Notice and Unilateral Notice – are meant to serve different purposes. An Agreed Notice is meant to protect an interest about which there are no concerns as to its validity, either because its existence is accepted by the registered proprietor of the burdened title or because it arises from an order of a court.[21] As such, full details of the third-party right are disclosed on the register unless an exemption request is granted.[22] By contrast, although a Unilateral Notice may be challenged, the applicant does not need the consent of the registered proprietor to register the interest, nor need he lodge details disclosing full details of the right.[23] Consequently, a Unilateral Notice is an effective way of keeping confidential matters off the register and may be chosen, or suggested by professional advisers, even though the applicant could have registered an Agreed Notice. Indeed, it may well be that certain proprietors in granting third-party interests – eg landlords granting short leases or owners granting options – should specify in the contract of grant that the third-party right holder should *not* apply for an Agreed Notice, precisely to keep matters confidential.[24]

B. The Priority Rules

The LRA 2002 seeks to simplify issues of priority by laying down clear rules about the circumstances in which a registered proprietor can be subject to third-party interests. It institutes a statutory scheme of priorities that replaces the less

---

[20] Assuming the interest protected is otherwise valid under the general law, section 32 LRA 2002. This is very different from the old 'caution' of the LRA 1925.

[21] Land Registration Rules 2003 (LRR 2003), R 80.

[22] LRR 2003, R 136.

[23] Of course, the registrar must be furnished with sufficient details to accept the validity of the right purported to be registered, sections 35 and 36 LRA 2002.

[24] For example, would a landlord of a mixed-use shopping centre with several units be happy to have the details revealed of the different rents payable by the various tenants?

organized system of the Land Registration Act 1925.[25] In essence, the rules are marginally different according to whether there is a first registration of title or whether there is a subsequent disposition of a registered title and this mirrors the use of two Schedules for overriding interests. The position in respect of first registrations is similar to the law of the LRA 1925 (with necessary modifications), but the position in respect of registered dispositions (dealings) of a registered estate is re-cast in a rather more radical way and may well be the source of problems.

1. First registration of title

Under sections 11 and 12 LRA 2002, the first registered proprietor of a freehold or leasehold estate[26] with title absolute is 'subject only' to the following interests, provided that they affect the estate at the time of the registration (eg are otherwise valid and have not been waived *inter partes*). First, interests protected by an entry on the register – eg those protected by a Notice – being those translated from the Land Charges Register of the Land Charges Act 1972 and those former overriding interests revealed to the Registrar under the duty to disclose or apparent from the title deeds. Second, those interests which override under Schedule 1 LRA 2002, having not been entered on the Register through disclosure. Third, interests acquired by reason of adverse possession of which the proprietor has notice, although if the adverse possessor has not completed 12 years' adverse possession at the time of first registration, this is likely to mean no more than the ability to apply to be registered as proprietor under the new scheme of the LRA 2002.[27] Fourth, if the registered proprietor is not entitled to the land solely for his own benefit (eg he is a trustee of land), then as regards the person beneficially entitled, the proprietor is subject to those rights of which he has notice.[28]

---

[25] Under this Act, priority was expressed in terms of 'voidness' and utilized, rather than codified, existing common law principles. Thus, it might have been relevant to assess whether 'the equities were equal' in the application of the 'first in time' rule: see Law Comm. Report No 271 para 5.1 et seq.

[26] For leaseholds, section 12 LRA 2002 also specifies that (unsurprisingly) the leasehold is subject to implied and express covenants and obligations in the lease. If the leasehold is registered with 'good leasehold' title, the priority rules are the same, save that (again unsurprisingly) the leasehold does not have priority over any interest affecting the title of the lessor to grant the lease, s 12(6).

[27] Assuming 12 years' adverse possession has been completed prior to first registration, the interest will be an overriding interest if the adverse possessor is in actual occupation within the meaning of Schedule 1. In the unlikely event that the possessor is not in such occupation, then this provision ensures that the proprietor is bound if he has notice of the adverse possession, not being able to escape its consequences through his own act of first registration. Persons who have not completed 12 years' possession and thus are forced to apply under the new scheme are unlikely to acquire title given the way the scheme works.

[28] Registration with *qualified* or *possessory* title enjoys the same priority save that, for qualified title, the enforcement of a third-party interest excepted from the effect of registration is preserved. For possessory title, the priority of any interest affecting the estate at the time of registration is preserved. If absolute title to a leasehold is not possible (perhaps the superior freehold is not registered), then *good leasehold* is as strong as absolute title, save that registration does not secure priority over any matter affecting the title of the lessor to grant the lease.

These provisions are uncontroversial and are unlikely to give rise to serious difficulties. However, there are two points of note. First, the priority rule applies to all first registrants, irrespective of whether they were purchasers or donees of a gift. This is as it should be, given that (as explained above) first registration of title does not signify a change in ownership and should not change *pre-existing* priorities.[29] Second, however, the provisions on adverse possession may lead to an unexpected inconsistency. If, at first registration, an adverse possessor already has completed 12 years' adverse possession of the previous unregistered title, established common law principle means that he has a better title than the paper owner. This entitlement will override the first registered proprietor *if* the proprietor has notice (section 11) or if the adverse possessor is in actual occupation of the land sufficient to establish an overriding interest within para 2 Schedule 1. Of course, most adverse possessors will fall into one of these two groups. However, a claimant who has completed 12 years' adverse possession but is not within either of these provisions appears to have no priority over the first registered proprietor. The Act, surprisingly perhaps, contains no protection *per se* for the adverse possessor who had completed the period required for adverse possession while the land was unregistered, despite the general view that first registration should not alter pre-existing priorities.[30] This is peculiar, especially considering that, if the land were already registered when the adverse possessor completed 12 years' adverse possession and this occurred before the entry into force of the Act,[31] the adverse possessor *would* have a right to be registered as proprietor against the existing proprietor without having to chance the new machinery specified in Schedule 6 to the Act.[32] It is surprising that priorities gained by an adverse possessor against an existing owner prior to the Act are

---

[29] The applicant's relative priority would already have been decided when they acquired the title under the rules of unregistered conveyancing. It would have mattered at that time whether they gave value or not. In the same way, any adverse rights granted by the first registered proprietor before registration will continue to be effective against that proprietor after registration, whether otherwise protected or not, simply because a grantor cannot derogate from his own grant. Thus, an option which is unregistered but granted by the first registered proprietor remains effective after registration against that proprietor, as would merely personal rights. It is only on a subsequent disposition that these rights might lose their priority.

[30] If the registered proprietor disposed of the estate despite the fact of 12 years' possession being completed before 13 October 2003, the new proprietor is bound only if the interest is one which overrides within Schedule 3 (discoverable actual occupation).

[31] If 12 years has not been completed by the time the Act entered force, then the issue is immaterial because in such cases the Act provides that the adverse possessor merely may apply to be registered, thus triggering the provisions of Schedule 6. The likely outcome is objection by the registered proprietor and an end to the adverse possession.

[32] Schedule 12, para 18(1). This preserves existing priorities. However, if the existing proprietor transfers the estate, the adverse possessor who completed 12 years before the Act will not have priority over a transferee for value unless in actual occupation.

preserved if the land is already registered, but not if it is unregistered. It has been suggested that an adverse possessor finding themselves in such a situation at first registration (admittedly rarely) would be able to apply for rectification of the register, presumably on the ground that there is a mistake in the register because the applicant for first registration actually had no title to register.[33] This would at least be consistent with the view that first registration should not change existing priorities. However, the ability to rectify in such circumstances is untested and the legislation concerning priorities does seem clear and unequivocal. Sections 11 and 12 are categorical that a first registered proprietor takes the land 'subject only' to the matters specified therein.

2. Registered dispositions: dealings

The great strength of the priority rules in the 2002 Act as they apply to registered dispositions of registered titles[34] – which of course will form the bulk of dealings with commercial and residential property – is that they are simplified and self-contained. The *basic rule* found in section 28 and operating as a default is that all pre-existing third-party proprietary rights will take priority over a registered disposition simply because they pre-date the estate registered. However, this basic rule will give way to the *special priority rule* found in section 29 LRA 2002 if the disponee is a purchaser, as will be the case in the majority of transactions.[35] This has the double merit of making it clear that, absent a purchaser under a registered disposition, there is nothing to debate save the pre-existence of the third party's property right,[36] but also that a purchaser is in a special, privileged position because he gives value.[37] The special rule is that a purchaser who completes the registration of their sale, lease or mortgage[38] will have priority over all pre-existing rights in existence at the time of registration[39] *except* for a valid interest which is protected by a Notice or other entry on the register, or which is a valid registered charge, or which is unregistered but overrides under

---

[33] In much the same way that the grantor of a right is bound by it irrespective of the LRA 2002.

[34] For example, sales, leases, mortgages.

[35] Testamentary devises are likely to be the most common non-purchase transfers.

[36] Thus, if the purchaser takes only an equitable interest, there is no need to ask whether the 'equities are equal' as the prior right has priority. Likewise, if there is no purchase or the purchase is not completed by registration: see *Sainsbury's Ltd* v *Olympia Homes Ltd* [2005] EWHC 1235 (Ch) [2005] Conv 447.

[37] Professional advisers might well choose to construct transactions as purchases in order to take advantage of this special rule. In case this is thought improper, see the notorious *Midland Bank Trust Co v Green* [1981] AC 513.

[38] This includes the granting of non-registrable legal leases for seven years or less, s 29(4) LRA 2002.

[39] Rights arising subsequently cannot have priority over the registered proprietor unless he granted them.

Schedule 3, or which is excepted from the effects of registration.[40] Putting aside the last of these,[41] in simple terms, in order to have priority against a purchaser, a third-party interest must either be protected by an entry on the register or fall within Schedule 3 as an interest which overrides.

It is clear that this is meant to be a simple and all-encompassing system of statutory priority. A purchaser is meant to be able to take a conveyance of an interest in the land – eventually an e-conveyance – with the certainty that by inspecting the register (and lease where appropriate) and making sensible enquiries to discover Schedule 3 overriding interests, he will not be affected by the priority of any third-party interest of which he was unaware. Once again, of course, this is an expression of the 2002 Act's fundamental tenet that there must be transactional certainty in an e-conveyancing climate. Nevertheless, the re-drafting of the provisions concerning overriding interests in order to support this goal is not entirely uncontroversial and there may well be problems in the application and interpretation of Schedule 3. These are discussed below, but before that we need to appreciate the significance of expressing the relationship of purchaser and third party as one of 'priority' rather than absolute supremacy.

It will be remembered that under the 1925 Act, the equivalent provision declared that a purchaser took the estate 'free from all other estates and interests whatsoever' unless protected by an entry on the register or as an overriding interest.[42] This was regarded as a voidness rule as there was no doubt that an unprotected interest could not survive a transfer of the burdened estate to a purchaser. Under the 2002 Act, an unprotected interest (that is one neither registered nor within Schedule 3) is *postponed* to the interest under the disposition. It is not declared void and the Act is equivocal in a way that the 1925 legislation was not. The very clear meaning is that the unprotected third-party right remains valid, in the sense of existing in relation to the land, but that it cannot be exercised against the interest of the purchaser if he has duly completed a registered disposition. It means also that the postponed interest *can* be exercised against an interest (ie a person with such an interest) that does not benefit from the priority rule. There are good reasons for this, but also a potential problem.

By expressing the priority rule in terms of postponement rather than voidness, section 29 makes it clear that there are a number of legitimate circumstances when the third party's postponed right should not lose its enforceability, and of

---

[40] Or, in respect of leaseholds, is a burden incidental to the estate.

[41] The 'excepted interests' are a very minor hangover (possibly now defunct) arising from dealings with qualified title.

[42] Sections 20 and 23 LRA 1925.

course it can retain enforceability only if it is not void despite the registered disposition. For example, if the registered proprietor of a freehold (R) enters into a restrictive covenant with X, but X fails to protect the covenant by registration,[43] when R grants a 10-year lease by registered disposition to Y, Y has priority over the covenant and it cannot restrain his use. However, when the lease expires, X may enforce the covenant against R because it is no longer postponed to the 'interest under the disposition' – the lease.[44] Likewise, if a mortgagee (M) takes a registered charge over H's freehold, the mortgagee will have priority over W, a co-owner by constructive trust who is *not* in discoverable actual occupation within Schedule 3,[45] but if the mortgage is redeemed, or the security is realized through sale and possession, W continues to be able to assert her interest against H or the balance of the proceeds of any sale. Of course, in both of these cases, it might be thought that the effect of the priority rule is easily explained because the purchasers (Y and M) can be seen to be purchasing a *different* interest from that which the registered proprietor held and thus it seems appropriate that the third-party interest should not be void against the original proprietor. In this sense, to express the rule in terms of postponement and priority merely confirms the position under the 1925 Act because it reflects the requirements of the general law. It might even be thought that the continued existence of the claims in such cases can be explained because they are enforceable *in personam* against the grantor or constructive trustee, rather than that the interests themselves retain proprietary character: that is, a grantor cannot escape from their own grant.

However, this analysis does not cover all cases. Assume that R grants the same restrictive covenant to X, which is again unprotected, but later R sells the freehold to P by registered disposition. The covenant is unenforceable against P because P has priority and the covenant is postponed to the interest under the disposition – section 29 LRA 2002. What happens, however, if P sells the land to P2, but in the interim X has registered the covenant? At the time of registration of the second sale, the covenant appears to be protected and, having been merely postponed rather than voided, was not destroyed by the first sale. A literal reading of section 29 would suggest that the covenant now binds P2. This may not be a problem for P2, who would have discovered the covenant by inspecting the register, but it may well be for P whose sees the value of his land diminished when

---

[43] Protection should be by Notice and although overriding status under Schedule 3 para 2 (actual occupation) is not inconceivable, it is hardly likely.

[44] In addition, of course, R was the grantor so there is contractual liability.

[45] Such interests may not be the subject of a Notice, section 33 LRA 2002.

he tries to sell to P2 because of the restrictive covenant.[46] It might be objected that the Land Registry would not entertain the registration of a Notice in such circumstances, or at least would remove it following an objection from P, but it is not clear on what grounds this could occur because the covenant does exist – it is merely postponed.[47] Likewise, even if the covenant remains unregistered – either because no application to register is made, or one is made and refused – if P then *gives* the land to G, or dies and devises the land to B by will, a literal reading of section 28 would suggest that both G and B would be bound by the covenant because they are not purchasers and the covenant pre-dates their interests and was only 'postponed' by the earlier sale to P.

At present, of course, these remain hypothetical problems, but there is little doubt that section 29 will be an issue in litigation in due course. One interpretation that would avoid the problem identified above and effectively treat an unregistered interest as becoming void on the occasion of a sale is to argue that a purchaser with priority (in these examples P) transfers to a further disponee only that estate which he held, whether by sale or gift or inheritance. As such, the disponee receives that which the purchaser had – an estate with priority. This is, of course, to accept that titles remain relative rather than absolute – a view generally eschewed by the LRA 2002 – but it would appear to be the only solution if we wish to avoid the unfortunate consequences that could follow from regarding the 'special' position of a purchaser literally as one merely of priority.

C. Interests Which Override

It is not the purpose of this analysis to rehearse the arguments in favour of, or against, retaining a category of non-registered but binding property rights in a system of registered title. Suffice to say that this author believes that there are powerful policy arguments in favour of ensuring that some pre-existing rights bind all transferees of land irrespective of registration. The more pertinent question, given the law we have and the policy of the LRA 2002, is where to draw the line and which interests to exclude from such protection. To that end, it is necessary to examine whether the alleged reduction of overriding interests by the LRA 2002 (particularly in Schedule 3) will make a significant difference in practice to the operation of the registered land system. The apparent narrowing of the scope of overriding interests is a much lauded aspect of the 2002 Act – at least from

---

[46] P, of course, paid a price for the land as if it were not burdened by covenant. If the covenant was against building, the difference in values would be severe.

[47] It could be argued that the covenant should not be registered because it is unenforceable against P, but the point of registration is not to make it enforceable against P but against P2.

those who see overriding interests as a threat to security of title and e-conveyancing – but it is not at all clear that there were significant problems in this regard or that the 'solutions' will make much practical difference.

1. Exclusions

Schedules 1 and 3 exclude from overriding status a number of matters that would have overrode under the old law, save that generally if a person already held an overriding interest on 13 October 2003 (the entry into force of the LRA 2002), that status will continue. Rights which no longer qualify for automatic protection include: the rights of adverse possessors per se; the rights of a person in receipt of rents and profits; equitable easements and profits; in rare cases impliedly created legal easements;[48] and three types of short legal lease.[49] In reality, however, none of these is problematic and barely caused problems under the old law. Some concern has been expressed above about adverse possessors out of occupation, but most are likely to be in actual occupation within the meaning of the Schedule and their entitlement or accrued rights are likely to be protected for that reason. Likewise, not only are equitable easements and profits relatively rare, the intention in 1925 was that they should be registered in order to be protected and so the LRA 2002 merely returns the situation to one of orthodoxy by effectively reversing *Celsteel v Alton*.[50] The removal of the overriding status of the rights of persons in receipt of rent and profits (not also being persons in actual occupation) could affect some intermediate landlords under a head lease, as might the removal of overriding status for the special (and rare) short leases. Yet again, however, both rights commonly arise in situations where it is very likely that professional advice has been taken and registration of the interest by means of a Notice will be very normal. Finally, there may be some surprise that in certain situations impliedly created legal easements will not enjoy overriding status, for that seems to cut against our notion that legal rights are pretty well indestructible.[51] As we shall see, however, it may be that this exclusion is more apparent than real and, in any event, very few transactions taken under competent advice will generate impliedly created legal easements.[52]

---

[48] See below text accompanying footnote 53.

[49] A reversionary lease takes effect more than three months after granted, a lease granted out of right-to-buy legislation, and certain leases granted to former secure tenants under preserved right to buy.

[50] [1985] 2 All ER 562.

[51] Expressly created easements may be 'legal' only if entered on the register and so, by definition, will be protected by the register entry. If they are not so registered, they default to equitable status, s 27 LRA 2002.

[52] Their creation should be excluded by the terms of any (every!) conveyance. The exception may be future prescriptive easements.

In other words, while it is true that a number of matters have been excluded from overriding status where previously they were included within the old section 70(1) LRA 1925, in reality we will have to search hard to find anyone adversely affected by these changes.

2. Re-defining overriding interests

The 2002 Act re-defines the old conception of overriding interests in three areas, although once again interests which overrode before the Act came into force generally are not affected.[53] First, it is now the case that only legal leases for seven years or less will override, but this is no more than the counterpart to the rule that legal leases over seven years must be registered with their own title. There is no real problem here, although it is true that lawyers are advising clients to grant business leases of no longer than seven years in order to avoid compulsory registration.[54] Second, it is no longer true that every circumstance in which a person is in 'actual occupation' will trigger overriding status for that person's interest. This requires a fuller analysis as it is important to appreciate that this change does appear to rebalance priorities in favour of a purchaser when compared with the position under the LRA 1925.

In respect of a first registration of title, Schedule 1 provides simply that a person's interest shall override by reason of actual occupation, so far as relating to the land occupied and excluding an interest arising under the Settled Land Act 1925.[55] The exclusion of rights under settlements mirrors the LRA 1925,[56] but there is an additional condition which reverses the decision in *Ferrishurst v Wallcite*[57] by restricting the priority of the claimant's right to the land they actually do occupy.[58] In reality, this is but a small matter, again affecting very few interests, and in substance Schedule 1 mirrors the position under the old law. For dealings with a registered estate, however, Schedule 3 para 2 appears to make some substantive changes of more significance. As well as incorporating the exclusion of

---

[53] There are other relatively minor changes to the operation of overriding interests not dealt with elsewhere in this chapter. We should note that the very special and uncommon interests specified in paras 10–14 and 16 LRA 2002 will override for 10 years only from the entry into force of the statute. During this time, they must be entered on the register to ensure their priority against a future purchaser. No fee will be charged.

[54] There seems to be no reason for this, other than to avoid the extra fees (surely often passed on to the tenant?) and extra work. A rational reason would be to avoid disclosure of the terms of the lease to other tenants in multi-unit developments where different tenants may have negotiated different terms.

[55] Schedule 1, para 2.

[56] Section 86(2) LRA 1925.

[57] [1999] 2 WLR 667.

[58] Thus occupation of one flat in a building would give priority to the rights over that flat but not the entire building; see *Ferrishurst*.

settlement interests and the reversal of *Ferrishurst*,[59] Schedule 3 provides that actual occupation does *not* give rise to overriding status unless either the actual occupation would have been obvious on a reasonably careful inspection of the land prior to the disposition, or (assuming actual occupation) the disponee has actual knowledge of the interest for which protection is claimed. The point of these changes is, of course, to protect the purchaser from interests about which he was not aware or could not suspect. This seems perfectly reasonable, especially as there is no requirement that a purchaser should actually inspect (although a prudent one will), and no escape if the purchaser inspected and did not discover the occupation if he should have.

The test is objective. However, there are concerns. First, we might disagree fundamentally with the policy that weighs the scales in favour of the purchaser in this manner. It is *not* axiomatic that a purchaser *should* prevail over an occupier simply because the occupier (or his interest) was undiscoverable. We might think that there are some interests worthy of priority irrespective of whether the purchaser was aware of them.[60] The 2002 Act here appears to take a different view, but it remains to be seen whether in the interpretation of this legislation the judiciary holds firm to a pro-purchaser policy. The history of the 1925 property Acts is replete with examples of constructive interpretation that appears to thwart the purpose of the legislation in order to achieve a result more consonant with social or economic needs.[61] Second, the Schedule does not permit consideration of *why* the right holder may have been undiscoverable in her occupation. If the right holder has hidden themselves away, few would argue that we should protect the purchaser, but what if the undiscoverability of the occupier is because of action – innocent or otherwise – by a third party? In *Chhokkar v Chhokkar*, the reason for the purchaser's inability to discover the right holder had nothing to do with Mrs Chhokkar and everything to do with the seller who hid all evidence of her existence.[62] It is unfortunate that the reasons for any 'undiscoverability' are not overtly relevant in deciding questions under Schedule 3 para 2, although we can speculate that Chancery judges might well silently consider

---

[59] In addition, there is no overriding status if the right holder fails to disclose their interest in response to an enquiry, when it is reasonable to so disclose. This seeks to mirror the position under the 1925 Act, but it raises the tantalising prospect that it is sometimes legitimate to conceal an interest from a purchaser when questioned. The paragraph implies that there are circumstances when it is reasonable not to disclose if asked and so overriding status can be retained despite the purchaser being misled by the right holder.

[60] The Act accepts this with respect to the other, relatively low-impact overriding interests specified in paras 10–14 and 16 of Schedule 3.

[61] For example, s 34(2) LPA 1925 does not seem to support the imposition of a trust in cases of implied co-ownership and there is always *Celsteel v Alton*.

[62] It was, of course, the seller who stood to gain from a trouble-free sale.

them when applying the Schedule to the facts of the case before them. Third, we do not know yet when the disponee will be taken to have 'actual knowledge' of the interest, or what amounts to 'a reasonably careful inspection' so as to render the occupation undiscoverable. These are not conceptually certain phrases and the only way to clarify the meaning of para 2 Schedule 3 is through judicial interpretation. In this sense, the law change generates uncertainty and will generate litigation as parties – mainly purchasers – seek to avoid overriding interests by arguing that they have escaped Schedule 3. Previously, there was little or no room for argument and no convincing evidence that this certainty was causing any practical difficulties. There are very few reported cases under the old law where a purchaser was caught by an *undiscoverable* overriding interest (as opposed to one that was undiscovered)[63] and it is difficult to see why it was necessary to do anything at all. Undoubtedly, it fits well with the ethos of the LRA 2002 and it 'solves' one of the 'problems' caused by the existence of overriding interests, but there is the suspicion that this is the triumph of form over substance. All in all, it may well be that this re-definition of the 'actual occupation' provision has been for little practical effect, except to introduce uncertainty and generate litigation. This is not in the interests of purchasers, especially mortgagees who can deal with most eventualities provided the law is clear.

The third substantive issue around Schedule 3 concerns the treatment of impliedly granted legal easements and profits.[64] As we have seen, equitable easements are required to be registered to achieve priority over a purchaser of a registered estate[65] and all new expressly created legal easements will by definition have been entered on the register.[66] Easements created by prescription, or implied into a conveyance through necessity, common intention, the rule in *Wheeldon v Burrows* or section 62 of the LPA 1925 may be substantively registered,[67] but also can qualify for overriding status under para 3 of Schedule 3.[68] Once again, however, the matter is not straightforward and since 13 October 2006,[69] implied

---

[63] None is cited by the Law Commission and this author has found four or five. See *The Reform of Property Law and the Land Registration Act 2002: A Risk Assessment,* chapter 6 in *New Perspectives on Property Law, Obligations and Restitution,* edited by A Hudson (Cavendish Publishing, 2004) or also at [2003] 67 The Conveyancer & Property Lawyer p 136.

[64] The analysis will concentrate on easements, as there are doubts about the precise circumstances (if at all) in which profits can be impliedly created. Examples are rare.

[65] Unless they were overriding when the 2002 Act came into force.

[66] Else they will be equitable, s 27 LRA 2002. Note that expressly created legal easements in short leases are required to be registered, even though the lease (being for seven years or less) is not.

[67] For example, after being disclosed on an application for registration of the burdened estate.

[68] They also qualify under Schedule 1 para 3 at first registration, save that the problematic extra conditions applicable to Schedule 3 do not apply.

[69] A three-year transitional period expired on this date during which all impliedly granted legal easements were protected.

legal easements will override only if they satisfy one of the additional conditions found in the Schedule. Unfortunately, this paragraph has not been drafted with the reader in mind and it is not so much impenetrable as indecipherable. It is meant to provide[70] that impliedly granted legal easements will override if, but only if: they are registered under the Commons Registration Act 1965; or they have been 'exercised' at any time within one year prior to the transfer over which priority is claimed; or they would have been obvious on a reasonably careful inspection of the burdened land; or they are within the actual knowledge of the disponee. A careful reading of the paragraph may well reveal this meaning (on a good day), but putting aside this concern in the hope that courts will interpret the paragraph in the light of its intended purpose, there remain two issues. First, once again we have questions of interpretation that can be settled only by litigation. What is 'actual knowledge', how extensive must use of the easement have been to qualify as 'exercised' and what is 'obvious on a reasonably careful inspection'? Second, actually it is quite difficult to think of situations when an impliedly granted easement would *not* qualify under this paragraph. Commons Act Registration is a specialist matter, but at least one of the other three conditions is likely to be satisfied as a matter of course. No doubt, there could be a case outside of the provision – perhaps even within the next 50 years – and one could invent scenarios in order to illustrate how the provision would work. But the reality is that it is hard to see what type of easement is going to fall out of overriding status because of these provisions – not only because the provision encompasses virtually all impliedly granted easements, but because impliedly granted easements are rare anyway. The point may well be that the legislation will protect a purchaser in rare cases, but we should ask why it was necessary to go to these lengths, with such a complex provision, which has abandoned certainty, in order to protect the 'once in a blue moon purchaser'. It cannot be in the general interest for parties to have to litigate simply to clarify a provision which in the vast majority of cases will lead to the same result as that which existed under the 1925 Act.

D. Protected Interests

As has been discussed above, registration by means of the entry of a Notice on the register of title is intended to become the default mechanism for protecting third-party rights. It is already true that some third-party rights cannot exist as legal interests without such registration,[71] and by virtue of section 93 LRA 2002,

---

[70] See Law Commission Report 271 para 8.23 et seq.

[71] For example, expressly created profits and easements, even if contained in unregistrable dispositions such as short leases.

when e-conveyancing is in operation fully, many interests will not exist *at all* unless entered on the register at the time of creation.[72] When combined with the duty of disclosure, the registrar's power to enter Notices and the reduction in the number and extent of overriding interests (even if this is not as substantial as might first appear), it is clear that the 2002 Act does indeed signal a sea change in the deliberate protection of third-party rights.[73] There is no concept of 'minor interest' in the 2002 Act and this is perfectly in accord with both the philosophy and the reality of the legislation. Similarly, the process of registering third-party rights has been simplified and the effects of registration have been clarified. Of course, there are circumstances in which a registrant can 'play the system' by opting for a Unilateral Notice instead of the Agreed variety and thereby defeat the public information aspects of the legislation, but this is a small point and may not prove significant if the 'exempt document' provisions are applied sympathetically to protect applicants' legitimate commercial concerns. Further, while there is no convincing evidence from the 1925 Act that spite or fraudulent registrations are common, s 77 (1)(b) LRA 2002 provides that the *application* for entry of a Notice must be made with reasonable cause. All in all, therefore, the Act can be regarded as providing successfully for the efficient and effective deliberate protection of third-party interests. It may even be, as the Law Commission hopes, that this will reduce the impact of overriding interests as property professionals come to appreciate the value and simplicity of disclosing and registering third-party interests.

E. Conclusion

The Land Registration Act 2002 deploys numerous strategies in relation to third-party interests in land. Most of these are transaction oriented, in the sense that they are designed to protect a purchaser from any right that he could not have discovered by inspecting the register or making reasonable inspections and enquiries. When coupled with the certainty of protection for an adverse interest when it is registered, the paramount aim is to create a climate in which e-conveyancing can flourish. The main challenge in this regard has been overriding interests, and the Act tackles this by downplaying their significance as a feature of the land registration system and by apparently minimizing their impact

---

[72] Thus, for many third-party rights, there will be no distinction between 'legal' and 'equitable' interests because the only valid interest will be one created by registration. According to s 93, transactions specified for e-conveyancing 'only has effect' [sic] on such registration.

[73] Certain rights are excluded from protection by means of a Notice – s 33 LRA 2002. Even here, however, there is consistency because such rights are either protectable by well-established other means, or are within discoverable overriding interests, or will not defeat a purchaser who overreaches.

in practice. Indeed, the public relations was impressive and on paper the Act does seem to achieve this. However, it is arguable that most of the changes made to the definition and scope of overriding interests is marginal and cosmetic. Some third-party rights are indeed excluded, but they are not common. Some will cease to override over a period of time, but they are anachronistic and rarely oppressive.[74] For the remainder of the reforms, the jury remains hung. It may be that the reforms of the LRA 2002 will result in a radically different system in terms of protecting third-party interests, but if at all, this is on a long, slow fuse.

---

[74] It may be otherwise with chancel repair liabilities, *Aston Cantlow* v *Wallbank* [2003] 3 WLR 283.

3

COMMUNITY OF PROPERTY, JOINT OWNERSHIP, AND THE FAMILY HOME

Elizabeth Cooke

A. Introduction

Consider two generalizations.

In 1955 Otto Kahn-Freund remarked:

> Since in our societies, marriage is the basis for the normal family, it follows that marriage must have a profound effect on the property of the spouse . . . It is difficult to imagine any system of law which in its regulation of the impact of marriage on property could completely ignore these elementary social facts, i.e. confine itself to a strict rule of 'separation of property' in the sense that marriage has no effect on the property of the spouses at all.[1]

Grace Blumberg, in her Californian text on matrimonial property, 2003, states:

> In the western world, the basic ownership unity has been the conjugal, or husband – wife, dyad. Apparently rooted in Germanic and Visigothic law, community property principles spread all over Europe and many of the areas colonized by Europeans, such as South Africa and Latin America.[2]

These statements sound very unfamiliar to an English lawyer. Why can English law not cope with the idea that marriage might have a profound effect – or any effect – on the property of a spouse?[3] How does marriage affect property rights in other jurisdictions? And why is everyone out of step except us?

---

[1] O Kahn-Freund, 'Matrimonial Property Law in England' in W Friedmann (ed), *Matrimonial Property Law* (Toronto: Stevens & Sons, 1955) 267–8.

[2] G G Blumberg, *Community Property in California* (4th edn, New York: Aspen, 2004), 1. A funny linguistic quirk is that Americans speak of 'community property' whereas Europeans refer to 'community *of* property'.

[3] It has none, save that property rights are in issue on divorce and on death.

This chapter attempts to answer some of those questions, and in doing so explores two areas: first, the European systems of community of property, and second, the recurrent proposals that English law should be reformed so as to provide for automatic joint ownership of the family home (this is not the same as community of property, as will be seen).

In doing so, the writer draws on material from a project funded by the Nuffield Foundation, entitled 'Community of Property: a regime for England and Wales'.[4] The project set out to examine European community of property regimes primarily with a view to gaining insights which might assist with the reform of the very troubled law relating to family property in this country. The aim was to cast light, if possible, upon the law relating to financial provision on divorce – in a state of flux as usual – and also upon the formulation of provisions for financial relief on the breakdown of cohabitation, in the hands of the Law Commission at the time of writing. The final findings of the project are presented in *Community of Property: a regime for England and Wales*.[5]

This chapter, however, is about land law, because what we have discovered in the course of the project has sparked reflections, both technical and substantive, about the way we organize ownership, joint ownership, and family property. It is suggested that in comparison with community of property, English law's concept of joint ownership is very weak; this may be what we want, but it is worth being aware of alternative approaches. More importantly, it is suggested that choices made in 1925 and throughout the twentieth century about the structure of co-ownership and the nature of registration would make it very difficult to move to a position where marriage, or any other relationship, could by itself have an effect upon property ownership. This is disturbing because it sets us apart from our European neighbours.[6] And it is the source of misunderstanding, because

---

[4] The team members are the writer, Professor Anne Barlow (University of Exeter), Dr Therese Callus (University of Reading), with research assistants Augustina Akoto and Peter Petkoff. I gratefully acknowledge their research, and their influence upon the thinking in this chapter. An earlier version of it was delivered as a paper to the Property and Trusts section of the Society of Legal Scholars at its conference at the University of Strathclyde in September 2005.

    More information about this project can be found at <http://www.rdg.ac.uk/law/research/cooke-cttyprop.htm>; readers are particularly referred to the writer's translation, to be found at that web address, of J Bernard, *Choisir son contrat de marriage*, 2002; one of the series: *Les memos: conseils par des notaires*, which is a very helpful summary of the various options available in France.

[5] E Cooke, A Barlow, T Callus (Bristol: The Nuffield Foundation, 2006). Copies are available free of charge thanks to the Nuffield Foundation's funding and can be obtained on request to e.j.cooke@reading.ac.uk; a pdf version is available at the website referred to in n 4 above. There is inevitably duplication between this paper and chapter 3 of that report.

[6] The distinctiveness of English matrimonial property law are causing considerable problems for the European Commission's efforts to harmonize rules of private international law; see the Green Paper on matrimonial property regimes COM (2006) 400 published in July 2006.

many people in this jurisdiction think that marriage does affect property ownership, and many members of the public who know that it does not, think that it
should do so.

B. Community of Property

Community of property systems come in two forms, immediate and deferred.
When a legal system operates immediate community of property, this means that
at the point of marriage or registered partnership, some or all of the property of
the couple becomes community property. Thereafter, until the dissolution of the
community, the property is owned jointly by the couple (regardless of paper or
registered title). When the community is dissolved by divorce or by death, the
community is split 50/50, and there is very little discretion to vary this.[7]

Deferred community of property, by contrast, has no effect upon property rights
within marriage; couples retain separate ownership of their assets as they do in this
jurisdiction.[8] But at the point when divorce occurs or the partnership ends,
some or all of their property is treated as community property and, as in the
immediate systems, divided equally. Deferred community of property creates
rights *in personam*, obligations rather than property rights, and is not discussed
further in this chapter (although its relevance to English law in the light of recent
developments, and in particular the case law about equal division of matrimonial property following *White v White*,[9] will be obvious to those familiar with
family law).

Immediate community is found in The Netherlands, France, Belgium and a
number of other European jurisdictions,[10] as well as in South Africa and eight
American states.[11] The jurisdictions differ as to how much property the community encompasses. Most regimes catch property acquired after the marriage
(hence the name of the French regime, *communauté réduite aux acquests*), and
most but not all exclude property acquired by gift or inheritance after marriage.
The Netherlands includes absolutely everything owned by the two individuals,
before or after the marriage; the South African system is almost as comprehensive.

---

[7] The availability of discretionary variation differs between jurisdictions, and is seen particularly
in the Nordic jurisdictions, but is in any event limited. On the Nordic and German community
systems, see J Scherpe, 'Pre-nuptial agreements in Europe' [2007] *International Family Law*.

[8] This includes the ability to own assets jointly out of choice; as we shall see, this is not the same
as owning them in community of property.

[9] [2001] AC 596.

[10] Austria, Italy, Portugal, Spain.

[11] These are the states that took their legal system from Spain rather than from the common law,
as a result of their colonial origins.

For the rest of this chapter, the phrase 'community of property' is used to refer to the immediate community regimes.

The community regimes – both deferred and immediate – are default systems, in the sense that they operate upon the couple's property unless they opt out by contract, before or during the marriage or partnership.[12] Contracting out is controlled, in a number of senses. Thus in most European jurisdictions[13] a pre-nuptial contract has to be notarized, which means that it is scrutinized and validated by a notary; in some jurisdictions, contracting out during the marriage actually requires scrutiny by the court.[14] In some countries there is freedom – subject to the scrutiny just mentioned – to contract into whatever regime, including separation of property, the couple may choose;[15] in some, there is a limited range of options.[16]

C. Community of Property and its Impact upon Creditors

The writer recalls a friend, of her mother's generation, who had been a housewife and homemaker throughout her married life, saying, 'I have nothing, except what my husband gives me.' This is the inevitable consequence of the traditional housewife marriage: it is encapsulated in Sir Jocelyn Simon's famous aphorism:

> . . . the cock bird can feather the nest precisely because he does not have to spend most of his time sitting on it.[17]

---

[12] For convenience, this chapter will refer just to marriage from now on, but most European jurisdictions now have available a registered partnership system, and most apply to the registered partnership the same community regime applied to marriage, whether deferred or immediate (one exception is the French PaCS).

[13] But not the Nordic countries.

[14] For example in France: *Code civil* art. 1397; cf the Spanish civil code, article 1317.

[15] B Beignier, *Les régimes matrimoniaux* (Paris: puf, 1999), 4: 'Les régimes matrimoniaux ont plus de variétés que l'arc-en-ciel n'a de couleurs.' France is perhaps the most liberal of the community of property jurisdictions in allowing couples to create their own version of community, allowing them to vary the range of assets upon which it bites and the proportions in which the community is to be divided on death. Equally, couples may contract into separation of property; or into the German 'accruals' system whereby what is divided, at the end of the relationship, is the increase in each party's wealth during the marriage.

[16] South Africa: J A Robinson, S Human, A Boshoff, *Introduction to South African Family Law* (2002) 108–9. In some jurisdictions where the default regime is deferred community it is possible to contract into immediate community (eg Greece: C Hamilton, A Perry (eds) *Family Law in Europe* (London: Butterworths LexisNexis, 2002) 335; in others (eg Sweden) this is not an option.

[17] 'With all my Worldly Goods . . .', Holdsworth Club lecture, University of Birmingham, 20 March 1964, p 14.

This is the situation that community of property prevents.[18] It is based on the notion that the marriage relationship[19] has consequences in terms of property ownership. Jurisdictions that operate community of property as a default regime fall squarely into Kahn-Freund's model.[20]

The results of this can be quite startling. A Dutch lawyer we interviewed in the course of our research project gave the example of a client whose mother lent her money to buy a very expensive violin. The client was married, and so the violin, once purchased, became part of the community of property and was half her husband's.

More dramatic still is the effect of community of property on third parties.

Case A

> Henry and Wanda are married; they are joint owners of the family home. Henry fails to pay a huge business debt.

H and W are English.	*H and W are Dutch*
The creditor can obtain any of the usual enforcement orders, including a charging order against H's beneficial interest in the house – but Wanda's share of its value is safe.	*(or live in any other jurisdiction where the default regime is immediate community) and have not contracted out of the default regime.* The creditor can obtain [the local equivalent of] a charging order and claim the whole value of the house. The property is part of the community of property and therefore the whole of its value is available to meet debts contracted by either.

Take Henry and Wanda, married in England, joint owners of their family home. Henry contracts a huge business debt, which he cannot pay; his creditor sues him, obtains judgment for the debt, and obtains a charging order against the house. Because this is Henry's debt, the creditors can apply to the court for the

---

[18] A number of jurisdictions, in particular the Scandinavian countries, moved from immediate to deferred regimes as part of the process of the emancipation of women. This makes more sense now, when it is normal for mothers to be in employment, than perhaps it did in the 1920s, for example, when the change was effected in Sweden.
[19] Or registered partnership; see n 9 above.
[20] N 1 above.

house to be sold,[21] and may well succeed in getting an order for sale.[22] On sale, once any prior mortgage debt is paid, half the net proceeds, representing Henry's share, will be available to Henry's creditor to pay off the debt, but obviously Wanda's share is safe and Henry's creditor cannot touch it.

By contrast, under an immediate community regime, and assuming the family home is part of the community,[23] once any prior mortgagee is paid, the creditor can access the *whole* of the net proceeds to satisfy Henry's debt. The signature of one spouse engages the whole of the community and makes it available to meet a debt, and this is the case whether the individual items of property – land or whatever – were bought jointly or singly.[24]

Case B

> Henry and Wanda are married.
> The family home was bought in
> Wanda's name.
> Henry fails to pay a huge business debt.

H and W are English.	*H and W are Dutch*
The creditor can obtain any of the usual enforcement orders, but unless he can show that H has a beneficial interest in the house, cannot obtain a charging order against it; if H has an interest, the house is available to meet the debt but only to the extent of H's interest.	*(or live in any other jurisdiction where the default regime is immediate community) and have not contracted out of the default regime.* The creditor can claim the value of the house and obtain [the local equivalent of] a charging order. The property is jointly owned by virtue of the marriage *and* the whole of its value is available to meet debts contracted by either.

---

[21] Under sections 14 and 15 of the Trusts of Land and Appointment of Trustees Act 1996.

[22] Absent family circumstances, for example the presence of children, which may persuade the court not to order a sale for the time being: *Re Evers' Trust* [1980] 1 WLR 1327.

[23] This would be automatic in The Netherlands, where the default regime is one of universal community, but would be the case in France, under the default regime, only if the house was acquired after the marriage.

[24] See articles 1413 ff of the French *Code civil*; and this is the rule in all immediate community systems. For South Africa, see J A Robinson, S Human, A Boshoff, *Introduction to South African Family Law* (2002) 121 ff. California Family Code, section 910: 'Except as otherwise expressly provided by statute, the community estate is liable for a debt incurred by either spouse before or during marriage . . .'

Note that the same result follows if the house was purchased in Henry's name alone, or indeed in Wanda's name alone. Unless the couple has contracted out of the community regime operative by default in their jurisdiction, the house is part of the community of property, and is available to Henry's creditors.[25] Consider Case A and Case B, above, where the contrasting positions are set out.

Indeed, the availability of property as a source of credit is one of the objectives of community of property. Immediate community is a way of giving property to spouses who otherwise have nothing. It is explicitly designed as a protection for the economically weaker spouse, typically the housewife. It is intended to enable her to participate in the wealth built up by the husband. It gives her an entitlement to the family property on the death of her husband – aside from the inheritance to which she is automatically entitled under most European legal systems. It gives her a credit rating which she would otherwise not have.[26]

The corollary of this is that community of property carries a huge risk – if one spouse contracts a debt that cannot be paid, both, in effect, must pay it out of the family's resources. This property is *truly* joint, for richer for poorer, in (financial) sickness and in health. Therefore in a jurisdiction operating an immediate community of property regime, anyone running their own business will, if properly advised, contract out of the community regime and maintain separate assets (or opt into a deferred community regime), so as to safeguard their partner.

It is arguable therefore that community of property should be referred to, for the sake of clarity, as 'community of property and obligations', or perhaps even 'community of liability'. It is a way of enforcing the sharing of property and the sharing of liabilities – subject, of course, to contracting out.

This is not a family law paper and it is not the intention to go into the merits and demerits of community of property as a system of managing family wealth. Suffice it to say that the research project carried out by the writer and her colleagues into community of property did not, in its conclusions, recommend the adoption of immediate community of property in this jurisdiction;[27] there is no possibility of the community of liability aspect being found desirable or acceptable. Nevertheless, it is worth spending some time looking at community of property through a land

---

[25] Assuming, at the risk of labouring the point, that it is one of the items of property that are caught by the regime in question. It would be included in the community in The Netherlands; in France, if it was bought before the marriage it would remain Wanda's own property and not fall into the community.

[26] B Beignier, op cit n 15 above: for both spouses, community of property 'augmente sensible-ment leur crédit, ce qui au bout du compte est un bienfait'.

[27] See the project report, n 5 above, in particular ch 3.

lawyer's spectacles, as a form of joint ownership, and contrasting it with joint ownership as found in this jurisdiction.

D. Technical Contrasts

There is simply nothing like immediate community of property in English law; indeed, it took a while for the writer and the project team to realize just how different community of property is from our concept of joint ownership.

Blackstone referred to beneficial joint tenancy as a 'thorough and most intimate union of interest and possession'.[28] One feels that if this was Blackstone's idea of intimacy he may have been missing something; certainly the joint tenancy is nowhere near as joint or as intimate as community of property. The latter involves:

- community of obligations/liability
- no separate or severable share
- joint management and control of the property, so that neither owner can deal with the property separately.[29]

Thus there is no potential for a joint owner in community of property to dispose of his or her share of the property, in the way that an owner of land in joint tenancy can do (thereby creating a tenancy in common). The only way to effect such a severance would be to contract out of the community regime, wholly or partly, or to bring it to an end by divorce, or indeed to reach an agreement with one's partner to contract out of the community regime and into separation of property.

1. Inheritance

Community of property does *not*, however, involve the distinctive feature of the joint tenancy, namely the right of survivorship. Indeed, it occurs in jurisdictions which do not give complete testamentary freedom. Death brings the community

---

[28] W Blackstone, *Commentaries on the Laws of England* (1st edn, London 1765–1769) Vol II, p 182.

[29] In most European jurisdictions there are restrictions upon a sole owner's power to deal with the family home even where there is no community regime or where the home happens to fall outside the community. Thus in France even a sole owner of the family home, ie where the home is not part of the community, nevertheless cannot dispose of it without his or her spouse's consent, and dispositions made without consent are voidable for a year thereafter: *Code civil* art 215. The corresponding protection for spouses in English law is weak, being dependent upon registration (Family Law Act 1996, s 30); on this see the recommendations in ch 5 of the community of property project report, n 5 above.

to an end; on Henry's death, a French Wanda would be entitled to her half of the community, plus that share of Henry's estate (his separate property plus his half of the community) to which she is entitled by law,[30] but depending upon the presence or absence of children, other relatives would have an entitlement to the rest of Henry's estate.[31]

A recent innovation in California is CPWROS – 'community property[32] with right of survivorship' – which combines joint tenancy with community of property. This seems to have been introduced by popular demand, because of the helpful feature of joint tenancy as the 'poor man's will'; there was a wish to combine community of property – very much the norm for married couples, despite the risk associated with it, and very much ideologically valued – with the ability to transmit property to a surviving spouse without the need to make a will.[33]

2. Community of property, civil law and common law

As an aside, but still looking at the mechanics of community of property: how does community of property come to exist in the US? It is, of course, a civil law concept; it is found in eight US states whose legal heritage derives as much from Spain as from England and which were therefore in a position to pick and choose elements from each. They operate a largely common law system of land law; and, of course, there is no 1925 legislation in these states. Thus legal tenancy in common remains an option and co-ownership does not automatically give rise to a trust. Community of property[34] is simply a further option, alongside joint tenancy and tenancy in common. The US states offer rather more flexibility in contracting out of the community regime than do the European jurisdictions, and a married couple can choose to take a jointly owned property on any of these bases without going through the rigmarole of changing their marital regime. Among the motives for owning in community of property are taxation on death – community of property offers a significant capital gains tax advantage.[35]

---

[30] Note that recent reforms have made the French system much more generous to the surviving spouse: *loi du 3 décembre 2001*.

[31] Yet another quirk is that in France, it is possible to construct a community regime in which the proportions into which the property is divided on death are varied. It is possible to contract for a regime in which the community is divided 75/25, or even 100/0, on death. In that event, there is effectively a *ius accrescendi*.

[32] As the Americans say.

[33] California Civil Code 682.1.

[34] Or CPWROS in California.

[35] Where land is owned in community of property the entire value is re-based on death; where it is owned in joint tenancy or as tenants in common, only the deceased's half is re-based.

3. Registration

If we think about the consequences of community of property for a registration system, we find a contrast in terms of information, and another contrast in terms of purchaser protection.

First, then, while community of property does not actually require a particular form of land registration, it sits more happily with non-English and non-Torrens systems. In Case A above, joint ownership is obvious from the documentary title to the property. It is not at all obvious in Case B. Community of property there-fore involves a more flexible view of registration than the one prevalent in the English and Torrens registration systems; it involves an acceptance that the regis-ter may not tell the whole story.

This is not perceived as a problem in European registration systems. One reason is that title registration systems generally follow the German model and are nega-tive rather than positive. This means that registration does not automatically confer title, for example after a void transfer; there is no equivalent of section 58 of the Land Registration Act 2002.[36] Another reason is that a surprising (to us) number of European jurisdictions operate systems of deeds registration rather than of title registration. Thus France and The Netherlands have deeds registra-tion systems; so does South Africa; so do all the US states. One of the features of deeds registration is that one has to accept that changes in title not effected by registrable deeds are not apparent from the register.[37] In most such systems there is protection for purchasers in good faith inadvertently purchasing property sold wrongfully without the concurrence of a spouse – although equally, there is an expectation in community of property systems that purchasers check the marital status of vendors. In some jurisdictions nuptial contracts are entered on the land register for the protection of lenders.

That takes us to the second point of contrast. The effect of community of prop-erty in the registration system has a completely different dynamic from that found in the interaction of ordinary joint ownership with registration. The emphasis in the latter system is upon protecting purchasers from unexpected joint ownership. For if an apparent sole owner is in fact a joint owner in equity, then he has less security to offer than would appear, and is a far less good risk than the register appeared to indicate.[38]

---

[36] One of the best explanations of this is the recent paper by the Scottish Law Commission, *Discussion Paper on Land Registration: Void and Voidable Titles* Discussion Paper No 125 (Edinburgh, The Stationery Office, 2004); discussed by E Cooke at [2004] Conv 482.

[37] E Cooke, *The New Law of Land Registration* (Oxford: Hart Publishing, 2002) 18 ff.

[38] The very basics of *William and Glyn's Bank Ltd v Boland* [1981] AC 487.

By contrast, in a community of property jurisdiction, the risk to creditors arises from a marriage *out* of community, where a pre- or post-nuptial contract excludes the community regime. In that instance, the property of a married couple which looks as if it is owned in community and therefore available in its entirety to a creditor is in fact only partially available. Hence the need for protection arises not from the *presence* of co-ownership but from the *absence* of community; hence the provision in some countries for nuptial contracts to be noted on the land register.[39]

E. Policy Contrasts

Why has community of property never been a feature of English law? For historical reasons it did not evolve here. Why did no one, apparently, think about it around the time of the Married Women's Property Act 1882? So far as this writer is aware it was not considered, perhaps because English land lawyers have not always been well informed about civil law institutions. Whether or not that was the case, the nineteenth-century English lawyers would have had as their paradigm for family property the family settlement, with its emphasis on providing for the eldest son and thereafter for future generations. The settlement structure had its own mechanisms for providing for widows, but shared ownership was not among them; and community of property, if it had been considered at all, would have been utterly inimical to this particular legal mindset. Given those social conditions in the nineteenth century, then, it is not surprising that community of property was not considered as an option at the one obvious point when it might have been introduced.

Aside from the absence of any community regime, consider two other contrasts in policy.

First, a land law point: the English version of joint ownership takes a remarkably individualistic form. Joint tenancy is not very intimate, and attempts to make it so have failed. Tenancy by entireties – an unseverable version of beneficial joint tenancy[40] – was abolished in 1925. Lord Denning attempted, with a splendid sense of history and tradition but wholly without authority, to bring back a form of unseverable joint tenancy, but he failed.[41] And the courts lean towards a finding that a joint tenancy has been severed, and turned into tenancy in common, whenever possible, holding that a notice of severance is effective if it is received at

---

[39] This is not an issue in systems of *deferred* community, of course.
[40] Still available in some US jurisdictions, where of course 1925 did not take place.
[41] *Bull v Bull* [1955] 1 QB 234.

the other's address, even if he does not read it, even if the sender, having changed her mind, picks it up and throws it away, even if the dog eats it.[42] There is live debate as to whether or not beneficial joint tenancy should be abolished.[43] In contrast with community of property, joint ownership in this jurisdiction is scarcely joint at all; perhaps we should not hasten to abolish the slightly more intimate form that we have managed to preserve.

Second, a point which lies at the intersection of land law and family law. Although no one would seriously suggest the introduction here of community of property, in its full sense of community of property and obligations, there have been realistic suggestions that marriage, and perhaps cohabitation, should give rise, not to community of property but to automatic joint ownership of the family home – just one limited aspect of community of property. These suggestions extend over many years – they were at their loudest in the 1970s, from the Law Commission and others,[44] but have been made again more recently.[45] The Scottish Law Commission also made this suggestion in the 1980s,[46] but did not pursue it.[47]

So far, these suggestions have not made any progress towards implementation. The difficulty is a sort of blind spot: English law has never been able to take hold of the idea that ownership of land might be determined by a relationship. Thereby hang all our difficulties with the common intention constructive trust.[48] There lies the judiciary's apparent fixation with contribution as a source of proprietary rights;[49] there lies much of the difficulty in the allocation of property post divorce. In divorce cases, the courts have adopted the idea of equal division of property in

---

[42] *Kinch v Bullard* [1999] 1 WLR 423.

[43] M Thompson, 'The drawbacks of beneficial joint tenancies' [1987] Conv 29; and the reply by Prichard [1987] Conv 273.

[44] O Kahn-Freund, '*Matrimonial Property, Where do We Go from Here?*' Unger Memorial Lecture, 1974; quoted in B Hale, D Pearl, E Cooke, P Bates, *The Family, Law and Society* (5th edn, London: Butterworths LexisNexis, 2002) 161; Law Commission Working Paper No 42, *Family Property Law*, 1971; a national survey of married couples and divorced people, carried out by the Office of Population Censuses and Surveys (J E Todd and L M Jones, *Matrimonial Property* (HMSO, 1972) found that of a sample of 1877, 94 per cent of respondents agreed that 'the home and its contents should legally be jointly owned by the husband and wife irrespective of who paid for it' (ibid para 22); perhaps the most powerful advocacy of automatic joint ownership for spouses is found in the Law Commission's report on *Matrimonial Property* Law Com No 175 (London: HMSO, 1988).

[45] A Barlow and C Lind, 'A Matter of Trust: the Allocation of Property Rights in the Family Home' (1999) 19 *Legal Studies* 468.

[46] 1983, Scottish Law Commission: *Consultative Memorandum on Matrimonial Property*.

[47] *Report on Matrimonial Property* (Scot Law Com No 86, 1984).

[48] S Gardner, 'Rethinking Family Property' (1993) 109 LQR 263; contrast A Bottomley, 'Women and Trust(s): Portraying the family in the gallery of the law' in S Bright and J Dewar (eds) *Land Law: Themes and perspectives* (Oxford: OUP, 1998).

[49] *Lloyds Bank v Rossett* [1991] AC 107, per Lord Bridge, etc.

excess of need, but insist on doing so on the basis that each party has contributed equally to the marriage, whether by earning or homemaking.[50] This gives rise to problems in cases where contribution has patently not been equal.[51] There would be no such problems if we could see entitlement arising on the basis of the marriage itself. And the very existence of the spouse's statutory and registrable right of occupation of the matrimonial home arises from a determination not to accept that marriage can be a source of proprietary rights.[52]

F. Automatic Joint Ownership of the Family Home: is it Achievable?

The suggestion of automatic joint ownership may not go away. It is interesting to note that Lord Lester's Civil Partnership Bill in 2003 contained a provision that the civil partners' home should be jointly owned.[53] The research project conducted by the writer and colleagues includes a substantial empirical study of the views of adults in England and Wales, in which we sought to test the acceptability of automatic joint ownership, and there would appear to be some support for automatic joint ownership. The study conducted by Anne Barlow and her colleagues into the perceptions of the effect of cohabitation found that many people believe that marriage and cohabitation have the same legal effects, and that many people think that these relationships either do or should give rise automatically to joint ownership of property.[54]

A system where marriage and civil partnership give rise to joint ownership at least of the family home would have much to commend it, and would meet public expectations far more than does the system of separation.[55] People like the idea. But the technical consequences have to be thought through properly.

---

[50] *White v White* [2001] AC 596.

[51] Hence the further development and confusion arising from the House of Lords' decision in *Miller v Miller; McFarlane v McFarlane* [2006] UKHL 24; see E Cooke, '*Miller/McFarlane*: law in search of discrimination' [2006] CFLQ 1.

[52] *National Provincial Bank Ltd v Ainsworth* [1965] AC 1175; Family Law Act 1996 s 30.

[53] 2001 Relationships (Civil Registration) Bill (subsequently withdrawn following the government's promise to consider legislation for civil partnerships).

[54] A Barlow, S Duncan, G James and A Park, *Cohabitation, Marriage and the Law* (Oxford: Hart Publishing, 2005).

[55] If we are to take seriously public perception of the lack of legal distinction between marriage and cohabitation, there is an argument that any such change in the law should extend to cohabitants as well, or at least to cohabitants with children. The difficulty with this is the uncertainty inherent in the definition of cohabitation. In many cases it is clear-cut, but the grey area would generate huge problems. Accordingly this option is not considered further here. It would, of course, be perfectly practicable to introduce *deferred* community of property for unmarried cohabitants. But it would

It is readily apparent that any proposal of automatic joint ownership involves a choice: should it be legal or equitable? This is not an issue in the civil law jurisdictions, obviously. Here, legal ownership of a registrable estate is not possible without registration;[56] thus our registration system makes automatic legal joint ownership impossible, unless by some computer wizardry it were possible for registration of marriage or of civil partnership to trigger re-registration of any estates in land held by the parties. This can probably be ruled out for the foreseeable future.

The only practicable option is therefore equitable joint ownership. The difficulty faced here is the law's policy – firmly expressed in the 1925 legislation and in case law throughout the last century – of minimizing the powers, and the effect on third parties, of equitable owners who do not also hold the legal estate. The curtain behind which equitable interests are supposed to be hidden is so thick and effective that the proprietary effect of equitable ownership vis-à-vis third parties is minimized.

Thus it is not possible, as things stand, for an equitable joint owner who does not have legal title to restrain or control the legal owner's powers of disposition, unless there is a restriction on the register[57] or, for married persons, a notice recording a right of occupation.[58] Again, the dominance of the register, not only over legal ownership but also as the only source of owner's powers or of restraint of those powers, means that automatic joint ownership without a change in the register is limited in its effect.

Moreover, an equitable joint owner has very little protection against third parties seeking to take the property free of their interest, as buyers or as mortgagees. This is the result of the combination of the fact that trust interests cannot be protected by notice on the register,[59] and the conveyancing practice of seeking waivers from adult occupiers of premises so as to nullify the protection given by para 2 of Schedule 3 of the Land Registration Act 2002. Again, our conceptions of joint ownership, and our concessions to joint occupation, are extremely individualistic, as well as being heavily slanted towards the protection of purchasers. This may need a re-think, unless we are interested in a form of joint ownership that does not affect third parties.

---

not be realistic to suggest such a reform for cohabitants without also introducing some form of community of property for married couples.

[56] The combined effect of sections 6 and 7, 27 and 58 of the Land Registration Act 2002.
[57] Section 26 Land Registration Act 2002.
[58] Section 30 Family Law Act 1996. The right of occupation may be protected thus by a spouse who is also an equitable co-owner (s 1(9)) even though the intention behind the creation of the registrable right of occupation was to protect a non-owning spouse.
[59] Section 33 Land Registration Act 2002.

There is another side to this coin too. Not only would joint ownership, in the form available as the law stands, give limited protection to those it is supposed to benefit, it could well be opposed by commercial and financial interests – who would have to have a voice in any consultation about a proposed change to automatic joint ownership. Consider the position of creditors. Secured creditors have been effectively protected by the courts from the risks arising from most instances of unexpected joint ownership.[60] But automatic joint equitable ownership of the matrimonial home would prejudice creditors in two ways.

First, secured creditors are not protected against an unexpected joint owner in the case where the charge secures a loan that is not linked with the acquisition of the property. A mortgagee whose charge secures business debts, and was granted after acquisition and where a co-owning spouse is in occupation, may find itself unexpectedly bound by the spouse's overriding interest.[61] The property which it thought was solely owned is in fact jointly owned and only half the equity is available to meet the debt.

Second, an unsecured creditor may have relied upon the fact that the debtor was a homeowner, knowing that if the debt was not met it would be able potentially to resort to the value of the house through a charging order. Hidden and automatic joint ownership is a substantial prejudice to such creditors.

The community of property jurisdictions have managed a neat play-off. The system is acceptable to financial interests such as lenders because of the element of joint liability. The housewife spouse who would otherwise be without property gets a credit rating, but the lender gets enhanced protection. English law gives joint owners their severable shares and protects them from each other's creditors but thereby makes automatic joint ownership rather more controversial, and probably unacceptable to the financial interests who have constituted land law's darlings for the last century or so.

---

[60] *Abbey National BS v Cann* [1991] AC 56, HL; *Bristol & West BS v Hening* [1985] 1 WLR 778, CA; *City of London Building Society v Flegg* [1988] AC 54, HL; etc.

[61] This assumes that the waiver system has not worked. The creditor would then have a remedy in misrepresentation against the debtor, which would probably be useless in the circumstances.

The waiver system is a horribly imprecise tool. It is therefore used here as an argument both that joint equitable owners have very little protection against third parties (because the system usually works) and that creditors are at risk from unexpected equitable interests (because it sometimes doesn't).

G. Conclusions

Two substantive conclusions are offered, both arising from the very individualistic nature of English land law and from its bias towards the safety of purchasers, in particular of financial institutions.

First, we should bring an element of scepticism to proposals, persistent though they are, for automatic joint ownership of the family home. These are not flights of fancy by family lawyers; they would bring our land law into line with a number of other jurisdictions and would bring the law into line with the expectations of much of the population. The difficulty is that joint ownership would give rather restricted protection to those whom it is intended to benefit; and without the element of community of liability it would probably be opposed by financial institutions. Any proposal for automatic joint ownership of the home of married couples and civil partners would have to engage with these difficulties, and the difficulties go to some very fundamental elements of our land law and registration systems. The writer doubts that these can be overcome in the foreseeable future.

Second, the study of community of property may lead one to feel less enthusiastic (if one ever was) about the abolition of the beneficial joint tenancy. The Californian experience has been to extend its availability. Take away the technical reasons for and against it, it may actually meet an emotional need. Sharing property, as we have seen, has its attractions for couples. If this is the best we can do as an 'intimate' form of property ownership, we should not get rid of it.

Finally, the study of community of property leaves us with the realization of how very unusual English law is. This goes for both land law and family law. We stand virtually alone in Europe in not having community of property in either its immediate or its deferred forms;[62] and we are a long way distant from those jurisdictions that have been able to see marriage, and now registered partnership, as a source of proprietary rights in land and other forms of family wealth. Grace Blumberg's statement that the basic ownership unit is typically the dyad does not work for us. As we have seen, one reason why that is likely to remain the case is

---

[62] The assertion that we do not have deferred community of property is perhaps slightly controversial following the House of Lords' introduction of the idea that, once needs have been met, a divorcing couple's property is to be divided in accordance with the 'yardstick of equality; see n. 9 above. But if this is deferred community, it is only for the rich; and it is scarcely reasonable to regard as a community system one which has no clear definition of the community property. Equally, although a facility for contracting out is not a logical corollary of a community of property system, all such systems have it but we have not.

the fact that we persist with this in the oddity of our land law (the dual system of legal and equitable ownership), and the fact that our registration system is fundamentally different from continental European systems.[63] In Europe, our legal system is odd. We might do well to contemplate this further, as a general proposition, as we move steadily closer to our European legal neighbours.

---

[63] This feature has been reinforced, if anything, by the reforms effected in the Land Registration Act 2002. One of the watchwords of the reform was the idea that we must have 'title by registration, not registration of title'. Title by registration is a feature of the Torrens registration systems, whereas the European systems seem much closer to the registration of title.

4

(MIS)INTERPRETING THE TRUSTS OF LAND AND APPOINTMENT OF TRUSTEES ACT 1996

Rebecca Probert

The growing body of cases on the Trusts of Land and Appointment of Trustees Act 1996 makes it timely to consider its impact. In particular, how has it influenced the resolution of disputes between co-owners and creditors? Under the Act it is not possible to hold that the interests of a creditor are automatically to be preferred to those who occupy the family home. The Act implies that a clear distinction is to be drawn between applications by a trustee in bankruptcy and applications by a creditor, since different sets of rules apply to each.[1] Under section 15 the courts are required to have regard to a number of factors in considering whether sale should be ordered at the instigation of a creditor. These factors are not listed in any order of priority, and there is no indication that any of them is to be given more weight than any other. There can be discerned in the case law, however, three ways in which the interests of a creditor may still prevail. First, the courts may emphasize the importance to be attached to the interests of a creditor, taking the view that, while all the factors listed in section 15 are equal, some are more equal than others. Second, the other factors listed in section 15 may be interpreted so restrictively that they have little application in most cases: the interests of the creditor thus prevail because there is nothing in the balance to weigh against those interests. The third possibility is that, on the facts of any given case, the interests of the creditors may prevail once all of the relevant factors have been given sufficient weight and a genuine balancing act has been carried out by the courts. If this third approach is taken, it is possible that the interests of a creditor will *not* prevail on the facts of a particular case – whereas if either the first or second approach is taken it is almost certain that they will.

---

[1] As pointed out by J Neuberger in *The Mortgage Corporation v Shaire* [2000] 2 FCR 222.

At first it appeared that the courts would adopt the third approach. In *The Mortgage Corporation v Shaire*, Neuberger J gave consideration to each of the factors listed in section 15 and carried out a balancing exercise that gave at least some weight to each.[2] Since then, however, a combination of the first and second approaches has been adopted, despite the lack of any legislative sanction for this pro-creditor stance. As a result, in practice, there is little difference between the cases decided immediately before or after the 1996 Act, as the second part of this chapter will demonstrate.

I would suggest that the third approach best fits what was intended by the Law Commission and Parliament, in proposing and enacting what became the 1996 Act. Opponents of this view might argue that the courts have consistently held that the interests of creditors should prevail, and that no change of policy was intended when the 1996 Act was enacted. In order to address this argument, we need to take a closer look at the recommendations of the Law Commission and the background against which they were formulated.

A. The Background to the Act

It was initially suggested that cases decided under section 30 would continue to be relevant.[3] In *The Mortgage Corporation v Shaire*,[4] Neuberger J advocated a more cautious approach:

> Where one has concluded that the law has changed in a significant respect so that the court's discretion is significantly less fettered than it was, there are obvious dangers in relying on authorities which proceeded on the basis that the law was more fettered than it now is. I think it would be wrong to throw over all the earlier cases without paying them any regard. However, they have to be treated with caution, in light of the change in the law, and in many cases they are unlikely to be of great, let alone decisive, assistance.[5]

In deciding that the earlier case law remained relevant, the judge relied on a number of factors, including the views expressed by the Law Commission when recommending reform. Academic commentators made the same point in noting that 'there is room for the old case law to creep back in'.[6] Yet the fact that the

---

[2] This analysis was followed in *Chan Pui Chun v Leung Kam Ho* [2002] BPIR 723 at first instance. This aspect of the decision was not appealed.

[3] *TSB Plc v Marshall* [1998] 3 EGLR 100.

[4] [2001] Ch 743.

[5] P 761.

[6] L M Clements, 'The Changing Face of Trusts: The Trusts of Land and Appointment of Trustees Act 1996' (1998) MLR 56, p 63. See also N Hopkins, 'The Trust of Land and Appointment of Trustees Act 1996' (1996) 60 Conv 411.

Law Commission stated its view that 'the court's discretion should be developed along the same lines as the current "primary purpose" doctrine', that that doctrine 'gets the balance more or less right' and that the aim of setting guidelines would be to 'consolidate and rationalise the law'[7] – all statements suggesting that the earlier case law would continue to be relevant – does not mean that *all* cases decided under the 1925 legislation remain relevant. It is important to note exactly when these recommendations were formulated, and in particular the state of the law at the time that they were formulated. The report was published in 1989, two years before the decision in *Re Citro*[8] that at common law[9] the interests of the trustee in bankruptcy should prevail unless the circumstances were 'exceptional', and four years before *Lloyds Bank v Byrne* decided that this approach was equally applicable to applications by creditors.[10]

Re Citro marked a change in the test applied by the courts. Prior to *Re Citro*, the courts stressed that they had a discretion in deciding whether or not to order sale under section 30. The test applied by the courts in deciding what order to make was first formulated in a contest between co-owners in *Re Buchanan-Wollaston*:[11]

> . . . the court of equity . . . must look into all the circumstances of the case and consider whether or not, at the particular moment and in the particular circumstances when the application is made to it, it is right and proper that such an order shall be made. In considering a question of that kind . . . the court is bound . . . to ask itself the question whether or not the person applying for execution of the trust for sale is a person whose voice should be allowed to prevail.[12]

This flexible approach was held to be equally appropriate in cases involving applications by a trustee in bankruptcy.[13] Thus in *Re Bailey (a bankrupt)*[14] we find Megarry V-C giving due consideration to the interests of the different parties:

> One has to weigh, on the one hand, the claims of the trustee in bankruptcy and the creditors; against those, one must put into the scales all that can properly be put there on behalf of the other spouse of the marriage and any children.[15]

---

[7] Law Commission, *Transfer of Land: Trusts of Land*, Law Com No 181 (1989), para 12.9.

[8] [1991] Ch 142.

[9] As distinct from the statutory criteria set out in the Insolvency Act 1986, which was not applicable in *Re Citro* because the relevant events took place before the Act came into force.

[10] [1993] 1 FLR 369; *Barclays Bank v Hendricks* [1996] 1 FLR 258; *Bankers Trust v Namdar* [1997] EGCS 20.

[11] [1939] Ch 738.

[12] P 747.

[13] *In re Soloman (A Bankrupt)* [1967] Ch 573; *In re Turner (A Bankrupt)* [1974] 1 WLR 1556; *Re Densham* [1975] 1 WLR 1519; *Re McCarthy (A Bankrupt)* [1975] 1 WLR 807; *Re Bailey (A Bankrupt)* [1977] 1 WLR 278.

[14] [1977] 1 WLR 278.

[15] P 283.

This test was intertwined with the question of whether the property was held for a purpose that was collateral to the statutory duty to sell. If it could be shown that the property had been acquired for a collateral purpose militating against sale (for example the provision of a family home or the retention of the property for other purposes[16]) then sale would normally be refused while that purpose was continuing. Yet the very circumstances that had led to the application for sale being made might indicate that even if there had once been a collateral purpose, it had come to an end – for example if the property had been purchased as a home by a couple whose relationship had subsequently broken down.[17] This did not mean that sale had to be ordered – as Goff J noted in *Rivett v Rivett*,[18] the court 'still had a discretion, although it was of a much more limited character, and the Court had to order the sale unless, having regard to all the circumstances, it was of the opinion that a sale would be inequitable'.

One factor that weighed heavily with the courts in deciding whether to order sale was the fact that the trustee in bankruptcy had a statutory duty to realize the assets: in *Re Turner* this was held to tip the scales in favour of ordering sale.[19] In fact, in virtually all cases involving an application by a trustee in bankruptcy, sale was ordered.[20] The exception was *Re Holliday*, in which sale was postponed until the youngest child reached the age of 17, partly because of the difficulties the wife would face in re-housing herself and her three children and partly because it was 'highly unlikely that postponement of the payment of the debts would cause any great hardship to any of the creditors'.[21]

While Goff LJ in *Re Holliday* referred to sale being ordered at the request of a trustee in bankruptcy unless there were 'very special circumstances',[22] and Walton J in *Re Lowrie*[23] observed that sale tended to be ordered unless the circumstances were 'exceptional' (such as those demonstrated in *Re Holliday*), these observations did not form part of the test applied by the courts. As Slade LJ noted in

---

[16] *Re Buchanan-Wollaston* [1939] Ch 738.
[17] *Jones v Challenger* [1961] 1 QB 176; *Rawlings v Rawlings* [1964] P 398; *Jackson v Jackson* [1971] 1 WLR 1539; *Bernard v Josephs* [1982] Ch 391.
[18] [1966] EGD 706.
[19] [1974] 1 WLR 1556; applied in *Re Densham*.
[20] There was, of course, a difference between ordering the sale of the property and ordering that a trustee in bankruptcy should take possession of the property: as J Goff noted in *Re McCarthy* [1975] 1 WLR 807, an order for possession would result in the family having to leave the property more speedily than if there were an order for sale. It was accordingly more onerous and 'should not be made unless the facts justify it'. In most cases, therefore, there would be some period of time in which the parties could look for new accommodation.
[21] Per David Cairns LJ p 425.
[22] P 415.
[23] [1981] 3 All ER 353.

Thames Guaranty Ltd v Campbell,[24] it was 'by no means a foregone conclusion' that sale would be ordered at the instance of a trustee in bankruptcy.

> The discretion of the court is a real one and in considering whether or not to order a sale, it must weigh the conflicting legal and moral claims of the creditors on the one hand and those of the wife on the other, taking all relevant facts, including the existence of children, into account.[25]

It is clear that the courts continued to regard the appropriate test as being to 'ask whose voice in equity should prevail' rather than holding that sale should be ordered unless the circumstances were exceptional.[26]

In *Re Citro* the observation in *Re Lowrie* – that the interests of a trustee in bankruptcy usually prevailed save in exceptional circumstances – was transformed into the test to be applied by the court: sale should not be ordered unless there were exceptional circumstances. There is a subtle but important shift here. In the earlier cases, the interests of the competing parties are being weighed against each other, and the court has a genuine discretion. On the facts the interests of the creditors may prevail, but this is not inevitable. Post *Citro*, however, the interests of the creditors are assumed to be of overwhelming importance, and little consideration is given to the interests of those occupying the family home unless the circumstances can be shown to be exceptional. It is against the background of the former that the recommendations of the Law Commission should be read: they were endorsing the flexible test formulated in *Re Buchanan-Wollaston*, not the more restrictive approach that was later adopted.

It is also worthy of note that two members of the Court of Appeal in *Re Citro* were unhappy with the result. Bingham LJ noted that the trial judge had

> treated *In re Holliday* as entitling or obliging him simply to balance the interests of the creditors against those of the wife, the creditors' prima facie entitlement to their money being simply one element in the scales – and not a particularly weighty one at that.

He went on to acknowledge the attraction of such an approach:

> I would willingly adopt this approach if I felt free to do so. It is in my view conducive to justice in the broadest sense and it reflects the preference which the law increasingly gives to personal over property interests. I do not, however, think it reflects the principle which, as I conclude, clearly emerges from the cases, that the order sought

---

[24] [1985] QB 210.
[25] P 239.
[26] *In re Toobman (a Bankrupt)* (1982, unreported); *First National Securities v Hegerty* [1985] FLR 80; *Chhokar v Chhokar* [1984] FLR 313; *Wollam v Barclays Bank plc* (1988, unreported); *Martin v Nash* (1989, unreported).

by the trustee must be made unless there are, at least, compelling reasons, not found in the ordinary run of cases, for refusing it.[27]

So Bingham LJ was clearly acting under the perceived constraint of authority – despite the fact that the case law had consistently emphasized the discretion of the court. He was also dubious about the test of 'exceptional circumstances', suggesting that it was 'in the absence of statutory guidance, more stringent than was warranted'.[28] The other judge, George Waller LJ, simply dissented, concurring with the trial judge's order that sale should be postponed until the youngest child of each of the two families involved had reached the age of 16.

Thus a comment by the deputy judge in *Re Lowrie*, approved by Walton J when the case came before the Chancery Division, was held by the Court of Appeal in *Re Citro* to represent the test to be applied to applications by a trustee in bankruptcy and was further applied to applications by creditors in the cases of *Lloyds Bank v Byrne*, *Barclays Bank v Hendricks*, and *Bankers Trust v Namdar*. Accordingly, in deciding how section 15 was intended to operate, it is necessary to take into account that the Law Commission's recommendations were formulated against a more flexible judicial approach. Cases decided after those recommendations were published in 1989 should be treated with even greater caution than those decided before that date: it cannot be assumed that the Law Commission would have endorsed the approach adopted in *Lloyds Bank v Byrne* and subsequent cases.

There are two further reasons why the cases decided under section 30 of the Law of Property Act may mislead more than they assist: they are unlikely to be an appropriate guide to the weight to be attached to the factors listed in section 15[29] and, more fundamentally, they may constrain the judicial imagination in determining the actual meaning of those factors. As the Law Commission pointed out, the starting point that there was a duty to sell 'confined the development of judicial doctrine to the formulation of reasons why sale should not take place'.[30] The primacy of the duty to sell had to be outweighed by an equally strong counter-factor. This meant that the contest between the trust for sale and the collateral purpose was a stark one: the collateral purpose could displace the primacy of the trust for sale, and sale might be refused if the purpose was ongoing. Indeed, in *Abbey National Plc v Moss*[31] it was suggested that sale would be refused if the

[27] P 161.
[28] P 160.
[29] See also N Hopkins, 'The Trust of Land and Appointment of Trustees Act 1996' [1996] 60 Conv 411.
[30] Para 3.5.
[31] [1994] 1 FLR 307.

purpose was ongoing: according to Peter Gibson LJ, 'where the collateral purpose has not come to an end the Court will ordinarily not allow the trust for sale to defeat that purpose'.[32] It followed that the factors that would indicate a collateral purpose would be narrowly defined, since a finding that there was a collateral purpose would have a powerful effect. By contrast, under section 15 there is a range of factors to take into account. The fact that the property is being used for the purpose of providing the family with a home does not indicate that sale should be refused: it is merely a factor to be taken into consideration. The courts could thus be more generous in their interpretation of the factors listed in section 15 than they were in their recognition of collateral purposes.

B. The Interpretation of Section 15

With these points in mind, the following section will review the varying ways in which the courts have been interpreting section 15, and suggest how its provisions could be developed along lines that are more consistent with the intentions of Parliament.

One preliminary point is that a more consistent approach to each of the factors in section 15 needs to be developed. At present there seems to be no consensus on the meaning of the factors listed in section 15 – save in the importance to be attached to the interests of creditors. Often a different interpretation is adopted in intra-family disputes to that where the family is in conflict with a third party. It is reasonable to expect a different result to occur depending on whether the case is one that involves a third party or not. But a distinction needs to be drawn between the *meaning* of each of the factors listed in section 15 and the *weight* attached to each factor in any given case. The latter may vary according to the context, but the former should not. It is, for example, legitimate to hold that the purpose of providing a family home has to yield to the interests of the creditors on the facts of the case. But the mere fact that the dispute involves a creditor should not lead the courts to construe the specific factors in s 15 more narrowly, as they have been doing.

1. The importance of creditors' interests

It is clear that the courts have continued to regard the interests of creditors as the key factor in deciding what order should be made. Thus in *Pritchard Englefield (a firm) v Steinberg*,[33] while the judge acknowledged that 'the former paramountcy

---

[32] P 316.
[33] [2004] EWHC 1908 (Ch).

of a creditor no longer exists', he went on to say that 'it is a factor, which requires consideration' and in fact did not give explicit consideration to any other factor.[34] Similarly, in *Bank of Ireland v Bell*,[35] Peter Gibson LJ stressed that 'a powerful consideration is and ought to be whether the creditor is receiving proper recompense for being kept out of his money, repayment of which is overdue'.[36] *Bell* was endorsed by a differently constituted Court of Appeal in *First National Bank v Achampong*,[37] which deployed noticeably more emotive language in referring to the interests of the creditors than in discussing the welfare of the family.[38] The pro-creditor stance of the courts was noted in *Edwards v Lloyds TSB Bank Plc*,[39] which commented that the earlier cases of *Shaire*, *Bell* and *Achampong* all 'bring out the point that, if there is a creditor of a husband or wife and the creditor's interest is to be taken into account . . . it is unsatisfactory for the court simply to say that it declines to make any order for sale'.[40]

Delay by the creditors in instigating the proceedings is not ignored by the courts, but instead is read as having been a positive advantage to the occupiers. Thus in *Bell* Peter Gibson LJ observed that 'it hardly lies in Mrs Bell's mouth to complain, given that she has had the benefit of continuing to occupy the property without paying any interest to the bank, which largely funded the purchase of the property'.[41] It remains to be seen whether innovations in the context of bankruptcy cases – the requirement that the home should be sold within three years or will revert to the bankrupt[42] – will affect this perception that delay is inevitably beneficial to the occupant.

2. Intentions and purposes

It is convenient to consider paragraphs (a) and (b) of section 15(1) together, since the courts so often elide intentions and purposes without considering how the two might differ. They are, of course, distinct: Parliament would hardly enact

---

[34] On the facts it was arguable that the property was acquired to provide the owner's mother with a home for life, a purpose that was still being carried out. The fact that the mother had lived there for 40 years was held only to justify postponing sale for up to two months to see whether she could find a buyer willing to purchase the lease subject to her life interest – which the court thought was unlikely. If contracts were not exchanged within that period then the sale was to take place with vacant possession.

[35] [2001] 2 FLR 809.

[36] Para 31.

[37] [2003] EWCA Civ 487.

[38] 'The effect of refusing a sale is to condemn the bank to wait – possibly for many years – until Mrs Achampong chooses to sell' [para 62].

[39] [2004] EWHC 1745 (Ch).

[40] Para 30.

[41] Para 32. See also *Achampong* para 62.

[42] Enterprise Act 2002.

two provisions to the same effect. The terminology of section 15 supports Pascoe's suggestion that the 'intentions' referred to in s 15(1)(a) crystallize at the time that the trust is created, and that the purposes to which the property is subsequently put can be taken into account under s 15(1)(b).[43] The first part of this distinction is generally accepted – as Arden LJ noted in *W v W*: 'Parliament has used the word "intention" which speaks naturally to the intentions of persons prior to the creation of the trust'.[44] The circumstances in which the court will hold that another purpose has emerged are rather less clear – as Arden LJ's judgment in that case further demonstrates.[45]

The intentions of the parties may be expressed – either formally[46] or informally[47] – or implied from the circumstances of the case. Since section 15(1)(a) refers to 'intentions' in the plural, it is legitimate for the court to find that the parties who created the trust had a variety of intentions in regard to the property. Thus in *Holman v Howes*,[48] a house was purchased after the parties had divorced as the ex-husband hoped that this might lead to a reconciliation. The court found that his intention was, first, to provide a home for himself, his ex-wife and their child with the hope that they would reconcile, but, second, that in any case his former wife was to have 'the use and occupation of the Property for so long as she wished'.[49]

This case should be contrasted with that of *Telecom Plus plc v Hatch*,[50] where only one intention – and indeed only one purpose – was discerned by the court. The facts of this case were slightly unusual. The family had got into financial difficulties and the husband's employer – Telecom Plus – had purchased the family home from the mortgagee in possession to prevent Mr and Mrs Hatch from being evicted. It might be assumed that the court would hold the intentions of Telecom Plus were to provide a family home for Mr and Mrs Hatch and their children, or at least that this was the purpose for which the property was being held. This, however, was not the court's interpretation of the situation. David Richards J found that '[b]oth the intentions of the persons creating the trust . . . and the purposes for which the property subject to the trust was to be held, was . . . quite

---

43 S Pascoe, 'Section 15 of the Trusts of Land and Appointment of Trustees Act 1996 – A Change in the Law?' [2000] Conv 315, p 318.

44 Para 23.

45 See further section 3 below.

46 Gray and Gray suggest that s 15(1)(a) is 'primarily relevant to trusts created by express disposition or by will, particularly where the trust takes the form of a "trust for sale"' [1135].

47 See, for example, *Holman v Howes* [2005] All ER (D) 169.

48 [2005] All ER (D) 169.

49 Para 65.

50 [2005] EWHC 1523 (Ch).

clearly that the property should stand as security for the amount which Telecom Plus plc provided for its purchase'.[51] It was consequently in keeping with this intention and purpose that the property should be sold and the amount repaid. In this case Telecom Plus was not, of course, a creditor but the registered owner of the property, so its interests could not be taken into account under section 15(1)(d). The very narrow interpretation of 'intention' and 'purposes', however, meant that Telecom Plus's interests prevailed despite this technicality.

The courts do not, however, always distinguish between the intentions that the parties had at the time the property was purchased and the purposes that developed over time. In *Bank of Ireland v Bell* it made sense to hold that the original intention of the parties was that the property should be used as a family home, since it was purchased after the birth of the parties' son. But should the court find that the original intention of the parties was to provide a home for as yet unborn children, as it did in *Edwards v Lloyds TSB Bank Plc*?[52] It would make sense if the courts were to draw a distinction between the matrimonial and the family home: the initial intention of the parties that the house should be their matrimonial (or quasi-matrimonial) home may give way to the purpose of providing a home for the family once children have been born.

It should not, however, be necessary for the parties to spell out either their intention that the property should be a matrimonial home or the fact that it is now a family home, despite the suggestions to this effect in *W v W (Joinder of Trusts of Land Act and Children Act Applications)*.[53] In that case Arden LJ suggested that in determining 'the purposes for which the property subject to the trust is held' the court does not simply look at the factual use to which the property is being put, but must consider whether the parties actually *agree* that this is a purpose:

> For the purposes of s 15(1)(b), purposes could have been formulated informally, but they must be the purposes subject to which the property is held. The purpose established at the outset of the trust which, on the judge's finding, did not include the provision of a home for children, could only change if both parties agreed. There was no evidence from which the judge could find that the mother agreed to the additional purpose spoken to by the father.[54]

It is difficult to imagine that – at least prior to the litigation – the mother would not have agreed that the purpose of the property was to provide a home for her children, born in 1989 and 1992 respectively. Her agreement could surely have been inferred from the fact that, when she was pregnant, the property was

---

[51] Para 37.
[52] Para 29.
[53] [2004] 2 FLR 321; [2003] EWCA Civ 924.
[54] Para 24.

remortgaged to finance an extension to accommodate the expected child. To insist on a specific agreement between the parties is unrealistic in view of the dynamics of family life. The decision is particularly harsh in light of the fact that this restrictive interpretation was formulated in the context of an intra-family dispute: it is to be hoped that it is not carried over into the context of a dispute with a creditor.

The elision of 'intentions' and 'purposes', and of the matrimonial home with the family home, has led to section 15(1)(b) being construed more narrowly than was intended. The departure of a spouse or partner means that the property can no longer be regarded as the (quasi-) matrimonial home, but this should not affect the fact that it is still the family home if it is occupied by the children of the family. Yet neither the approach nor the terminology adopted by the courts on this point has been consistent. In some cases the courts have held that the purpose of providing a family home comes to an end with the departure of one of the adult members of the family, even if the home is still occupied by young children. Thus in *Bank of Ireland v Bell* Peter Gibson LJ held that the purpose of providing a family home 'ceased to be operative once Mr Bell had left the property',[55] although Mr Bell's son was only nine at this time. By contrast, in *Edwards v Lloyds Bank* it was said in relation to the provision of a *matrimonial* home:

> In part that purpose has gone, because the marriage is over and the husband is no longer living in the house, but in part the purpose still survives, because the house is still the home for Mrs Edwards and the two children.[56]

In many cases the purpose of providing a family home will overlap with the interests of the minor children who are occupying the property as their home. The courts have shown themselves unwilling to recognize that a 'family home' may exist where the family in question does not consist of at least one adult (preferably two) and minor children. In *Achampong* the home was occupied by the wife, her elder daughter, and her grandchildren. The purpose of providing a matrimonial home, it was decided, had ceased with the departure of the husband. In addition it was held that:

> Insofar as the purpose of the trust – and the intention of the Achampongs in creating it – was to provide a family home, and insofar as that is a purpose which goes wider than simply the provision of a matrimonial home, I am unpersuaded that it is a consideration to which much if any weight should be attached. The children of the marriage have long since reached adulthood. One of them is no longer in occupation. It is true that the elder daughter, Rosemary, is a person under mental disability and remains in occupation but to what extent that fact is material to her continued

---

[55] P 815.
[56] Para 29.

occupation of the property and therefore to the exercise of any discretion under section 14 is not apparent.[57]

Yet a finding that the property is held for the purpose of providing a family home should not depend on the *nature* of the family in occupation of the home. Indeed, even in the case of a childless couple, it can still be said that the property is held for the purpose of providing the remaining occupant with a home. That purpose may not prevail against the other factors listed in section 15, but it should at least be a matter for consideration. Otherwise, childless spouses may actually be worse off under section 15 than under the insolvency regime. Their rights and needs are not a special consideration for the court; if the other party has left and there are no children then under the current approach none of the factors listed in section 15(1) will apply.

There are, it should be noted, two cases in which the courts have held that the purpose of providing a home for one of the parties survived the relationship. Both were, however, slightly unusual, since in both cases the court decided that there had been explicit promises to this effect. In *Holman v Howes*[58] the ex-husband attempting a reconciliation 'accepted that he needed to do something to encourage [his former wife] to go along with his plans'[59] and 'clearly assurances of some kind were given to the Claimant' which the judge decided 'must have been assurances that come what may the Claimant was to be entitled to stay in the Property for so long as she wished'.[60] Similarly, in *Chan v Leung*[61] the parties had specifically agreed that the property would not be sold unless both of them agreed. As the judge noted, this agreement had 'more of the flavour of a commercial negotiation than one normally finds between parties setting up home together in anticipation of married bliss'. The reason for this element of arm's-length bargaining was that Miss Chan's confidence in Mr Leung had already been dented – he had previously been imprisoned for bribery – and she wanted the security of knowing that she would be able to remain in the property even if the relationship had broken down. Both cases are accordingly more akin to the express agreement in *Re Buchanan-Wollaston's Conveyance* than to the cases involving family breakdown where the parties have been less explicit about their intentions. Yet if the occupation of the family home by one of the parties can be agreed to be a purpose by the parties, there is no reason why it could not be inferred to be a relevant purpose in an appropriate case.

---

[57] Para 65.
[58] [2005] All ER (D) 169.
[59] Para 64.
[60] Para 65.
[61] [2003] 1 FLR 23.

Returning to the topic of multiple purposes, and the point at which any individual purpose comes to an end, there is similarly a problem with the assumption that the purpose of providing a family home comes to an end if one of the adult members of the family uses the home as security for a debt. This was held in two cases decided under the old law: *Barclays Bank v Hendricks* and *Bankers Trust v Namdar*. In the first Laddie J noted that the collateral purpose that the house was to be retained as the matrimonial home 'had ceased to exist both because Mr Hendricks was no longer living there and, more importantly, because Mr Hendricks' interest as co-owner had been charged to the bank'.[62] These words were echoed by the Court of Appeal in *Namdar*. It is likely that the strictness of this approach was motivated by the desire to avoid the effect of *Abbey National v Moss*, which had held that if the collateral purpose was still subsisting, sale should be refused. If there was no collateral purpose then the obstacle to sale would be removed.

Quite apart from the legitimacy of relying on cases such as *Hendricks* and *Namdar* – for the reasons explained above – to decide that using the house as security for a debt brings the collateral purpose to an end is difficult to justify. It means that it will always – and perversely – be decided that the purpose of providing a family home has been extinguished in the very cases where it is most important to show that the property is still being used for this purpose – namely where the property has been mortgaged to a third party who is now claiming sale. The idea that there can be only one purpose for which the property is held, and that a new purpose drives out an earlier purpose, is consistent with neither the spirit nor the terms of the Act. The Act was, after all, intended to confer a broad discretion on the court, and explicitly refers to the *purposes* – in the plural – for which the land is held on trust. It would be preferable to accept that a property can be held for more than one purpose, and that the fact that it is being used as security does not preclude it being used as the family home, since this reflects the reality of the situation.

3. Interests of children

Prior to the enactment of the 1996 Act, it was a matter of debate how the courts should take into account the interests of children. The Court of Appeal in *Re Holliday* preferred the suggestion that the presence of children was 'a factor incidentally to be taken into account so far as they affect the equities in the matter as between the parties entitled to the beneficial interests in the property', as suggested by Buckley LJ in *Burke v Burke*,[63] rather than as prolonging the collateral purpose for which the property was held.

---

[62] P 263.
[63] [1974] 2 All ER 944.

The Law Commission's initial suggestion was that '[a]rguably, in line with other legislation, the welfare of the children should be the first consideration'.[64] This tentative suggestion did not appear in the final report, but there was no indication as to why it had been dropped. It might have been because of opposition among consultees to the principle or because the decision in *Suter v Suter* suggested that such a formulation would have little effect.[65]

It is clear, nonetheless, that the Law Commission expected more weight to be given to the welfare of children as a result of the changes it proposed. It stated that the welfare of children was to be 'expressly defined as an independent consideration'[66] rather than being dependent on whether the purpose of the trust was to provide a family home or matrimonial home, 'to ensure that the interests of children are not linked to the interests of particular beneficial owners'.[67] More explicitly, it noted that while the guidelines were not intended to fetter the discretion of the court:

> Clearly, the terms of these guidelines may influence the exercise of the discretion in some way. For example, it may be that the courts' approach to creditors' interests will be altered by the framing of the guideline as to the welfare of children. If the welfare of children is seen as a factor to be considered independently of the beneficiaries' holdings, the courts may be less ready to order the sale of the home than they are at present.[68]

Were the intentions of the Law Commission shared by the legislature? It is often difficult to discern the intentions of Parliament on a certain topic, particularly when *Hansard* reveals only the most cursory debates on a particular point. In this case it should be noted that no member of the legislature expressed concern that the interests of creditors were not accorded sufficient importance by the new formulation, while a number welcomed the fact that the family home would now be recognized as a home rather than merely an asset.[69] In the House of Lords, Lord Meston, for example, wished to 'particularly welcome the formulation of a court's powers in Clause 14 of the Bill and the formulation of the relevant matters for consideration by the court in Clause 15, especially the express reference to the welfare of any minor child. It seems to me that that will assist in preserving the home for children so far as may be practicable'.[70]

---

[64] Law Commission, *Trusts of Land* (London: HMSO, 1985) WP No 94, para 10.9.

[65] *Suter v Suter* [1987] 3 WLR 9 had held, in the context of the Matrimonial Causes Act 1973, that the use of the word 'first' did not mean that the welfare of the children should be 'paramount'.

[66] Para 12.9.

[67] ibid.

[68] P 23, fn 143.

[69] *Hansard* (HL) vol 569 col 1720 (Lord Mishcon), col 1725 (Lord Browne-Wilkinson), 1 March 1996.

[70] *Hansard* (HL) vol 569 col 1724, 1 March 1996.

In fact, little attention has been paid to the interests of minor children occupying the home. In *Bell* the court noted that the son was nearly 18, and that accordingly his interests 'should only have been a very slight consideration'.[71] Yet the legislation gives no indication that the age of the minor is relevant. The approach of the court in *Bell* seems to confuse the length of time for which the welfare of the son would have been a relevant factor with his actual interests. It is important to disentangle the two issues. A 17-year-old may be sitting important public examinations that will determine his or her future: it is arguably more important that sale should be delayed in such a case than it would be if the children were younger.

The courts have shown themselves more willing to imagine the hardships that may be caused to the creditors kept out of their money than how the welfare of children might be affected by the loss of the family home. In *Achampong* the judge held that although the interests of the infant children – the grandchildren of the owners – were relevant, 'it is difficult to attach much if any weight to their position in the absence of any evidence as to how their welfare may be adversely affected if an order for sale is now made'.[72]

Even in *Edwards v Lloyds Bank*, where sale of the property was delayed at least until the youngest child reached the age of 18, the welfare of the children was not discussed in depth, the judge going no further than saying that their interests were 'certainly relevant'.[73] The only other case in which the welfare of the children had any influence on the outcome of the case was *Telecom Plus plc v Hatch*. Here the son of Mr and Mrs Hatch was almost 18 but according to his father had been 'diagnosed as suffering from clinical depression'.[74] The court held that a short extension was appropriate – although as the extension deemed appropriate was a mere four weeks it cannot be claimed that the welfare of the son was given much weight.[75]

One of the most restrictive decisions to date is that of the Court of Appeal in *W v W (Joinder of Trusts of Land Act and Children Act Applications)*,[76] which involved a dispute between an unmarried couple as to whether the home should be sold. The case had two unusual features: first, it was the mother who had left the family home that she had shared with her cohabitant and whose request for sale was granted by the judge at first instance; second, this was the reverse of her original

---

[71] P 816.

[72] Para 65.

[73] Para 29.

[74] Para 38.

[75] The parties were allowed eight weeks to 're-settle themselves' rather than the 28 days that the judge would otherwise have allowed.

[76] [2004] 2 FLR 321; [2003] EWCA Civ 924.

claim that sale should be deferred until the youngest child reached the age of 18 (her assumption then having been that she would be the one to remain in the family home with them). The court at first instance had ordered that the property should be sold, and the Court of Appeal endorsed this result.

For the court, it was a matter of balancing 'the two most important competing considerations, namely the mother's need for realization of her only capital in order to acquire a home, and the competing interests of the girls who, as the father has throughout emphasized, have known no other home'.[77] How did the court manage to isolate these two factors from the list in section 15? Consideration of (a) and (b) was excluded on the basis that the provision of a family home was neither the intention of the parties (because the children were born after the acquisition of the property) nor an agreed purpose.[78] No independent consideration was given to the father's wishes and circumstances under s 15(3).[79]

The fact that the father had applied for an alternative order under the Children Act may have meant that the Court of Appeal did not feel the need to interpret section 15 in a way that would ensure that the home remained available for the occupation of the children. Yet there was no need to swing to the other extreme. Arden LJ interpreted the criteria listed in s 15 of the 1996 Act in a way that will make it more difficult for the interests of children to be taken into account in future cases – and in cases involving third parties there will be no recourse to the adjustive regime provided by the Children Act.

If the residence order had been granted to the mother, and it had been the father applying for an immediate sale of the property, would the court have given as much weight to his wish for sale as it did to the mother's 'need for realization of her only capital in order to acquire a home'?[80] One suspects not. The particular – and unusual – facts of this case may have influenced the decision of the court in favour of one woman, but the reasoning affects the likelihood that the property can be retained for mothers and children in other cases.

4. The wishes and circumstances of the beneficiaries

Where an application is made for the sale of the property – whether by a co-owner or by a third party – the court is also directed to take into account 'the circumstances and wishes of any beneficiaries of full age and entitled to an interest in possession in property subject to the trust or (in case of dispute) of the majority

---

[77] Para 18, per Thorpe LJ.
[78] See further above.
[79] See further below.
[80] Thorpe LJ para 18.

(according to the value of their combined interests'.[81] It was decided in *The Mortgage Corporation v Shaire* that this factor should be taken into account by the court when considering any application other than one relating to either section 6(2) (an explicit exclusion) or section 13 (in which case section 15(2) would apply). It is clear from the Law Commission's report that this is what was intended: the draft bill listed this alongside the other factors that now appear in section 15(1).[82]

In *W v W*, counsel for the father tried to argue that the circumstances and wishes of the mother in favour of sale were balanced out by the circumstances and wishes of the father against sale, since each had an equal interest in the property. Arden LJ, however, thought that it was 'open to the judge to have regard to the wishes of the mother and to her circumstances, and to give that factor such weight as he thought fit'.[83] It is true that the list of factors in section 15 is not exhaustive, and that the court can have regard to all the circumstances of the case. But given the fact that section 15(3) was clearly intended to recognize the wishes of *all* those who had a beneficial interest in the property, it seems inappropriate to consider the wishes of only one on the basis that the court has a discretion. After all, under the terms of the legislation, if the beneficiary has a 51 per cent share, then his or her wishes will prevail:[84] as a matter of logic the wishes of a beneficiary with a 50 per cent share should be given as much weight as those of the other beneficiary or beneficiaries. This is not to argue that the mother's wishes should not have been taken into account, merely that the court should have given weight to the wishes of the father as well. Arden LJ's expansive approach on this point is also at odds with her restrictive interpretation of s 15(1)(b) elsewhere in the case: if the judge can take into account all the circumstances of the case, why should the scope of s 15(1)(b) be constrained by the fact that the parties have not specifically agreed what the purpose of the property is to be?

C. Conclusion

As Miller has noted: '[t]he task of tilting the balance in favour of the occupier will not be easy, but it must have been the intention that the balance would be tilted more in favour of the debtor's co-owner and family than is the case on an application for an order for sale by a trustee in bankruptcy where exceptional

---

[81] Section 15(3).
[82] Law Commission, *Transfer of Land: Trusts of Land* (London: HMSO, 1989), Law Com No 181, p 44, clause 6.
[83] Para 26.
[84] See, for example, *Chan v Leung*.

circumstances must be shown to avoid an order for sale'.[85] This is not, however, what has happened in practice. Are there any cases decided under the 1996 Act that would have been decided differently under the previous law? The most generous decision to date is that of *Edwards v Lloyds Bank*, but it is hard to escape the suspicion that the factor that justified a delay in this case was not the presence of two children in the home, nor the fact that the debt had been incurred by the wife's ex-husband, who forged his wife's signature after their relationship had come to an end, but rather the fact that delay would not be prejudicial to the creditors. The judge pointed out that the debt was less than the value of the interest over which the bank had an equitable charge,[86] and that their security was in fact secure. A parallel can be drawn with the bankruptcy case of *Re Holliday*, the key similarity being the security of the debt rather than the security of the children occupying the family home.

It could be argued that it is necessary to avoid double counting in the evaluation of the interests listed in section 15. If, for example, the court attaches weight to the intention that a property was to be used as a family home, to the fact that it is still used for this purpose, *and* to the welfare of the children who occupy it, does this give too much weight to the single fact that the property in contention is a family home? If each factor listed in section 15 is accorded equal weight, then the interests of creditors will often have to yield to the combined force of the factors that the property was intended for use as a family home, is still being used for this purpose, and is occupied by minor children whose welfare would be affected by the sale. In order for the interests of creditors to prevail in such a case, the courts must either define the former in such a way that it trumps the other three put together, or it must refine the other three out of existence, so that three become two or even one. In practice it has done both, as the above discussion has shown.

Yet the court has a discretion under section 15: its role is not simply that of totting up the factors listed and mechanically weighing them so that (a) plus (b) plus (c) will always outweigh (d). As the Law Commission stated, the court's powers under the 1996 Act would 'be framed with sufficient breadth to permit a genuinely flexible approach'.[87] The courts have not taken up this opportunity.

Radley-Gardner has suggested that the pro-creditor stance of the courts in considering applications under section 14 is due to a realization that a more generous approach would merely result in more applications being made to bankrupt

---

[85] G Miller, *The Family, Creditors and Insolvency* (Oxford: OUP, 2004) 89.
[86] Initially £15,000 but had risen to approximately £40,000 because of interest and costs.
[87] Para 3.6.

the mortgagor.[88] In the wake of the decision in *Alliance and Leicester plc v Slayford*,[89] which held that the use of this alternative was not an abuse of process, 'even if a more flexible approach had emerged under section 15, it would have been a paper tiger, easily undercut by recourse to the insolvency regime'. This does, however, miss an important point, namely that the matrimonial home is afforded *some* protection under the statutory insolvency scheme, at least in the first year of the bankruptcy. It is only after this period has expired that sale must be ordered – unless, of course, the circumstances are exceptional. The co-owners against whose wishes sale has been ordered under section 14 would no doubt have been glad of a year's delay.[90]

If Radley-Gardner is right and the courts' interpretation of section 15 has been intended to bring applications under the 1996 Act into line with the approach taken upon insolvency, it is a little ironic that co-owners are now actually worse off if an application is brought by a creditor under section 14 than if the insolvency scheme applies. This was not what the Law Commission or Parliament intended. It may in turn have its own impact on the options that creditors choose to pursue: if possession of the family home can be achieved more or less immediately by bringing an application under the 1996 Act, this may be preferable to taking steps to bankrupt the owner. Of course, there is not always a real choice between taking steps to bankrupt the co-owner and making an application under section 14, as the co-owner may not, in fact, be insolvent. In such a case it seems particularly inappropriate to apply the test formulated in the more extreme case of bankruptcy.

In the light of this, I would argue that it is incumbent upon the courts to develop the scope of section 15 as it was intended to operate by the Law Commission. The analogy with the bankruptcy jurisdiction should be abandoned. The courts should recognize that co-owners can have multiple intentions and purposes; that a new purpose – such as the provision of security – does not necessarily drive out the old; that families can take many forms; and that nowhere in section 15 is there any indication that the interests of a creditor should prevail. Perhaps then a fairer balance can be struck between creditors and members of the family.

---

[88] O Radley-Gardner, 'Section 15 of TLATA, or The Importance of Being Earners' (2003) 5 Web JCLI.

[89] (2001) 33 HLR 66.

[90] See, for example, *Telecom Plus plc v Hatch* (eight weeks) and *Pritchard Englefield* (two months).

5

LANDLORDS, DISABLED TENANTS AND THE RISING TIDE OF EQUALITY LAW

Anna Lawson

A. Introduction

In the UK, obligations not to discriminate against disabled people were imposed on landlords, for the first time, by the Disability Discrimination Act 1995 (DDA). A necessary distinction was made between the landlords of employers and of service providers on the one hand, and those who let premises directly to disabled people on the other. Landlords in the former category were prevented from withholding their consent unreasonably to requests by their tenants (seeking to comply with their own obligations not to discriminate against their disabled employees or customers) to make physical alterations to the property.[1] At that time, however, the DDA imposed no equivalent duty on landlords in the residential sector: landlords whose tenants might themselves be disabled and in need of physical alterations in order to use and access their homes.

The provisions of the DDA relevant to landlords of disabled tenants, often referred to as the 'premises provisions', are sections 22–24. As originally enacted, these simply prohibited the unjustified less favourable treatment of disabled people by persons managing or disposing of premises. Although these were useful provisions, which have already given rise to some important decisions,[2] in

---

[1] Ss 16, 27 and 28W.

[2] See, for example, *North Devon Homes v Brazier* [2003] EWHC 574 and *Manchester CC v Romano* [2004] EWCA (Civ) 834. See also *Rose v Bouchet* [1999] IRLR 463. See generally, A Lawson, 'Selling, Letting and Managing Premises: New Rights for Disabled People?' [2000] Conv 128 and J Shepherd, 'The Impact of the Disability Discrimination Act 1995 on Housing' [2000] JHL 65.

contrast with other areas of the DDA (such as employment and the provision of goods and services) they imposed no duty to make reasonable adjustments.

In 1999 the Disability Rights Task Force[3] recommended that the premises provisions be amended to include a duty to make reasonable adjustments to practices, policies and procedures and to provide auxiliary aids and services. The Government accepted these recommendations and gave them effect through s 13 of the Disability Discrimination Act 2005 (DDA 2005) which introduced new sections 24A–24L into the 1995 Act. These additions are extremely welcome but will not be considered in depth here.

The prime focus of this chapter, then, is not the duty to take reasonable steps to adjust policies, practices, procedures and terms or to provide auxiliary aids and services. It is, rather, another, much more controversial, change introduced by the 2005 Act: a change in the nature of the rights of a disabled tenant to make disability-related physical alterations to their home. This change was effected by provisions, termed here the physical alterations provisions, which were described in the House of Lords as 'possibly the most complex'[4] and also as 'some of the most important parts of the Bill'[5] – impressive attributes given the complexity and range of the Bill in question!

In the next section, the history of the 2005 physical alterations provisions will be outlined. Section C will assess the nature and scope of the new duty they impose on landlords not to withhold consent unreasonably to relevant requests by tenants. It will be suggested that this new duty adds little, if anything to the pre-existing duties imposed on landlords by general property law statutes. Section D will examine some of the much more significant changes introduced by the physical alterations provisions. These relate to enforcement and mark a re-positioning of the right of a disabled tenant to make reasonable disability-related adaptations to their home. Instead of being situated in the context of mainstream property law, where it has hidden unnoticed and untested for many years, it has now been given a more prominent place in the realms of equality law. Finally, in section E, some attention will be given to the problem of access to communal and external areas. It will be argued that this, too, is an issue crying out for inclusion in equality legislation. Without it, indeed, the effect of the 2005 physical alterations provisions will be largely undermined.

---

3 *From Exclusion to Inclusion*, 1999, London: Department for Education and Employment.
4 House of Lords, Hansard, 28 February 2005, col 77 per Baroness Hollis.
5 ibid, col 78, per Lord Ashley.

B. History of the 2005 Physical Alterations Provisions

1. The problem

These provisions emerged from recognition of the difficulties faced by thousands of disabled people living in rented accommodation. The English Housing Survey of 2001–2002 indicated that some 9 per cent of disabled tenants, approximately 18,000 people, were living in unsuitable, inaccessible conditions because their landlords had refused to allow them to make physical adaptations to their homes.[6] It should be stressed that, in these cases, there would have been no obligation on landlords to bear the financial cost of the alterations. That cost would be borne either by disabled tenants themselves or by the State through grants such as the disabled facilities grant.

Thus, without the landlord's consent to the making of physical alterations of the premises, thousands of disabled tenants were being denied the opportunity to adapt their homes in order to make them accessible. In such circumstances, disabled people experience 'immense hardship that remains largely unseen'[7] but which causes their exclusion from 'everyday life in the outside world'[8] and their house to become 'a prison rather than a home'.[9] The fundamental importance of suitable housing was recognized by the Disability Rights Task Force which opened its chapter on housing and the environment with the following passage:

> Adaptations to housing are a matter of equal opportunities in the most basic aspects of human life. In a well adapted house, a disabled person can move about, cook, or go into the garden, turn on lights, have a shower or bath or put a child to bed – when and how they want to, with minimum help from other people. Without adaptations, these people may be condemned to isolation, frustration and humiliation.[10]

---

[6] *Report of the Joint Committee on the Draft Disability Discrimination Bill 2003*, April 2004, para 313, London: Stationery Office. See also Office of the Deputy Prime Minister, *Housing in England 2001/2: A report on the 2001/02 Survey of English Housing*, (London: Stationery Office, 2003).

[7] House of Lords, Hansard, 17 January 2005, col GC 179 per Baroness Wilkins.

[8] ibid.

[9] House of Lords, Hansard, 6 January 2005, col 684 per Lord Ashley.

[10] *From Exclusion to Inclusion*, above n 3, p 79. The quote is taken from F Heywood, *Managing Adaptions*, (Joseph Rowntree Foundation, 1996). See further on the issue of inaccessible housing, M Harrison, and C Davis, *Housing, Social Policy and Difference*, (Bristol: The Policy Press, 2001); J Ackroyd, *Where do you think that you are going?* (London: John Grooms, 2003); DRC *Housing: Issue paper prepared for DAN* (London: DRC, 2004); DRC *Independent Living – Real Choice; Real Control; Real Independence – The equal citizenship of disabled people* (London: DRC, 2005).

Accordingly, along with its recommendations relating to reasonable adjustments and auxiliary aids and services, it recommended as follows:

> Recommendation 6.27: There should be no duty on those disposing of premises to make adjustments to the physical features of the premises. However, in civil rights legislation, they should not be allowed to withhold consent unreasonably for a disabled person making changes to the physical features of the premises.

2. Protection afforded by property law statutes

The Disability Rights Task Force's recommendation initially appeared to be accepted by the Government,[11] but it did not find its way into the original version of the Draft Disability Discrimination Bill 2003. Its omission was due to the fact that, in the Government's view, the problem was already addressed by provisions of mainstream property law which had not been considered by the Disability Rights Task Force.[12] These provisions are contained in the Housing Acts 1980 and 1985 and in the Landlord and Tenant Act 1927.

In the private rental sector, under s 81 of the Housing Act 1980, it is an implied term of protected and statutory tenancies that the tenant should not make improvements to the premises without the consent of the landlord and that that consent must not be unreasonably withheld. The same term is implied into secure tenancies (in the public sector) by virtue of s 81 and also s 97 of the Housing Act 1985. The Housing Act 1988 introduced the concept of assured tenancies and made it virtually impossible to create new protected or statutory tenancies after 15 January 1989. No term requiring improvements to be subject to the reasonable consent of the landlord is implied into assured tenancies.

Outside the context of protected, statutory and secure tenancies, where a lease (other than a few specified types including agricultural and mining ones) provides that improvements[13] are subject to the landlord's consent, s 19(2) of the Landlord and Tenant Act 1927 generally requires that that consent must not be unreasonably withheld. This 'famous'[14] subsection played a pivotal part in the debates about the need for legal change.

---

[11] Department for Education and Schools, *Towards Inclusion: Civil Rights for Disabled People*, (London: Stationery Office, 2001) para 3.83.

[12] See, for example, *Report of the Joint Committee on the Draft Disability Discrimination Bill*, above n 6, para 311; and Department for Work and Pensions, *The Government's Response to the Report of the Joint Committee on the Draft Disability Discrimination Bill*, (London: Stationery Office, 2004).

[13] 'Improvements' for these purposes is given a broad interpretation to cover alterations generally – see s 81(5) Housing Act 1980 and (in the context of s 19(2)) *Balls Bros v Sinclair* [1931] 2 Ch 325 and *Lambert v Woolworth and Co Ltd* [1938] Ch 883.

[14] House of Lords, Hansard, 20 January 2005, col GC315 per Lord Morris.

The Government's view that the difficulties faced by disabled tenants needing to make physical adaptations to their homes was adequately addressed by mainstream property law, and the consequent omission from the Draft Bill of any relevant provisions, was criticized in the report of the Parliamentary Joint Committee on the Draft Disability Discrimination Bill.[15] There was concern that, despite the fact that since 1927 hundreds of thousands of disabled people would have lived in unsuitable conditions as a result of their landlords' refusal of consent to physical adaptations, no disability-related cases had been brought under the Landlord and Tenant Act. Some possible explanations for this startling dearth of cases are suggested in the following pronouncement of the Disability Rights Commission (DRC):

> The current system has failed to protect them since they cannot get assistance from the DRC or access an appropriate conciliation process. Moreover there has been no statutory guidance for landlords, disabled people or the courts on when it is reasonable to grant or refuse consent in the case of access improvements a disabled tenant is proposing to make and what conditions landlords might reasonably attach to consent.[16]

These barriers to legal redress could be tackled only by situating the right to make reasonable access-related physical alterations in the realms of anti-discrimination legislation rather than in those of property law.

3. The emergence of the physical alteration provisions

The Disability Discrimination Bill, when it was introduced into the House of Lords on 25 November 2004, still contained no physical alterations provisions. It was only after vigorous debate on the question during the Bill's second reading,[17] its committee[18] and its report[19] stages, that it was finally amended to include such provisions in clause 16.[20] Section 16 inserts a new Part 5B (ss 49G and 49H) into the 1995 Act. Section 49G implies a term into relevant leases which is similar to that implied by the Housing Acts and which may be used by disabled tenants as an alternative to that implied by s 19(2). Section 49H brings disputes concerning disability-related alterations, whether they arise under the new s 49G, the Housing Acts or the Landlord and Tenant Act, within the domain of anti-discrimination legislation by extending to them various benefits associated with

---

[15] 24 April 2004, Ch 8 (London: Stationery Office).

[16] DRC, *An Initial Briefing on the New DDA 2005* (London: DRC, 20 April 2005).

[17] House of Lords, Hansard 6 December 2004, cols 674–710.

[18] House of Lords, Hansard 17 January 2005, cols GC175–190

[19] House of Lords, Hansard 3 February 2005, cols 444–7.

[20] House of Lords, Hansard 28 February 2005, cols 75–81.

the implementation and enforcement of the DDA. The effect of these provisions will now be analysed in more depth.

C. Section 49G and the Duty not to Withhold Consent Unreasonably

1. Leases allowing improvements subject to the landlord's consent

As discussed above, before the DDA 2005, under the Housing Acts 1980 and 1985 a term would be implied into all statutory, secure and protected tenancies preventing tenants from carrying out improvements to the leased premises without the consent of the landlord and requiring that consent not to be unreasonably withheld. In other leases, where there was a term allowing the tenant to carry out improvements with the consent of the landlord, s 19(2) of the Landlord and Tenant Act required that that consent should not be unreasonably withheld. The 2005 Act does not sweep away, replace or amend any of these pre-existing provisions. Through the new s 49G DDA, however, it does impose a duty on landlords, parallel to that imposed by s 19(2), to grant consent if it is reasonable to do so.

The new s 49G duty will not affect statutory, secure or protected tenancies.[21] The section makes no reference to s 19(2), however, with the result that there will be many cases in which either s 49G or s 19(2) could be argued. Some consideration has already been given to the scope of s 19(2) and an attempt will now be made to gauge the extent of the overlap between it and s 49G.

A pre-condition of the application of s 49G, like s 19(2), is that the tenant is entitled to make improvements to the leased premises with the consent of the landlord.[22] In addition, however, s 49G requires that the tenant, or any other person who will be lawfully occupying the premises, is disabled[23] and that the premises will constitute their only or principal home.[24] Further, s 49G applies only where the requested improvements are likely to facilitate the use of the premises by the disabled person in question.[25]

Thus, while s 19(2) applies to both commercial and residential leases, s 49G is limited to residential lettings. Further, it will be available only when there is a disabled occupant of the particular dwelling house and that occupant requests

---

[21] S 49G(1)(a).
[22] S 49G(1)(d).
[23] S 49G(1)(b). A 'disabled person' is defined in s 1 DDA 1995.
[24] S 49G(1)(c).
[25] S 49G(7).

physical alterations designed to facilitate their use and enjoyment of the property. It seems, then, that s 19(2) would apply to all cases in which s 49G could be invoked.

The essence of the duty imposed by s 49G is identical to that imposed by s 19(2) of the Landlord and Tenant Act 1927. It is a duty imposed on landlords not to withhold consent unreasonably to requests by tenants to make relevant improvements. Section 49G(2), however, contains a level of detail and protection which, though consistent with that contained in the Housing Acts, goes beyond that contained in s 19(2). Section 49G, for instance, specifies that an unreasonable refusal of consent to a request falling under the section[26] should be treated as an agreement to the improvements.[27] It also requires that where consent to a written request is withheld, the landlord must provide the tenant with reasons for that decision in writing.[28] More significantly, while the burden of proof in s 19(2) cases appears to be on the tenant,[29] s 49G places it on the landlord on the issue of the reasonableness of a refusal of consent or of conditions attached to its grant.[30]

Section 49G, then, imposes a duty on landlords, whose consent is required for improvements, to grant that consent to disability-related improvements where doing so would be reasonable. It sets out a regime very similar to that which regulates the granting of consent to physical alterations under the Housing Acts. Although this regime is also similar to that established by s 19(2) of the Landlord and Tenant Act, there are some differences, the most significant of which concerns the burden of proof. It would therefore be advisable for a disabled tenant, to whom both s 49G and s 19(2) applied, to bring their case under the former. Potential confusion may have been avoided had s 49G been drafted, along the same lines as the Housing Acts, so as to prevent s 19(2) applying to cases falling within its ambit.

2. Leases prohibiting improvements

Neither s 19(2) nor s 49G applies to leases which expressly prohibit the making of any alterations. Before the 2005 Act the only possible recourse for disabled tenants wishing to make disability-related alterations to premises let under such leases was the Unfair Terms in Consumer Contracts Regulations 1999.[31]

---

[26] Such refusals include grants of consent subject to unreasonable conditions (s 49G(4)) and a failure to either grant or refuse consent within a reasonable period (s 49G(3)(b)).

[27] S 49G(2).

[28] S 49G(3).

[29] A point made by the Law Society to the Joint Committee on the Draft Disability Discrimination Bill 2003 (see the report of the Joint Committee, above n 6, para 314).

[30] S 49G(5).

[31] SI No 1999/2083.

These are designed to give effect to the European Unfair Terms in Consumer Contracts Directive 1999,[32] and extend to terms in leases.[33]

According to reg 5(1):

> A contractual term which has not been individually negotiated shall be regarded as unfair if, contrary to the requirement of good faith, it causes a significant imbalance in the parties' rights and obligations[34] arising under the contract, to the detriment of the consumer.

Although it is possible that a disabled tenant may succeed in arguing that a term prohibiting alterations completely is unfair under these regulations, three major obstacles can be identified. First, no challenge may be made to terms in contracts created before the Regulations came into force. Second, challenges may not be made to terms which have been individually negotiated – a point which is worth making even though covenants prohibiting alterations are much more likely to be regarded as standard terms. Third, it is by no means certain that a term prohibiting alterations would be regarded as unfair. The most difficult type of case would be one in which there had been no reason to anticipate that the tenant might become disabled at the time of the contract but where this happened with the result that the premises would be unusable by the now disabled tenant in the absence of physical alterations.

The 2005 Act offers an alternative and much more promising means by which disabled tenants might attempt to secure physical alterations prohibited by their lease. Section 24D requires landlords to take reasonable steps to amend or waive a term in a lease if that term makes it impossible or unreasonably difficult for a disabled occupier to use the premises. According to reg 7 of the Disability Discrimination (Premises) Regulations 2006,[35] it will in certain circumstances always be reasonable for a landlord to amend a term prohibiting alterations so as to allow them to be made subject to reasonable conditions which may be specified by the landlord. The circumstances in question are ones in which a tenant has requested permission to make an alteration which it would, in all the circumstances, be reasonable for them to make and which would have the effect of preventing it being impossible or unreasonably difficult for a disabled

---

[32] Council Directive (93/13/EEC).

[33] *Khatun, Zeb and Iqbal v London Borough of Newham* [2003] EWHC 2326. See also Office of Fair Trading, *Guidance on Unfair Terms in Tenancy Agreements* (OFT 356 Sept 2005) available at <http://www.oft.gov.uk>.

[34] For further discussion of 'unfairness', see OFT *Guidance*, ibid, Parts 2 and 3, and *Director General of Fair Trading v First National Bank plc* [2002] 1 All ER 97.

[35] SI No 2006/887 reg 7(2) and (3). See also Disability Rights Commission 'DDA 1995 Code of Practice. Rights of Access: Services to the Public, Public Authority Functions, Private Clubs and Premises' (London: DRC, 2005) para 15.42. Compare the analogous approach taken by s 27(2) DDA.

occupant to enjoy the premises and any associated benefit or facility. Where these circumstances apply but the landlord is unable to alter a term without the consent of a third party, reg 6 provides that it will be reasonable for them to seek that consent but that it will not be reasonable for them to alter the term without it.

3. Leases silent on the issue of alterations

For the sake of completeness it is worth mentioning leases which make no reference to alterations. Such leases are not covered by either s 49G or s 19(2). In these cases the tenant may carry out alterations to the premises unless the alteration would amount to waste or constitute a breach of an express repairing covenant.

D. Section 49H and Enforcement Issues

1. Guidance on reasonableness

As the previous section has indicated, many tenants will be entitled to make alterations to the leased premises provided their landlord consents and the landlord will not be able to withhold consent unreasonably. For such tenants the way in which the reasonableness test is applied will be critical.

Before the 2005 Act, in relation to the term implied into protected, statutory, and secure tenancies, some statutory guidance was provided. In deciding whether consent had been unreasonably withheld, a court had to have regard, in particular, to the extent to which the improvement would be likely to make the leased premises, or any other premises, less safe for occupiers; to cause the landlord additional expense; or to reduce the market or rental value of the premises.

In the context of s 19(2), most of the cases on reasonableness concerned the sum required by the landlord by way of compensation for damage to the premises (or neighbouring premises owned by the landlord) or for diminution in their value. According to Woodfall, there was 'surprisingly little authority as to what other grounds for refusing consent may be upheld as reasonable'.[36] It seemed likely, however, that such cases would be decided by reference to similar principles to those applied, at common law, to cases concerning the reasonableness of a landlord's refusal to consent to an assignment.

In the context of assignments three 'overriding principles' were identified by Lord Bingham in *Ashworth Frazer v Gloucester CC*.[37] First, the withholding of consent

---

[36] K Lewison, J Brock, et al, *Woodfall's Law of Landlord and Tenant* (29th edn, London: Sweet and Maxwell, 1994) para 11.262.

[37] [2001] 3 WLR 2180 at 2182–3. For further discussion, see *Woodfall*, ibid, paras 11.140 and 11.141.

would not be reasonable if it was based on grounds irrelevant to the relationship of landlord and tenant with regard to the subject matter of the lease.[38] Second, the question was essentially one of fact depending on all the circumstances of the particular case.[39] Thus, according to Lord Bingham, 'care must be taken not to evaluate a decision made on the facts of a particular case into a principle of law'.[40] Third, the landlord need not prove that their reasons for withholding consent were justified provided that they were reasons which might have influenced a reasonable man in the circumstances.[41]

It is also worth noting that there were some indications that, though generally a landlord need consider only their own interests, a refusal to consent may be unreasonable if the consequent detriment to the tenant would be disproportionate to the benefit gained by the landlord.[42] There was a possibility that, had courts been confronted with a s 19(2) case concerning disability-related physical alterations, such disproportionate detriment reasoning would have been developed in favour of disabled tenants. It was by no means certain that this would occur, however. Even if it had, comparisons between aesthetic or sentimental reasons,[43] or even financial considerations, and access detriments to tenants would have been like comparing apples and Thursdays. It is not difficult to imagine a judge with a keen aesthetic sense deciding in favour of a landlord even though this would have required a tenant to find alternative accommodation. It is, for instance, easy to envisage a feature such as an access ramp triggering a similar response to that produced by a plate glass window on McKinnan LJ in *Lambert v Woolworth*:

> No court, as I hope and believe, will ever hold that under s 19(2) a landlord must consent to the hideous degradation of the front of his building . . . and be satisfied by a money payment for the loss of graceful eighteenth century buildings.[44]

As the law stood before the 2005 Act, then, there was no specific direction as to the weight to be given to securing access in housing for people with impairments

---

[38] *International Drilling Fluids v Louisville Investments* (Uxbridge) [1986] Ch 513 at 520 per Balcombe LJ; and *Houlder Bros v Gibbs* [1925] Ch 575 at 587 per Sargant LJ.
[39] *Bickel v Duke of Westminster* [1977] QB 517 at 524 per Denning MR.
[40] *Ashworth Frazer v Gloucester CC* [2001] 3 WLR 2180 at 2183. See also ibid at 2201 where Lord Rodger observed: 'Seeing that the circumstances are infinitely various, it is impossible to formulate strict rules as to how the landlord should exercise his right of refusal.'
[41] *Pimms Ltd v Tallow Chandlers Co* [1964] 2 QB 547 at 564 per Danckwerts LJ; *Shanly v Ward* [1913] 29 TLR 714.
[42] *Shepherd v Hong Kong and Shanghai Banking Corp* [1872] 20 WR 459, *Houlder Bros v Gibbs* [1925] Ch 575, *Leeward Securities v Lilly Heath Properties* [1984] 2 EGLR 54 and *Viscount Tredegar v Harwood* [1929] AC 72.
[43] The importance of which was stressed by the Court of Appeal in *Lambert v Woolworth* [1938] Ch 883 at 907 per Slesser LJ and 911 per McKinnan LJ.
[44] ibid at 911.

as compared with the property interests of others. Decisions in other areas of land law suggested that very little weight would be attached to the desirability of facilitating access for disabled people and that their claims to disability-related physical alterations might therefore be easily overridden. In *Drury v McGarvie*,[45] for instance, it was held that badly constructed gates did not amount to an obstruction of a disabled person's right of way across farmland to their home because they would not have constituted a 'material inconvenience' for a 'person of average strength and agility' or 'the ordinary, able-bodied adult'.[46] Article 8 of the European Convention on Human Rights increases the weight to be given to considerations such as access by disabled people, at least in cases where the disabled person is entitled to adaptations of property in which they already live and the landlord is a public authority.[47] Its effect is limited, however, and it is not at all clear that it will have a significant impact on very many disabled tenants, particularly in the private rental sector.[48]

The practical benefit of a code of practice, drawn up by the Disability Rights Commission, on factors to be taken into account in assessing reasonableness in these types of dispute is invaluable. Section 16(2), which inserts a new s 53A(1)(d) and (e) into the 1995 Act, authorizes the issuing of such a code. Significantly, according to the new s 53A(1)(e), such a code need not be limited to disputes concerning improvements under s 49G of the DDA but may also extend to disputes arising under s 19(2) of the Landlord and Tenant Act or under the Housing Acts of 1980 and 1985.

Such a Code has now been issued. On the question of the reasonableness of withholding consent to a proposed alteration, it acknowledges the relevance to s 49G and s 19(2) of the factors identified in the Housing Acts[49] (namely, the likely impact of the alteration on the safety of occupiers, on the expenditure of the

---

[45] [1993] SLT 987. See also *Middletweed v Murray* [1989] SLT 11, where a similar approach was adopted. For more general discussions of the treatment of disabled people in land law cases see R Edmunds and T Sutton, 'Who's Afraid of the Neighbours?' in E Cooke (ed) *Modern Studies in Property Law*, Vol 1, Property 2000, 2001, (Oxford: Hart Publishing) 133; and A Lawson, 'Land Law and the Creation of Disability' in A Hudson (ed) *New Perspectives on Property Law: Human Rights and the Family Home*, (London: Cavendish, 2003) 117.

[46] [1993] SLT 987 at 991.

[47] *R v Enfield LBC (Ex Parte Bernard)* [2003] HRLR 4.

[48] See further C Hunter, 'The (Lack of) Impact of the ECHR' [2003] *Journal of Housing Law* 17. See also *R v Havering LBC (ex p Johnson and Others)*; *YL v Birmingham CC and Others* [2007] EWCA Civ 26, ruling that a private entity, taking over a local authority residential care home, was not acting as a public authority for the purposes of the Human Rights Act 1998 and therefore not subject to its full force.

[49] Above n 35, paras 18.24 and 18.37.

landlord and on the value of the property or the rent which may be charged for it) and adds the following:

consent

the ability of the tenant to pay for the improvement

the scale of the proposed adaptations

the feasibility of the works

the length of the term remaining under the letting

the nature of the tenancy (eg the type and length)

the nature of the premises (eg their type, design, age, and quality)

the extent of any disruption and the effect on other occupiers of adjoining premises

the effect of, and compliance with, planning and Building Regulations requirements, and

the desirability or practicability of reinstatement of the premises at the end of the lease.[50]

The Code stresses that landlords must give 'due weight', in particular, to the needs of the disabled person in question.[51] This is likely to increase the weight which would otherwise have been attached to principles of access and inclusion and, thereby, to enhance the protection afforded to disabled people by s 19(2) and the Housing Acts as well as s 49G.

2. Conciliation

Section 49H(1) allows the DRC to establish a system of conciliation for 'a dispute of any description concerning the question whether it is unreasonable for a landlord to withhold consent to the making of a relevant improvement to a dwelling house'. Thus, provided the disputed improvement is one which would facilitate the use of the premises by a disabled person, it need not matter under which statute the dispute has arisen. All may be covered by the same conciliation service.[52]

3. Support for litigants

Section 49H(3) continues this extension of the benefits of anti-discrimination legislation to disputes which, though disability related, may not technically arise

---

[50] ibid, para 18.25.

[51] ibid, para 18.22.

[52] For a discussion of the advantages of conciliation in the context of anti-discrimination claims, see R Hunter and A Leonard, 'Sex discrimination and alternative dispute resolution: British proposals in the light of international experience' (1997) PL 298.

under the DDA. It inserts a new paragraph (aa) into s 7(1) of the Disability Rights Commission Act 1999. According to this new paragraph, the DRC will be able to assist disabled litigants in 'proceedings of any description to the extent that the question whether it is unreasonable for a landlord to withhold consent to the making of a relevant improvement to a dwelling house falls to be considered in the proceedings'. Thus, the legal and financial assistance of the DRC may be available to a disabled person seeking a disability-related improvement of rented premises even though the dispute has arisen in the contexts of the Housing Acts or of the Landlord and Tenant Act.

E. Communal Areas and External Access

The focus of this chapter has, until now, been on scenarios in which disabled tenants require physical alterations to be carried out inside their homes in order to facilitate access and use. What, though, of disabled tenants who require physical alterations to be made to property which is not actually included in the lease but which is connected with its use and enjoyment and which is owned by their landlord? What, for instance, of a person who needs a chair-lift in order to access an upper-floor flat as she can no longer use the communal staircase, or of a person who needs a grab-rail on an external flight of steps in order to access the building? This issue was described by Baroness Darcy as 'a particularly thorny question that is as vital to resolve as it is difficult'.[53]

Section 19(2) of the Landlord and Tenant Act applies only where the proposed improvements are to the premises comprised in the lease. Thus, in *Tideway Investment and Property Holdings v Wellwood*,[54] it was held not to apply where the installation of hot water systems necessarily entailed trespassing on property retained by the landlord. Under the Housing Acts 1980 and 1985, however, there is an argument that the implied term permitting improvements subject to the landlord's consent (and requiring that consent not to be unreasonably withheld) does extend to external or communal areas over which the tenant has been granted easements or analogous rights.[55] Nevertheless, the existence and extent of any such rights have not been tested and remain a matter of some speculation.

---

[53] House of Lords, Hansard, 20 January 2005, col GC 312.
[54] [1952] Ch 791.
[55] The argument is based on Housing Act 1980 s 85, Rent Act 1977 s 26 and Housing Act 1985 s 112(2). See the discussion of this issue by Jonathan Karas (Wilberforce Chambers) set out in *Review Group on Common Parts, A Review of the Current Position in relation to Adjustments to the Common Parts of Let Residential Premises and Recommendations for Change* (London: DWP, 2005) Annex 6 para 24.

Thus, the pre-2005 law offered little to a disabled tenant whose request for a disability-related alteration to a communal area (such as the installation of a grab-rail or improved lighting) or to the approach to their home (such as the installation of a ramp) was unreasonably refused by their landlord. On occasion, however, limited assistance might have been derived from the obligations imposed on landlords by s 11 of the Landlord and Tenant Act 1985. This requires landlords to keep in good repair areas over which tenants have easements and which are necessary for the use of the premises.[56] In *King v South Northamptonshire DC*[57] a disabled tenant relied on s 11 to require her landlord to repair the rear entrance to her home. She was unable to use the front entrance because of her mobility impairments. She therefore used the rear access but its state of disrepair caused her pain as well as inconvenience.

The 2005 duties to take reasonable steps to adjust policies, practices, procedures and terms and to provide auxiliary aids and services do extend to communal areas and external access which the lease entitles the tenant to use.[58] According to s 24E(1), however, it will never be reasonable for a landlord to have to remove or alter 'physical features'. The line between physical features and auxiliary services is thus an important one. Some clarification as to where it is to be drawn is provided in the 2006 Premises Regulations.[59]

Like s 19(2) of the Landlord and Tenant Act 1927, the new s 49G duty on landlords not to withhold consent to disability-related improvements unreasonably extends only to the premises included in the lease. It does not, therefore, require that landlords should consent to disability-related improvements to communal areas or external approaches where it would be reasonable to do so. The Joint Committee on the Draft Bill expressed considerable concern about this limitation and recommended its removal.[60] It referred to evidence it had received from those working in the field, including bodies such as the Disability Law Service, which had indicated that the majority of access-related problems which had come to its attention had related to the common parts of residential buildings.[61] The Government's response, however, was reluctant:

> We are not convinced that tenants should be able to make adjustments to common parts over which they have only limited rights or that a controller of premises should be required to allow a tenant to make changes to common parts. We believe that

---

[56] *Liverpool CC v Irwin* [1977] AC 239.
[57] [1992] 6 EG 152.
[58] Ss 24D1(a)(ii) and 24C(4)(a)(i) respectively.
[59] Above n 35, regs 4 and 5.
[60] Above n 6, paras 314 and 322–6.
[61] ibid para 323.

seeking to cover common or communal parts of premises in this way would pose quite severe problems on which we have not consulted . . .[62]

Amendments were tabled during the passage of the Disability Discrimination Act 2005 with the aim of extending s 49G to cover alterations to physical features in communal and external areas.[63] In the accompanying debates reference was made to the illogicality of the current position (which forbids the unreasonable refusal of consent to disability-related alterations if they happen to be needed inside the home but not if they are needed in order to reach it) as well as to its injustice. Lord Morris observed that 'a totally accessible flat may be of little use to a person who needs to but cannot negotiate even a short flight of steps to enter it'.[64] Despite rejecting the amendments, the Government recognized the existence of a problem[65] and established a committee to review the current position in relation to communal areas and to make recommendations as to how it might be improved.

The Review Group on Common Parts published its report on 23 December 2005.[66] It made two key recommendations. First, it recommended that the Government, without delay, should introduce non-legislative measures to provide clarity and assistance to those involved in relevant disputes. Such measures should include the allocation of additional resources to the disabled facilities grant to help resource undisputed alterations;[67] the publication of guidance for both landlords and tenants on good practice and the availability of relevant grants;[68] and the promotion of the use of alternative dispute resolution mechanisms by those unable to reach agreement.[69] Second, the Review Group recommended that the Government should consult further on the need for legislation on the matter and also on the suitability of the particular legislative provisions proposed in its report. Legislation, it considered, 'is likely to be the best long-term answer and one which will make a real difference to people's lives'.[70] The new provisions envisaged by the report would require landlords, if asked by

[62] Department for Work and Pensions, *The Government's Response to the Report of the Joint Committee on the Draft Disability Discrimination Bill*, above n 12, r 57.
[63] See, in particular, Amendment No 64 moved by Baroness Darcy (House of Lords, Hansard, 20 February 2005, col 311 et seq).
[64] House of Lords, Hansard, 20 February 2005, col 314.
[65] See, for example, House of Lords, Hansard, 20 January 2005 at col 320 per Baroness Hollis, echoing earlier sentiments expressed by Lord Rooker in debates on the Housing Bill (House of Commons, Hansard, 3 November 2004, col 370).
[66] Above n 55.
[67] ibid paras 5.8–5.11.
[68] ibid paras 5.12–5.13.
[69] ibid paras 5.14–5.17.
[70] ibid para 5.19. See now the proposals in *A Framework for Fairness* (London: DCLG, 2007) Ch 13.

a tenant who was disabled or was living with somebody (eg a child) who was disabled, to carry out disability-related adjustments to the common parts of the building if this would be reasonable. The cost of installation should be borne by the tenant but the cost of its maintenance should be spread among all the occupiers through a service charge.[71]

The thoroughness and efficiency of the Review Group are commendable and its recommendations are to be welcomed. Nevertheless, while it is obviously essential to ensure that the proposed legislation is appropriately drafted, it should not be forgotten that there is a price to be paid for delay in its implementation. In the words of Baroness Darcy:

> Disabled people cannot wait indefinitely for basic rights that everyone else takes for granted, which may have a huge impact on many aspects of their lives. The longer we leave the issue on the back burner, the more disabled people have to turn down job opportunities because there is nowhere accessible to live; the more they will suffer stress, anxiety and deteriorating health as their requests for adaptations prove abortive; and the fewer people will be able to be discharged from hospital and return to live in their community, because they cannot get something as simple as a ramp up to their front door.[72]

The problem is well illustrated by the recent case of *Williams v Richmond Court*.[73] This concerned an attempt by Mrs Williams, an 81-year-old tenant with mobility impairments, to install a stair-lift (at her own expense) in order to enable her to access her third-floor flat. The landlord refused to grant consent to this because of a contrary vote by the other tenants and the inconvenience it would cause them, because it would not be aesthetically pleasing, and because of the potential cost of repair. The Court of Appeal held that the DDA imposed no obligation on landlords either to make reasonable adjustments or to refrain from withholding consent unreasonably in relation to the physical features of the common parts of buildings. Accordingly, the landlord's refusal, however unreasonable it might have been, must be allowed to stand. It is therefore to be hoped that appropriate legislation, allowing the reasonableness of such decisions to be examined, emerges in the very near future.

Finally, it is worth noting that there is some ambiguity in cases which do not involve multiple occupancy but in which a disabled tenant wishes to make a physical alteration to the exterior of the leased premises in order to facilitate access. The Review Group was asked to consider the position relating to common parts.

---

[71] ibid ch 6.

[72] House of Lords, Hansard, 20 January 2005, col 314.

[73] [2006] EWCA Civ 1719. See also S Murdoch, 'A Stairlift Fraught with Problems' [2007] EG 201.

It interpreted 'common parts' to mean 'all those parts of a property and any associated land which the lessee or occupier has a right to use in common with others'.[74] It is not entirely clear whether the reference to 'others' here would cover cases in which the tenant had the right to use the area in question along with the landlord alone. The focus of the report, however, is firmly on cases of multiple occupation in which disabled tenants have rights to use communal areas along with other residents.[75] Cases in which there is no multiple occupancy, but in which the tenant accesses their home by means of an easement or licence over land retained by the landlord, are not explicitly considered. The latter type of case is likely to be less common than the former, but attention should nevertheless be given to the position of tenants in such circumstances who need to make disability-related alterations to the exterior access in order to be able to use their homes. They should certainly not be excluded from the scope of proposed legislative protection without careful consideration and convincing reasons.

F. Conclusion

The last decade has witnessed the appearance and multiplication of anti-disability-discrimination provisions in an area previously governed entirely by principles of mainstream property law. The first such provisions to enter the arena of residential property were the relatively gentle and easily contained sections 22–24 of the DDA 1995. These have now been joined by sections 24A–24L and, despite considerable initial reluctance on the part of the Government, by sections 49G and H. Thanks to these provisions, disabled people are now far more likely to be able to create a home in which they can cook, wash, and manoeuvre with safety than they might have been 10 years ago. Nevertheless, the current equality provisions do not go so far as to offer them any protection against the danger of becoming prisoners in their perfectly adapted homes because they are unable to negotiate non-adapted communal or external areas. Although the tide of equality law is rising, for such people it has not yet risen far enough and it is rising painfully slowly: too slowly, for many of them, to avert isolation, dependency and even institutionalization.[76]

As has been indicated above, the initial resistance to the inclusion of sections 49G and H was rooted in a belief that the problem was adequately addressed by the existing property law framework. A disabled tenant, like any other tenant, could

---

[74] Above n 55, p 5.
[75] See, for example, ibid paras 3.15 and 3.16.
[76] For examples of relevant calls received by the DRC Help Line, see ibid annex 5.

have challenged an unreasonable landlord under the Housing Acts or the Landlord and Tenant Act. The eventually successful argument that steps had to be taken in order to ensure that these theoretically available rights become practical realities for disabled people mirrors the argument which has led the United Nations to work on the elaboration of a Convention specifically dealing with the rights of disabled people.[77]

The emphasis of sections 49G and H is thus on making pre-existing rights available to disabled people in a meaningful way. Granting them similar rights over areas not included in their leases would, by contrast, represent a clear expansion of the rights conferred upon them by mainstream property law. Inevitably, therefore, such a prospect has triggered concerns as to its implications for the property rights of others, particularly of landlords.[78] In addition, frequent reference has been made to the need to exercise great care in any attempt to amend a statutory scheme as complex as that which applies in this field.[79] While both these concerns are entirely legitimate, they must not be permitted to obscure the plight of those who wait, imprisoned in their homes, for the tide of equality law to rise and to release them into the day-to-day life of their local communities. Equality principles have an important role to play in the property law of a society which genuinely values the participation and inclusion of disabled people. Such principles have not yet assumed what is to be hoped is their rightful place in the landlord and tenant law of England and Wales.

---

[77] See further G Quinn and T Degener (eds) *Human Rights and Disability – the current use and future potential of United Nations human rights instruments in the context of disability*, November 2002: UN (<www.ohchr.org/english/issues/disability/study.htm>); and A Lawson, 'The Draft UN International Convention on the Rights of Persons with Disabilities: Purpose, Progress and Potential' (a paper delivered at the Centre for the Study of Human Rights, London School of Economics, 9 March 2006).

[78] See, for example, House of Lords, Hansard, 20 January 2005, col 313 per Baroness Darcy; and the advice offered by the Review Group on Common Parts regarding Art 8 and Protocol 1 Art 1 of the ECHR, above n 55, para 6.17.

[79] See, for example, House of Lords, Hansard, 20 January 2005, cols 320 and 323 per Baroness Hollis.

6

PUT OPTIONS IN LAND: A NEGLECTED DEVICE?

*Richard Castle**

A. The Nature of Put Options

The put option is a well-known instrument in financial investment and its use there is widespread. Company shares are often the subject of put options.[1] In contrast, the put option in land is less well known. It has rarely come under the scrutiny of the courts, though its use in practice is widespread. A put option relating to land confers on the landowner the right to require the other party to acquire an interest in the land. In the past, courts tended to categorize options in land by reference to other concepts such as the conditional contract,[2] the irrevocable offer,[3] and the unilateral or 'if' contract.[4] All that was made redundant by the authoritative classification of options in land as unique contracts coming into existence at the time of their grant. That well-known reclassification was made by Hoffmann J in *Spiro v Glencrown Properties* [1991] Ch 537. It has been said[5] that *Spiro v Glencrown* reset the scene for the analysis of options. An option is one contract with potentially two stages. There appears to be no reason to

---

* Richard Castle was an associate in the Department of Land Economy, University of Cambridge and the author of the second and third editions of *Barnsley's Land Options*. He would like to thank Professor Peter Butt of the University of Sydney, Professor Kevin Gray of the University of Cambridge, and Castles solicitors of Hurstpierpoint, West Sussex for their help in the preparation of this chapter.
   1 See, for example, s 323 Companies Act 1985.
   2 *Griffith v Pelton* [1958] Ch 205 at 205.
   3 *United Dominions Trust (Commercial) Ltd v Eagle Aircraft Services Ltd* [1968] 1 WLR 74 at 81.
   4 *United Scientific Holdings Ltd v Burnley Borough Council* [1978] AC 904 at 928; *Sudbrook Trading Estate v Eggleton* [1983] 1 AC 444 at 477.
   5 R Castle, *Barnsley's Land Options* (3rd edn, London: Sweet & Maxwell, 1998) 14.

regard the put option in land as a separate category beyond the scope of *Spiro v Glencrown*. The requirement for writing imposed by section 2 of the Law of Property (Miscellaneous Provisions) Act 1989 would seem to apply. So provided all the terms of the put option are in writing:

- there is no need for extra paperwork on the exercise of the option in accordance with its terms
- notice of exercise unilaterally alters the relationship between the parties to one of buyer and seller
- all other principles relating to land options attach.

Special considerations do, however, apply to three aspects of put options in land, namely:

(1) the perpetuity period
(2) protection of the option by registration, and
(3) protection of the buyer–seller relationship by registration.

These three problem areas will be considered later. First, a fairly recent case on put options in land calls for full consideration. That case came before the Court of Appeal in Queensland, Australia and is *Denham Bros Limited v Freestone Leasing Pty Limited* [2004] 1 Qd R 500.

B. The Facts of *Denham Bros v Freestone*

The salient facts of *Denham v Freestone* are as follows.

(1) In 1982 Denham Bros agreed with the State Government Insurance Office (SGIO) of Queensland that SGIO would buy land and build a shopping centre on it, whereupon Denham Bros would lease the land from SGIO on specified terms.

(2) The scheme proceeded, and *Denham Bros* took the lease. The lease period was 15 years, and clauses 30A and 30B provided for successive five-year options to renew in favour of Denham Bros. Clause 33 of the lease read thus:

Should the Lessee not exercise its rights of renewal contained on clauses 30A and 30B hereof *THEN* immediately upon the expiration of the original term or the first option period hereby agreed to be granted whichever the case may be the Lessee shall purchase at the option of the Lessor the demised premises from the Lessor upon the same terms and conditions as is contained in Clause 14A and at the purchase price defined in Clause 31 hereof and in accordance with the terms and provisions hereof.

Clause 14A contained a covenant against assignment of the lease and enabled the lessor to require the lessee to buy the premises if a breach occurred. It also set the terms of the purchase. The price defined in clause 31 referred to the definition elsewhere of 'total capital outlay'. That definition included the moneys 'paid by the Lessor in the acquisition of the lands hereinbefore described and the construction and erection thereon of the works and extensions . . .'.

(3) In 1991 SGIO sold the reversion in the property to Freestone. No mention of the clause 33 option was made in the transfer.

(4) Denham Bros exercised the first of its options to renew the lease, but not the second. Freestone then gave notice to *Denham Bros* purporting to exercise Freestone's clause 33 option requiring *Denham Bros* to buy the premises. Subsequently SGIO by a deed of July 2002 assigned to Freestone 'all the rights title and interest of the Lessor under the said Lease including the Lessor's Option under Clause 33 of the said Lease'. A few days after that, Freestone notified *Denham Bros* of the assignment and of its exercise of the clause 33 option. As may be imagined, in the subsequent proceedings Freestone contended that the clause 33 option was binding on Denham Bros, whereas Denham Bros countered that it was not.

C. The Issues between the Parties

1. Indefeasibility by registration

Freestone claimed that the whole lease had the status of indefeasibility, on account of it being both registrable and registered. This proposition was founded on both Australian and New Zealand legislation, supported by case law.[6] On this question the court was split,[7] but the outcome of the case was not affected.

2. Attornment by deed of variation

In a further secondary argument, Freestone contended that a deed of variation of the lease amounted to an attornment, resulting in privity of contract between Denham Bros and Freestone. Denham Bros, it was said, had accepted Freestone as lessor and in effect had consented to the assignment of the reversion. Thereby Denham Bros had acknowledged Freestone's entitlement to all its rights under the lease, including those in clause 33. The court rejected this, on the basis that the variation was effected by deletion and replacement of specific clauses and

---

[6] *Denham Bros v Freestone Leasing* [2004] 1 Qd R 500 per Holmes J at 526.
[7] Contrast McPherson JA at 511 with Holmes J at 526.

nothing further.[8] Contrast the position in *Davenport Central Service Station v O'Connell* [1975] 1 NZLR 755 where the variation included a familiar clause in these words:

> In other respects the said lease and all of the terms covenants and conditions thereof shall remain in full force and effect.

That, said Holmes J, made the vital difference. It 'was an express and unequivocal agreement that the lessee should have the benefit of the covenants in the existing lease, so as to amount to a consent to an assignment'.[9]

3. Assignment of the benefit of the put option

A number of further points arose from the principal question about assignment of the benefit of the put option. They were:

- Was the benefit personal to the original lessor SGIO?
- Did the benefit pass automatically with the reversion? and
- Did the benefit pass by express assignment?

D. Was the Benefit Personal to the Original Lessor?

Denham Bros pointed to several aspects of the development scheme which involved SGIO exclusively. Among them were references to the sums paid for acquisition of the land and the costs of the works;[10] the inclusion of interest on moneys expended before the lease began;[11] and a provision for a certificate from 'the lessor' of the total outlay to be conclusive.[12] These factors, it was claimed, pointed to non-assignability of the option. Holmes J would have none of it. In the calculation of capital outlay 'the lessor' meant SGIO but in the put option it included assignees of the reversion. 'That does not mean that in either case there is ambiguity. There is simply a different meaning ascribed to the term in two different clauses.'[13]

A second aspect considered by the court was the possibility of an increased burden on the performing party by the assignment of the benefit of the obligation.[14]

---

[8] See Holmes J at 527.
[9] *Denham Bros v Freestone* 527.
[10] See *Denham Bros v Freestone* 515.
[11] See *Denham Bros v Freestone* 516.
[12] See *Denham Bros v Freestone* 516.
[13] Holmes J at 516–17.
[14] See *Denham Bros v Freestone* 517.

Denham Bros relied on a statement by Collins MR in *Tolhurst v Associated Portland Cement Manufacturers (1900) Ltd* [1902] 2 KB 660 at 668:

> The special right of ignoring altogether the consent of the person upon whom the obligation lies to the substitution of one person for another as the recipient of the benefit would seem in principle and common justice to be confined to those cases where it can make no difference to the person on whom the obligation lies to which of two persons he is to discharge it.

The cited passage was part of a commentary on basic contract principles. The judge was contrasting assignment of the burden of a contract (strictly novation, where consent of the benefited party is crucial) with assignment of the benefit (where consent of the burdened party is usually unnecessary). Only in cases where the burdened party has a special personal quality is his consent required.[15] The issue is whether the benefited party will be worse off if the assignment is without his consent, not simply whether the assignment will make the benefited party worse off. For the modern reader, Collins MR would have made himself clearer if he had said something like:

> In an assignment of the benefit of a contract, the consent of the person performing the contract can be ignored only if it can make no difference to him whether he performs it for one person or another.

Denham Bros was able to show that the substitution of Freestone for SGIO did make a significant difference to the obligation imposed on Denham Bros.[16] The court held that the possibility of a greater burden on the obligor was not conclusive of the obligation being owed to the original grantee and no one else. The question was of the 'true meaning and effect of the contract'.[17] Moreover the dealings concerned commercial property, not the provision of some personal skill.[18] And where, as in this case, the definition of lessor included the original lessor, its successors and assigns (a common enough provision in many commercial leases), the assignability became apparent. Even more, another clause declared that no subletting or licence would release the lessee from its liability to pay the rent and perform the other covenants

> . . . including in particular the obligations of the Lessee to purchase the demised premises from the Lessor *or the owner for the time being* in accordance with the provisions herein contained.[19]

---

[15] See *Tolhurst v Associated Portland Cement* [1902] 2 KB 668 at 669.

[16] *Denham Bros v Freestone* 515, 518.

[17] Holmes J in *Denham Bros v Freestone* at 518 citing the House of Lords decision in *Tolhurst v Associated Portland Cement* [1903] AC 414 at 417.

[18] *Denham Bros v Freestone* 518.

[19] *Denham Bros v Freestone* at 519 (underlining added in report).

The benefit of clause 33 was not personal to the original lessor and was therefore assignable.

E. Was the Benefit in Fact Assigned?

Freestone relied on *Griffith v Pelton* [1958] Ch 205, claiming that the benefit of the put option passed automatically with the assignment of the reversion from SGIO to Freestone. In *Griffith v Pelton* the lease defined 'lessee' in the customary way as including where the context allowed the lessee's personal representatives and assignees. It gave the lessee an option to buy the reversion. The original lessee assigned the lease to the plaintiff. The assignment document did not refer to the option, and subsequently the original lessee by deed expressly assigned the benefit of the option to the plaintiff. The personal representative of the original lessor was held to be bound by the option in the hands of the plaintiff. The original lessor and lessee were taken to have agreed that the benefit of the option would pass with the lease. If, however, the mere assignment of the lease was ineffective to pass the benefit of the option, the subsequent express assignment did the trick. *Woodall v Clifton* [1905] 2 Ch 257 was distinguished on the basis that it related to the burden rather than the benefit of a lessee's right to purchase the reversion.[20] *Woodall v Clifton* is authority for the proposition that a lessee's option to purchase the reversion does not touch and concern the lessee's estate in land, and so in the absence of intervening legislation does not bind a successor to the original lessor. Logically, a covenant relating to the lessor's interest cannot be said to touch and concern the interest vested in the lessee. The principle of *Griffith v Pelton* was applied in *Coastplace v Hartley* [1987] QB 948 where sureties covenanted with the lessors and their successors that the lessees would pay the rent. The lessors assigned the reversion without expressly assigning the benefit of the surety covenant. The benefit of the covenant passed even though it did not touch and concern the land.[21]

When *Coastplace v Hartley* came to be considered by the Court of Appeal in *Kumar v Dunning* [1989] QB 193, the judges considered that it was wrong on the 'touching and concerning' point.[22] Because the benefit of a surety covenant did 'touch and concern' the land, it ran with the reversion and so became enforceable by an assignee of the reversion. Accordingly it was unnecessary to consider the effect of *Griffith v Pelton*, apparently to the relief of Browne-Wilkinson V-C

---

[20] *Griffith v Pelton* [1958] 1 Ch 205 at 226 (Jenkins LJ).

[21] *Coastplace v Hartley* [1987] QB 948 at 959 (French J).

[22] *Kumar v Dunning* [1989] QB 193 at 201 (Browne-Wilkinson V-C with whom Croom-Johnson LJ and Neill LJ agreed).

who stated ('rather tersely', remarked Holmes J in *Denham Bros*[23]) that since he had considerable difficulty in understanding what *Griffith v Pelton* did decide, he would express no view on it.[24]

The real problem with *Griffith v Pelton* was that it ran together the notions of assignability and assignment.[25] The reasoning runs along these lines. The original lessor and lessee create a right in the hands of the lessee which is assignable. In normal circumstances they do not (perhaps they cannot) stipulate how the assignment is to be made. So they cannot invent a form of assignment (namely a standard assignment of the term) which by some magic wand carries with it an assignment of the benefit of the right. The riposte to this (as Wade suggests at [1957] CLJ 150) is that a standard assignment of the term passes to the assignee all the assignee's assignable rights under the lease, whether or not they touch and concern the land. The lease reveals the assignability or otherwise of the option. The instrument of assignment determines the scope of the assignment. Of course, for post-1995 leases in England and Wales, the problem does not arise. Section 3 of the Landlord and Tenant (Covenants) Act 1995 annexes the benefit of the lessor's covenant to the assignment of the lease. And if the option is a put option, the burden of the lessee's covenant will seemingly pass automatically with the lease unless the covenant is expressed (in whatever terms) to be personal either to the lessee or the lessor.[26]

In *Denham Bros v Freestone* one judge followed *Griffith v Pelton* and considered that the benefit of the put option would pass automatically with the reversion. The other two judges disagreed, holding that whilst the option was assignable in accordance with *Griffith v Pelton*, it was not in fact assigned until the express assignment of July 2002.[27] McMurdo P, the supporter of automatic passing of the benefit, stated:[28]

> In the absence of any proven contrary intention in the contract of sale between SGIO and the respondent for the sale of the land, I would be prepared to hold that, because of the terms of the lease, as in *Griffith v Pelton*, the benefit of the cl 33 option passed with the reversion, notwithstanding the omission of any reference to the assignment of that clause in the contract of sale . . .

On the other hand, Holmes J considered that the original parties could reach agreement about the assignability of a covenant but could not decide that a

---

[23] *Denham Bros v Freestone* 523.

[24] *Kumar v Dunning* at 207.

[25] See, for exmple, H W R Wade, 'Lease—option to purchase freehold—running of benefit' [1957] CLJ 148 at 150; and W J Mowbray, 'Who can exercise an option' (1958) 74 LQR 242 at 257.

[26] Section 3(6), Landlord and Tenant (Covenants) Act 1995.

[27] McPherson JA at 510 and Holmes J at 524.

[28] *Denham Bros v Freestone* 508.

particular event, namely the assignment of the term, could also effect assignment of the covenant. Further, she drew a distinction between assignment of a lessee's option to buy contained in an assigned lease and transfer of a reversion subject to a lease containing a put option.

> Holding that the assignment of rights under a lease includes assignment of rights under an option to purchase contained in the same document is rather a different thing from holding that the transfer of the lessor's interest in the fee simple could somehow incorporate and pass rights under the lease to which it was subject.[29]

Agreeing that the benefit did not pass automatically with the reversion, McPherson JA said:[30]

> Denham Bros as the original lessee and Freestone as the assignee of the reversion are mutually bound not by privity of contract but only by privity of estate. Consequently, unless the benefit of the covenant to purchase runs with the land, it would not, without more, have passed to the respondent Freestone automatically on the assignment to it of the reversion. The benefit of the covenant to purchase is nevertheless a chosen action which, like any other choice, is, as was recognised in *Griffith v Pelton* [1958] Ch 205, capable of being expressly assigned. That was what happened here when on 18 July 2002 the original lessor SGIO by Deed of that date assigned to Freestone the benefit of the covenant by the lessee *Denham Bros* contained in cl 33 of the lease.

All three judges dismissed the appeal and found that Freestone was entitled to exercise the put option against Denham Bros and had validly done so.

F. Some Reflections on *Denham Bros v Freestone*

Three lessons from *Denham Bros* stand out: first, the acceptance of put options into the general run of rights classed as options; second, the difficulty of the 'touch and concern' test; and third, the continuing scarcity of material on put options in gross.

In the three full judgments, the clause 33 option was only once referred to as a put option, and then only obliquely.[31] Even so, the clause 33 provision was a put option and absorbed by the court into the family of concepts called options. As for the difficulty of the 'touch and concern' test, it was recognized many years ago as being one where it is 'hard to discern the principles which should govern

---

[29] Holmes J at 523–4.

[30] *Denham Bros v Freestone* 510.

[31] McPherson JA at 510. It was also referred to once as a put option by Mullins J at first instance: [2002] QSC 307 at para 7.

where the dividing line is to be drawn'.[32] Note that neither at first instance nor on appeal did the court use the four-part test for 'touching and concerning' set out by Lord Oliver in *P & A Swift Investments v Combined English Stores* [1989] AC 632 at 642. The four conditions are that the covenant (1) must benefit the reversioner as reversioner, (2) must affect the nature, quality, mode of use, or value of the reversioner's land, (3) must not be personal, and (4) if for the payment of money, must be connected with something to be done on, to, or in relation to the land. By that test, the benefit of the put option in *Denham Bros* would seem clearly to touch and concern the land in Freestone's hands, and the express assignment of it was therefore otiose. For leases granted after 1995 in England and Wales the situation has been altered by statute. Now an assignee landlord is entitled to the benefit of all the tenant's covenants in the lease, except for any of those covenants which are expressed to be personal.[33] So if a case similar to *Denham Bros v Freestone* arose in England and Wales and the lease was a post-1995 lease, there seems little doubt that the benefit of the option would pass with the reversion.

Denham Bros related to a put option in a lease, where the likelihood is that the majority of put options arise. Much of the discussion in the case revolved around the position of the parties as lessor and lessee. So the decision can hardly be regarded as definitive on put options in gross. For them, problems about the transmissibility of benefit and burden remain. Put options in gross thus seem rather isolated, bereft of much direct analysis either in the courts or by academics. This chapter will return to the vexed question of put options in gross, their assignability and assignment, and the effect of the rule against perpetuity on them.

G. Guarantor Clauses in Leases

Put options in land are by no means as uncommon as might at first be supposed. This may be because the label 'put option' is seldom applied. In guarantor covenants incorporated in leases, it has long been the practice to require the guarantor to take a new lease if the lease is disclaimed by the tenant's trustee in bankruptcy or liquidator.[34] Similarly, authorized guarantee agreements under section 16 of the Landlord and Tenant (Covenants) Act 1995 are expressly

---

[32] Law Commission Working Paper No 95, *Landlord and Tenant: Privity of Contract and Estate: Duration of Liability of Parties to Leases*, (London: HMSO, 1986) para 3.6.

[33] Landlord and Tenant (Covenants) Act 1995 s 3.

[34] See, for example, RossCastle Letting Conditions clause 5.1:3 in M Ross, *Drafting and Negotiating Commercial Leases* (3rd edn, London and Edinburgh: Butterworths, 1989) 384; *Encyclopaedia of Forms and Precedents* (Vol 22, 5th edn, London: Butterworths, 1986) 750.

permitted to impose an obligation to take a new tenancy should the lease be disclaimed.[35]

Explicit adoption of put options is, however, relatively rare. They can be employed in complex developments as part of some grand plan.[36] Although there may be tax advantages in a put option, the parties must beware of being too clever by half and destroying the very protection they were trying to build.[37] Another positive use is in the planned withdrawal from a multi-use and multi-level complex.

H. Planned Withdrawal[38]

1. The possible scenario

Company A makes widgets at a large site which includes its head office and distribution centre. The buildings incorporate an underground car park and several two- and three-storey office blocks. The factory itself is an open-plan shed, surrounded by storage areas, both covered and open. The company intends to locate to several different sites, though suitable places have not yet been found. Company B would like to occupy the whole of Company A's current location. Company B is prepared to wait and to take the risk that Company A will never vacate all of its original place.

2. The legal possibilities

If Company A's interest is leasehold, its courses of action are likely to be restricted, not least by the terms of its lease and of any immediately superior lease.[39] If Company A's interest is freehold and it ultimately wishes to dispose of all that interest, a phased withdrawal by successive freehold transfers may be inhibited by the complex nature of the site, both horizontally and vertically. The preferred means of phased withdrawal is therefore likely to be by one or more leases of part, and the final instrument. The final instrument might be a transfer of Company A's entire interest or might itself be a further lease of whatever part has not already been leased. If every phase subsequent to the first can be the subject of a put option in favour of Company A, so much the better for Company A.

---

[35] Section 16(5)(c), Landlord and Tenant (Covenants) Act 1995.

[36] See, for example, *Allam Homes v Vocata* [2003] NSWSC 1052 available at <www.lawlink.nsw. gov.au>; and *Club of the Clubs Pty Ltd v King Network Group Pty Ltd* [2006] NSWSC 1138.

[37] See *Barnsley's Land Options* (3rd edn, p 197); *Ramsay v IRC* [1982] AC 300; *Furniss v Dawson* [1984] AC 474.

[38] The 'facts' in this section are projected from the study of a reasonably recent transaction in the south of England.

[39] *Hill v Harris* [1965] 2 QB 601.

Company B may of course be less happy because the initiative rests with Company A. As in the majority of commercial deals, the outcome depends upon what the parties want to achieve, the strengths of their bargaining positions, and their willingness to negotiate and compromise. One recent transaction in the south of England was structured in the following way.

- The parties entered into an agreement for a four-phase transition. The first phase was a lease of part. There was no premium for the lease and the rent was the rack rent.

- Simultaneously with the grant of the first lease the parties executed a supplemental agreement under which the landlord upon vacating a further defined area would serve notice on the tenant who would be required to take a supplemental lease of the defined area (the second phase).

- Similar provisions applied to vacation of the remainder of the property (the third phase).

- At that point, the supplemental deed required a variation of the three leases to a full repairing and insuring basis (the fourth phase).

The material parts of the supplemental deed were these.[40]

1.   BACKGROUND
1.1. The landlords and the tenant have today entered into a lease of part of the property ('the lease')
1.2. The parties have agreed to enter into this supplemental agreement to set out their future intentions with regard to the property
2.   AGREEMENT
2.1. The parties agree that as soon as the landlords have vacated the existing coldstore area as defined in the lease, the landlords will serve notice of their vacation on the tenant who will then enter into a supplemental lease ('the first supplemental lease') of the existing coldstore area comprising 580 square feet with an additional 2 car parking spaces at a rent of £8,200 a year. The service charge proportion in the first supplemental lease will be 6.3% and there will be no rent deposit otherwise the first supplemental lease will be on identical terms and conditions as the lease and will be outside the provisions of the Landlord & Tenant Act 1954
2.2. As soon as the landlords have vacated the first floor area comprising the remainder of the property, the landlords will serve notice on the tenant and

---

[40] Areas and measurements have been changed to preserve anonymity.

within one calendar month the tenant will enter into a supplemental lease ('the second supplemental lease') of the first floor area comprising 2,146 square feet with an additional 9 car parking spaces at a rent of £23,250 a year. The service charge proportion will be 17.8% and there will be no rent deposit otherwise this supplemental lease will be granted on identical terms and coterminous with the first supplemental lease and the second supplemental lease and will be outside the Landlord & Tenant Act 1954

2.3. Simultaneously with completion of the second supplemental lease the parties will enter into a deed of variation of the lease on terms to be agreed by the parties' solicitors acting reasonably to convert the lease and the first and second supplemental leases into full repairing and insuring terms without payment of a service charge (save that the landlord shall retain liability for the structure of the buildings marked A and C on the plan to the lease).

In passing, it should be noted that the scheme incorporated a number of option types: not only the put options set out above but also:

- a right for the landlords to terminate the agreement on default by the tenant or the happening of an 'insolvency event'
- rights for either side to bring the leases to an end if the property became unfit for use through the occurrence of an uninsured risk
- break clauses in favour of the tenant on specified conditions
- an express option for the tenant to renew for a further term of the same length as the original.

The presence of these additional options and the surrounding terms made the package less onerous than it might have seemed if the put options were considered in isolation.

I. The Perpetuity Rule and Put Options

Many of the provisions of the Perpetuities and Accumulations Act 1964 appear to have no application to put options. Section 9(2) reads:

> In the case of a disposition consisting of the conferring of an option *to acquire* for valuable consideration any interest in land, the perpetuity period under the rule against perpetuities shall be twenty one years, and section 1 of this Act shall not apply . . .[41]

---

[41] Emphasis added.

Since a put option is an option to dispose rather than an option to acquire, section 9(2) is clearly inapplicable. Likewise section 9(1) (disapplying the rule against perpetuities to a reversionary interest on a lease) speaks of 'the conferring of an option to acquire'. Accordingly the common law period of 21 years applies to put options unless for some reason a 'royal lives' clause is used[42] – though these are rare in commercial transactions.

What aspects of the 1964 Act, then, can apply to put options? Section 1(1) allows the specification of a perpetuity period of 80 years or less. Since this subsection is subject only to section 9(2) (see above) and to section 1(1) (special powers of appointment), there seems no reason why the grant of a put option might not limit its exercise to the 80-year period. The period should be referred to clearly as the perpetuity period applicable to the exercise, in view of the words in section 1(1) 'such number of years not exceeding eighty as is specified *in that behalf* in the instrument'.[43] The 'wait and see' provisions of the Act can apply to options but most unsatisfactorily they call for consideration of the common law rule.[44] The common law rule is that a disposition is void unless it must vest in interest within the period of 21 years after some life in being at the creation of the interest. The 1964 Act first suspends judgment where the conferring of an option would be void at common law on the ground that it might be exercised at too remote a time (s 3(3)), and then stipulates that the relevant lives are those of 'the person on whom the right is conferred' (s 3(5)(b)(v)) and 'the person by whom the disposition was made' (s 3(5)(a). In the case of a put option in gross, the landowner is 'the person on whom the right is conferred' and seemingly the covenantor is 'the person by whom the disposition is made'. Neither a corporation nor an animal can come within these provisions, which relate only to human lives.[45] So in summary (and attempting to make sense of a notoriously difficult statute), the position under the Perpetuities and Accumulations Act 1964 appears to be as follows.

(1) Subsections (1) and (2) of section 9 do not apply, since they relate to options to acquire, not put options.
(2) Section 1 (express period of 80 years or less) is capable of applying.
(3) A 'royal lives' clause could be effective but such clauses are rarely if ever found in commercial documents like grants of options.

---

[42] Megarry and Wade, *The Law of Real Property* (6th edn, (Harpum, C) London: Sweet & Maxwell, 2000) 350.

[43] Emphasis added.

[44] Megarry and Wade, n 42, p 308.

[45] J Morris and W B Leach, *The Rule Against Perpetuities* (2nd edn, London: Stevens & Sons, 1962) 63; *Re Kelly* [1932] IR 255.

(4) If both the landowner and covenantor are corporations and neither 2 nor 3 applies, the perpetuity period is simply 21 years from the date of the grant because there are no 'lives in being'.

(5) If the landowner is an individual and neither 2 nor 3 applies, the 'wait and see' provisions of section 3 apply, and the period is 21 years plus the life of the landowner (s 3(3), (4), and (5)(b)(v)).

(6) If the covenantor is an individual and neither 2 nor 3 applies, the position is as in 5 with the substitution of the covenantor for the landowner (s 3(5)(a)).

(7) If both parties are individuals and neither 2 nor 3 applies, the period is the longer of 5 and 6.

For completeness, it should be remembered that the rule against perpetuities has no application to contracts. So if both parties are corporations and the land does not change hands, an option can in theory remain effective indefinitely.[46]

J. Registration of Put Options

1. Options in gross

For put options in gross, the landowner has a right rather than an obligation. Where the land is registered, the right is not registrable as a notice under section 32(1) of the Land Registration Act 2002, which reads: 'A notice is an entry in the register in respect of the *burden* of an interest affecting a registered estate or charge' (emphasis added). In a similar vein, the Land Charges Act 1972 s 2(4)(iv) defines an estate contract as:

> . . . a contract by an estate owner . . . to convey or create a legal estate, including a contract conferring a valid option to purchase, a right of pre-emption or any other like right.

Although the curious decision of the Court of Appeal in *Pritchard v Briggs* [1980] Ch 338 indicates that section 2(4)(iv) may not mean what it says, the implication is clear: in unregistered titles, a land charge is a burden, not a benefit. In any event, a put option may not be an interest in land at inception. *Pritchard v Briggs* is authority for the strange proposition that a right of pre-emption does not become an interest in land until the landowner decides to sell.[47] If that is so, can a put option be an interest in land until the landowner decides to require the other party to buy? The arguments for *Pritchard v Briggs* being wrong, however, are powerful. It can be said to be inequitable, contrary to the 1925 legislation and

---

[46] See Megarry and Wade, n 42, p 349.
[47] See [1980] Ch 338 at 418 (Templeman LJ) and 425 (Stephenson LJ).

at variance with general principles of land law.[48] More than simply an example of 'hard cases make bad law',[49] it seems more to illustrate the proposition 'bad cases can make bad law' – the successful party's case appears entirely without merit. A later fixed-price option was allowed to prevail over a registered right of pre-emption. At all material times the successful party was aware of the earlier right.[50] People who in good faith on legal advice and with the approval of the Court of Protection had paid £14,150 for land were obliged to sell it for £3,000, incurring huge costs to boot.[51] Apart from the 1925 legislation, surely the creation of a put option is a 'contract for the sale or other disposition of an interest in land' required to be in writing by section 2 of the Law of Property (Miscellaneous Provisions) Act 1989.[52] Further, if the various statutory provisions are mechanisms to ensure that a purchaser does not take free of certain encumbrances, the beneficiary of put option in gross has no need to register. The practitioner should be able to persuade a Land Registry office that the put option can be entered in the property register by virtue of rule 5 of the Land Registration Rules 2003 SI 2003/1417 under which the property register of a registered estate must contain, where appropriate, details of

> easements, rights, privileges, conditions and covenants benefiting the registered estate and other similar matters.

And on the assumption that the benefit is assignable, a seller would be foolish not to reveal a put option to a potential buyer, whether the seller's title is registered or unregistered – not only to reveal the value of what he is selling but to ensure that any formalities for the effective transfer of the benefit of the option are complied with.[53]

2. Options in leases

Any attempt to frame a put option in favour of a lessee is likely to result in a right to renew the lease, a right to buy the reversion, or a break clause. In parallel with the position for options in gross, therefore, a put option in leases is inevitably for the benefit of the lessor. The rules relating to the assignment of the benefits of

---

[48] H W R Wade, 'Rights of pre-emption: interests in land?' (1980) 96 LQR 488.

[49] ibid p 488.

[50] See *Pritchard v Briggs* at 383 (Goff LJ) and Wade, n 48 at 489. Note also the semi-critical remarks of J Walton at first instance on the character of the ultimately successful plaintiff: *Pritchard v Briggs* [1980] 1 Ch 338 at 352, 353.

[51] *Pritchard v Briggs* at 424 (Stephenson LJ).

[52] See J Hoffmann in *Spiro v Glencrown* [1991] Ch 537 at 541; and Walton J in *Pritchard v Briggs* [1980] Ch 338 at 369.

[53] Note especially s 53(1)(c) Law of Property Act 1925 (requirement of writing) and s 136(1) (notice of assignment); and *Denham Bros v Freestone* [2004] 1 Qd R 500.

covenants in leases apply. It should also be noted that a put option is not among those matters which have to appear at the beginning of registrable leases by virtue of the Land Registration (Amendment) (No 2) Rules 2005 SI 2005/1982. Box LR9 (rights of acquisition, etc) refers to three subgroups: first, various contractual rights of the tenant; second, a tenant's covenant to surrender the lease; and third, a landlord's contractual right to acquire the lease. Thus a put option, being a tenant's covenant to take the reversion, is not required to be stipulated.

3. Registration of the buyer–seller contract

Registration of the contract which ensues from the exercise of an option is different from registration of the option itself, though if an option has been registered there is no need to register the subsequent contract separately.[54] Motivation to register the subsequent contract arising from a put option is weak, since the buyer is seemingly a reluctant party and the seller will hardly spring forward to burden his own land. If registration of any buyer–seller contract is rare, registration of one following the exercise of a put option is likely to be even rarer.

K. The Status of Put Options in Gross

It is suggested that the benefit of a put option in gross is capable of being an interest in land from its inception, and that it can pass automatically with the land. The exception is a put option which in some way is personal to the landowner. If the covenantor owes the obligation to the landowner personally, the benefit cannot pass to the landowner's successor in title.[55] The rationale for the general statement is as follows.

- At common law, the benefit of a positive covenant can run with the land.[56] In the case of a put option, the landowner has the benefit of a positive covenant.

- Similarly, at law the covenantor need not own any land at all.[57] In a put option in gross, the covenantor owns no relevant land.

- At common law, the covenantee and the assignee must each have had the same estate in the land benefited.[58] That will normally be the position with a put option in gross where the landowner has the fee simple and transfers it.

---

[54] *Armstrong & Holmes Ltd v Armstrong* [1993] 1 WLR 1482.
[55] See, for example, *P & A Swift Investments v Combined English Stores* [1989] AC 632 at 642.
[56] *Shayler v Woolf* [1946] Ch 320.
[57] *Smith v River Douglas Catchment Board* [1949] 2 KB 500.
[58] *Webb v Russell* (1789) 3 TR 393; *Rogers v Hosegood* [1900] 2 Ch 388.

Moreover section 78 of the Law of Property Act 1925 goes further, apparently transferring the benefit to lessees, underlessees and mortgagees. Section 78 says:

> A covenant relating to any land of the covenantee shall be deemed to be made with the covenantee and his successors in title and the persons deriving title under him or them, and shall have effect as if such successors or other persons were expressed.

- The section seems clear enough. Furthermore, it withstood the judicial scrutiny of positive covenants in *Rhone v Stephens* [1994] 2 AC 310 at 322 (Lord Templeman).

- Even if *Pritchard v Briggs* [1980] Ch 338 is good law, it can be distinguished on the basis that it related to the passing of a burden rather than a benefit. The status of a put option in gross in the hands of the landowner depends upon the principles relating to benefits in land, not burdens.

- Put options must surely have to be made in writing under section 2 of the Law of Property (Miscellaneous Provisions) Act 1989 relating to contracts for dispositions of interests in land. There is though something of a chicken and egg argument here. Does the requirement of writing come about because a put option is an interest in land, or does the instinctive feeling for writing confer the status of an interest in land on the put option? In any event, judges have felt that statutory mechanics do have a bearing on status.[59]

- The benefit of a put option in gross is analogous to interests in land like easements, restrictive covenants, and leasehold obligations integral to the leasehold relationship.[60] It is capable of satisfying the test for 'touching and concerning' set out in *P & A Swift Investments v Combined English Stores* [1989] AC 632, which itself can be seen as a wider test for interests in land generally. After all, there was no privity of estate between the parties in that case. It was therefore an example of the ancient common law principle that the benefit of a covenant relating to land becomes attached to that land and passes with it automatically.[61]

- *Swift* clearly implied that the benefit of a covenant affecting the present value of the land can subsist as an interest in land. As Hazel Williamson QC has said, the trend is towards eliminating academic distinctions in favour of common sense and a tacit recognition that the benefit of an interest in land

---

[59] See, for example, J Walton in *Pritchard v Briggs* [1980] Ch 338 at 369; and J Hoffmann in *Spiro v Glencrown* [1991] Ch 537 at 541.

[60] See Gray and Gray, *Elements of Land Law* (4th edn, Oxford: Oxford University Press, 2005) p 1565.

[61] See the excellent exposition in J E Adams and H Williamson ' "Touching and Concerning": from Spencer's Case to Swift' (1989) 8947 EG 24 at 77 and 8948 EG 22 at 22.

may lie in its investment value.[62] A put option in gross clearly affects the present value of the land and may well enhance its investment potential.

The burden of the covenantor's obligation under a put option in gross passes in accordance with contract law.[63] The burden is not attached to land. In addition to effective transfer by means of novation, the burden can transfer to the covenantor's personal representatives on his death or to his trustee or liquidator on insolvency.[64]

L. The Future for Put Options

In countries with a common law tradition, fashions in conveyancing come and go – witness the brief appearance of freehold flats in England and Wales,[65] the phenomenon of cross-leases in New Zealand,[66] and the use of strata titles in Australia.[67] Lockout agreements[68] and deposit guarantees[69] had their swift hours of fame. Often these fashions are prompted by tax saving or avoidance of planning control, and it may be that the incidence of stamp duty land tax will spur a move to greater use of options.[70] In the absence of something like that, the flexibility of solicitors alone is likely to ensure greater use of put options than formerly. The larger firms in the City of London have both the legal expertise and the know-how from financial markets to be able to use the put option in appropriate circumstances. Where those firms lead, others follow. The natural counterpart of the option is the conditional contract,[71] but often the option will be the simpler choice. Options can be used in isolation, and call options are

---

[62] (1989) 8948 EG 24.

[63] See Lord Templeman in *Rhone v Stephens* [1994] 2 AC 310 at 318: 'Enforcement of a positive covenant lies in contract.'

[64] See *Chitty on Contracts* (Vol 1, 29th edn, London: Sweet & Maxwell, 2004) paras 9–049, 9–050 and ch 20 (death and bankruptcy).

[65] Contrast E George, *The Sale of Flats* (2nd edn, London: Sweet & Maxwell, 1959) 7: 'A right of re-entry affecting freehold land appears to be subject to the rule against perpetuities, but this appears to be the only material drawback to the grant of a freehold,' with E George and A George, *The Sale of Flats* (5th edn, 1984) 22: 'Building societies have resolutely set their faces against lending on freehold flats and in consequence it must be accepted that all flat schemes for the foreseeable future must be leasehold.'

[66] A Alston et al, *Guide to New Zealand Land Law* (2nd edn, Wellington: Brooker's, 2000) 618.

[67] See A Bradbrook, S MacCallum, and A Moore, *Australian Real Property Law* (Sydney: The Law Book Co, 1991) 489.

[68] Following *Pitt v PHH Asset Management Ltd* [1994] 1 WLR 327.

[69] Schemes introduced in the mid 1980s by Legal and Professional Indemnity Ltd and Legal and General Assurance.

[70] See, for example E Slessenger, 'Renewed interest in options' [2005] 69 Conv 7.

[71] See *Barnsley's Land Options* (3rd edn) p 194 for a discussion of the differences between a conditional contract and an option, and the notion of the 'disguised option'.

especially useful for developers who are attempting to assemble a jigsaw puzzle of sites or who want to assemble a land bank without the costs and risks associated with outright purchase. The put option in particular is likely to form part of a fairly complex package, whether related to development, to planned withdrawal, or to some other objective. What lawyers should do is to have the put option available for use whenever circumstances call for its use. It should not become a passing fad, to be abandoned when some other trendy idea catches attention.

Part II

EQUITY AND THE LAW OF TRUSTS

7

UNCONSCIONABILITY IN PROPERTY LAW: A FAIRY-TALE ENDING?

Gary Watt

The tale of property law belongs to the science-fiction genre – it is part science, part fiction. In fact it is the ongoing story of efforts to supplant the fictions of law with the science of law. These efforts are keenly felt in connection with the idea of unconscionability. The most scientific approaches tell the story of equity in property law without resort to the idea of unconscionability. Sarah Worthington resort to the idea of exemplifies this approach in her monograph, *Equity*,[1] and F W Maitland takes a similar approach in *Equity: A Course of Lectures*,[2] in which he confines conscience to history.[3] There are, however, commentators who approve an aspirational version of equity in which good conscience is a transcendent extra-legal value to which appeal can be made through the language of unconscionability with a view to developing the law along 'better' lines. Margaret Halliwell is representative of this approach. In her monograph *Equity and Good Conscience* she contends that 'equity, or good conscience, operates as an anti-legal element *via* the judicial modification or supplementing of existing rules of law by reference to current conditions and circumstances'.[4] In an insightful paper to which further reference will be made,[5] Timothy Endicott also advances a vision of equity in which conscience operates as an external value with the power to

---

[1] S Worthington, *Equity* (Oxford: Clarendon Press, 2003).
[2] F W Maitland, *Equity: A Course of Lectures* (Cambridge: Cambridge University Press, 1909). Page references are to the 1936 revised second edition by Professor Brunyate, also published by Cambridge University Press.
[3] ibid pp 7–8.
[4] M Halliwell, *Equity and Good Conscience* (2nd edn, London: Old Bailey Press, 2004) 5.
[5] Timothy A O Endicott, 'The Conscience of the King: Christopher St. German, Thomas More, and the Development of English Equity' (1989) 47 University of Toronto Faculty of Law Review 549.

override posited law, albeit his vision places less weight than Halliwell's upon the shoulders of unconscionability per se. The present chapter argues that a scientific approach to property law should be favoured to ensure that outcomes of property dealings are generally predictable, but it contends that the language of unconscionability is still useful to describe conduct involving illegitimate use of legitimate rights. It is important, however, to keep the idea of unconscionability within proper bounds, especially in the context of property law. Accordingly, this paper will argue that the illegitimacy which makes conduct unconscionable varies according to the nature of the legitimate rights and powers that are being abused, with the result that the definition of unconscionability varies according to the particular legal context in which it is alleged. It is always necessary to state why conduct is unconscionable in the particular context, hence unconscionable conduct 'is not by itself sufficient to found liability'.[6] This supports Worthington's claim that there is no 'general theory of Equity'.[7] There is, however, scope to resort to *some* idea of unconscionability in every legal context in which legitimate rights are employed as the very instrument of abuse, so in this sense there is a 'general theory of equity' after all.

This chapter provides support for the retention of the idea of unconscionability in property law, but it is qualified support. For one thing, it is important to distinguish the legal idea of unconscionability from moral or religious ideas of conscience. If the retention of the language of unconscionability happens incidentally to perpetuate humane and aspirational virtues of conscience, that is well and good, but there is no room for the promotion of transcendental moral notions of 'good conscience' as a basis for enforcing and allocating rights in property. Christopher St Germaine was right to assert that 'where any Law is ordained for the disposition of lands and goods' it binds everyone under the law 'in the Court of Conscience, that is to say, inwardly in his Soul',[8] thereby stripping the Court of Chancery of any pretence to be a court of conscience and leaving no room at all for any extra-legal idea of conscience to disturb titles to property. Any judge who employs the language of unconscionability as a means of ditching property rules in favour of moral intuition is abusing the name of conscience. This chapter will demonstrate that the idea of unconscionability in property law is not an idea of conscience at all; it does not descend from the heavens like an angel. The idea of unconscionability does not descend from on high; it rises out of the law. It is true that equity sometimes ascends a little further than the common law, but only

---

[6] Sir Nicolas Browne-Wilkinson, *Presidential Address of the President of the Holdsworth Club*, Holdsworth Club, University of Birmingham, 1991, p 7.

[7] ibid p 17.

[8] *Two Dialogues in English Between A Doctor of Divinity and A Student in the Laws of England, of The Grounds of the said laws, and of conscience* (1532) ch XX.

because the common law has carried it most of the way. As the fable tells us, even a wren can fly further than an eagle if the eagle carries the wren as far as the eagle can go. An illustration of this dynamic relationship between equity and law is provided by equity's remedy of specific performance. The remedy is an exalted solution to the problem of breach of contract to sell land, but it does not appear spontaneously in a legal vacuum; it is resorted to only because the common law remedy of damages is inadequate and because it would be unconscionable for the defendant to offer an inadequate common law remedy by way of satisfaction for his breach. What makes the defendant's conduct unconscionable in such a case is not the infraction of any moral code or any social norm of acceptable behaviour, but the altogether mundane perversion of turning the law, which should be an instrument of justice, into an instrument of injustice.

Having demonstrated that the idea of unconscionability ascends out of particular laws, this chapter will stress the need to ensure that it does not rise so far as to lose touch with its origins. We do not wish the bird of unconscionability to be caged in the law, but its wings must be clipped. The argument of this chapter is that this can be achieved by taking care to ensure that there is no finding of unconscionable conduct where the defendant can show that his conduct was justified by norms or customs of conduct governing the particular context in which unconscionability is alleged or, better still, can show that his conduct was substantially (and not merely formally) justified by the substance of the parties' own contractual intentions.

Accordingly, the idea of unconscionability advanced in this chapter differs in at least two significant respects from the idea advanced by Halliwell in her monograph *Equity and Good Conscience*. First, she is committed to an idea of unconscionability which transcends particular legal contexts, whereas this writer contends that unconscionability is inevitably contextual, because it is bound to respect or 'follow' the particular law which it is alleged has been unconscionably abused. Second, whereas Halliwell considers that equity, perhaps especially in the context of unmarried cohabitation, 'prescribes optimum standards of behaviour in social relationships of trust' consistent with 'communal norms',[9] this author contends that identifiable social norms have a significant but opposite role. Judicial perceptions of social norms should never be a basis for a finding of unconscionability in support of an equitable claim, but defendants who can demonstrate that their conduct is consistent with an accepted social norm should on that basis be able to defend a finding of unconscionability.

---

[9] N 4 above p 153.

A. The Wolf in Sheep's Clothing

At first sight there is something comforting and humane in the thought that judges and lawmakers might be willing to admit exceptions to common law rules on the ground of conscience, but first impressions are misleading. History shows that the name of conscience is bloody with the lives it has claimed. It comes in sheep's clothing, but it has the bite of a wolf. Endicott regrets that the jurisprudence of Christopher St Germaine permitted the idea of conscience in Chancery to 'descend' into precedent,[10] but if we cannot be confident that judicial and executive expressions of conscience will ascend to the angels we might prefer a descent into precedent than a descent into despotism. This, according to Story's *Commentaries on Equity Jurisprudence*, is the worrying potential of a system of equity unbound by precedent:

> If indeed a Court of Equity in England did possess the unbounded jurisdiction . . . of correcting, controlling, moderating, and even superseding the law, and of enforcing all the rights, as well as all the charities, arising from natural law and justice, and freeing itself from all regard to former rules and precedents, it would . . . place the whole rights and property of the community under the arbitrary will of the judge, acting . . . according to his own notions and conscience, but still acting with a despotic and sovereign authority.[11]

Professor Birks even went so far as to compare judicial rule by conscience to the despotism of the Nazis.[12] He was criticized for making the comparison, but in a subsequent article he defended it on principle.[13] There his argument was that:

> Conscience, undisciplined by the apparatus of reason, is an alias for the will of those in power. They have only to believe that what they are doing is right, and conscience will justify them, at the same time blinding them to the possibility of error.[14]

Birks accepts that the 'great errors are mercifully rare', but notes that 'the lesser errors are of day to day concern'.[15] Certainly, the intuitive allocation of proprietary rights is not a great error in the category of genocide or unjustified invasion

---

[10] N 5 above 558.

[11] J Story, *Commentaries on Equity Jurisprudence* (W H Lyon, Jr, ed) (14th edn Boston: Little Brown & Co, 1918) Vol I § 19, at 21. Cited in *Grupo Mexicano De Desarrollo, S A v Alliance Bond Fund, Inc*, 527 US 308, 332–3 (1999).

[12] P Birks, 'Equity in the Modern Law: An Exercise in Taxonomy' (1996) 26 University of Western Australia Law Review 1, 17 (referring to A H Campbell, 'Fascism and Legality' (1946) 62 *Law Quarterly Review* 141, 147).

[13] P Birks, 'Annual Miegunyah Lecture: Equity, Conscience, and Unjust Enrichment' (1999) 23 Melb U L Rev 1.

[14] ibid at 21.

[15] ibid at 22.

of foreign territory, but it is an error nevertheless, and it is one which can have serious adverse consequences for the parties in individual cases. We might expect judges to be reluctant to admit any restraint upon the breadth of their judicial discretion, but many have echoed Birks' concerns. Thus Kirkby P has described unbounded notions of unconscionability in terms which hint at the wild beast lurking within. He observes that conscience, 'being so much a matter of personal opinion', needs to be 'tamed and classified according to established categories'.[16] Despite such warnings, one can discern in recent cases in the property jurisdiction of England and Wales a disconcerting relaxation of judicial attitudes towards the idea of unconscionability in property law, and certainly a disregard for the dangers which attend its use. Perhaps criticism is unfair; perhaps academic commentators are insufficiently sensible to the complexities of the judicial process and insufficiently sensitive to the burden upon judges to do what appears just to the parties before them. Richard Francis, the author of an early systematic text on equity, was far more trusting of what we nowadays term 'judicial activism'. He believed that no judge would 'dictate according to his Will and Pleasure' but, rather, would look to 'that infallible Monitor within his own Breast'.[17] Today we do not have such faith in the infallibility of the conscience caged within judicial ribs. No doubt we trust our judges to do what they believe to be right, but we doubt that they have any special monopoly on supra-legal notions of right and wrong, whether those notions are religious or moral. We recognize that they can do no more than promote their own reasonable notions of morality and society. Professor Birks opined that 'it ought not to be necessary to spend time showing that inscrutable intuition is the enemy of the rule of law',[18] but recent decisions have made it necessary again. Perhaps none more so than the decision of the Court of Appeal in *Pennington v Waine*.[19]

Mr Pennington was a partner in a firm of auditors acting for a private limited company in which Mrs Ada Crampton held a number of shares. She told Mr Pennington that she wished to transfer 400 of her shares in the company to her nephew, Harold. She signed a share transfer form to that effect and gave it to Mr Pennington. He placed the form on file and took no further action prior to Ada's death, except to write to Harold. In that letter he enclosed a form for Harold to sign his consent to become a director of the company, and the letter informed Harold that Mr Pennington's firm had been instructed to arrange for the transfer of the 400 shares and that Harold need take no further action.

---

[16] *Austotel Pty Ltd v Franklins Selfserve Pty Ltd* (1989) 16 NSWLR 582, 585.
[17] R Francis, *Maxims of Equity* (London: J Stephens, 1727).
[18] P Birks, 'Annual Miegunyah Lecture: Equity, Conscience, and Unjust Enrichment'.
[19] [2002] 1 WLR 2075.

Ada also informed Harold directly of her intention to transfer shares to him and of her desire that he should become a director of the company. However, when Ada died her will made no disposition of the shares in favour of Harold, so the question arose whether she had made an effective disposition during her lifetime. At first instance the court noted that there was no evidence that the gift had been intended to take effect in the future or subject to any condition precedent. Accordingly the court could have held the gift to be ineffective, but instead it held that the gift had been effective immediately the share transfer forms had been executed even though the forms were never delivered to Harold or to the company.

Having passed the share transfer form to her own agent it remained open to Ada to revoke her instructions to the agent for so long as she lived, and it is therefore most difficult to see on what basis she could be said to have disposed outright of her beneficial interest in the shares. Despite this fundamental problem, the Court of Appeal upheld the judgment at first instance. Their Lordships held that Ada's disposition had been effective on two grounds. One ground was technical. Clarke LJ held that the execution of the stock transfer form could take effect as a valid equitable assignment without the need for actual delivery of the stock transfer forms or the share certificates, provided the execution of the stock transfer forms were intended to take immediate effect. If his Lordship is right on that point, then from the moment the forms were transferred, Ada had actually done everything within her power that was required in order to divest herself of her beneficial interest in the shares. However, it is surely doubtful that a donor should be construed to have transferred beneficial ownership, whilst retaining legal ownership, in the absence of a clear intention to become a trustee of the transferred assets. The second ground was anything but technical. Arden LJ held that it would be unconscionable for Ada to resile from the transfer she had embarked upon. Arden LJ described unconscionability as a 'policy consideration'[20] that operates in favour of holding that a transfer has been perfected. It is submitted that this reasoning does not, with the greatest respect, withstand close scrutiny. Her Ladyship identified a number of specific facts which in her judgment would have made it unconscionable for Ada to have denied Harold his anticipated beneficial interest in the 400 shares. Those facts were as follows: first, Ada made the donation of her own free will; second, she signed the share transfer form and delivered it to Mr Pennington to secure registration; third, she told Harold about the gift; fourth, Mr Pennington told Harold that he need take no further action to perfect the gift; fifth, Harold signed a form by which he agreed to

---

[20] ibid at 2091.

become a director without limit of time, which he could not do without shares in the company.

If the first three facts, taken together or individually, were sufficient to bind Ada's conscience, it would surely never be safe for a competent person voluntarily to promise to make a gift, let alone to instruct their agent to take steps preliminary to making a gift. We must conclude, it is submitted, that the first three facts could have had no impact on Ada's conscience. This brings us to facts four and five. Fact four was no doubt a representation, but was it a representation upon which Harold had relied to his detriment so that Ada's conscience must be affected? That is most doubtful. There was nothing Harold could have done to perfect the gift in his favour, so his omission to do that which he could not have done can hardly be regarded as detrimental reliance. What then of the fifth fact? Here at last is a candidate. By accepting the directorship it is certainly arguable that Harold acted to his detriment in reliance on an expectation that he would acquire some shares in the company. Still, it is doubtful that the detrimental reliance was of such a degree as might irrevocably bind Ada's conscience to fulfil the gift. In any case, even if there had been a representation plus detrimental reliance thereon, this would normally be said to raise an estoppel binding on the conscience of the representor, yet their Lordships made no reference to the doctrine of estoppel, preferring instead to base their decision on an unencumbered notion of unconscionability. It is due to this omission to make any concession to legal science that the fiction of unconscionability was permitted to thrive in this case. It is respectfully submitted that it will not suffice to apply a vague idea of unconscionability in a context so dependent upon certainty as the transfer of beneficial ownership in shares. The court should have said what unconscionability *means* in this context[21] and why unconscionability arose on the facts of the case. Surely Ada's own intentions are not capable, without more, of creating a burden on her own conscience. Despite these concerns, Schiemann LJ agreed with Arden LJ's reasoning without discussion and Clarke LJ agreed that 'if unconscionability is the test . . . it would have been unconscionable of Ada, as at the time of her death (if not earlier), to assert that the beneficial interest in the 400 shares had not passed to Harold'.[22]

Arden LJ was no doubt sincerely motivated to achieve a just outcome for the parties in the case. To assist her in that mission her ladyship invoked equity's long tradition of protecting an intended donee from the rigours of equity's own maxim, 'equity does not assist a volunteer'. Her ladyship described the maxim as

---

[21] Following the advice of Lord Nicholls of Birkenhead in *Royal Brunei Airlines Sdn Bhd v Philip Tan Kok Ming* [1995] 2 AC 378, Privy Council at 392.

[22] [2002] 1 WLR 2075 at 2095.

a harsh wind blowing against a 'shorn lamb' (ie the donee) and she determined to 'temper the wind' to the lamb by finding some way to make the gift effective despite the inconvenient timing of Ada's death. Her ladyship was undoubtedly successful, but one is bound to conclude that the aid supplied to the donee came in somewhat woolly form. Her ladyship held that:

> There are . . . policy considerations which . . . militate in favour of holding a gift to be completely constituted. These would include effectuating, rather than frustrating, the clear and continuing intention of the donor, and preventing the donor from acting in a manner which is unconscionable.[23]

This resort to unconscionability is unhappy on several levels. First, how can the court claim to be simultaneously assisting and compelling the donor? A genuine bilateral or common intention between parties might conceivably bind the conscience of one to the other, but a unilateral intention of gift cannot bind the donor until it has been acted upon by the donor[24] (or, exceptionally, as in a case of estoppel, acted upon by the donee) in a way that makes the gift irrevocable. Second, if unconscionability is a policy consideration, it is undoubtedly a very broad one, equivalent perhaps to the policy of preventing the law from being brought into disrepute through misuse. Left at large like this it will be very hard to predict when the 'policy' of unconscionability might bite next, and how hard. A policy of preventing the common law from being brought into disrepute is very welcome, but unless it is employed as a last resort, or at least strictly controlled, it will do as much damage to the reputation of law as any strict common law rule. An unbounded policy of unconscionability can hardly be expected to follow its own precedents, let alone to 'follow the law'. It could take us back to the days when equity varied according to the length of the Chancellor's foot. Third, there is no indication of what unconscionability actually means in this context. Does it mean conduct which causes a loss to the intended donee? If not, then what? It is better to leave the shorn sheep to the wind than to cover it in a woolly idea of unconscionability. At least we can be confident that a shorn sheep is no wolf.

There is a stark contrast between the approach taken by the Court of Appeal in *Pennington v Waine* and the treatment of conscience by the Court of Appeal in *Re McArdle*.[25] In the latter case a testator left his residuary estate upon trust for his widow for life, remainder to his five children in equal shares. During the lifetime of the widow, one of the children, Monty, carried out improvements to a farm

---

[23] ibid at 2091.
[24] By execution of a deed of gift or by transfer of the subject matter of the gift to the intended donee.
[25] [1951] 1 Ch 669, Court of Appeal.

forming part of the testator's residuary estate. The testator's other children then
signed a document in the following terms:

> To Monty . . . in consideration of your carrying out certain alterations and improve-
> ments to the . . . Farm . . . at present occupied by you, we the beneficiaries under the
> will of William Edward McArdle hereby agree that the executors . . . shall repay to
> you from the said estate when so distributed the sum of £488 in settlement of the
> amount spent on such improvements.

When the widow died, the other children refused to accede to Monty's claim to
the £488. The Court of Appeal held that the transfer of the relevant part of the
residuary estate would be effective only if Monty (in fact Monty's widow by this
time) could establish that the signed document had been a binding contract or
a valid transfer of an equitable interest. The court held that it was neither. The
works of improvement had been completed before the execution of the document so that the consideration for the contract was entirely in the past, thus ren-
dering the contract legally unenforceable. However, the document had been in
form and intent a contract so the court refused to construe it as a valid equitable
assignment. Lord Evershed MR regretted that the other children had been able
'to evade the obligation which they imposed on themselves', but that, he said, 'is
a matter for their conscience and not for this court'.[26] Jenkins LJ added that, in
the absence of consideration or a perfected transfer, the donor of an imperfect gift
(each of the 'other children' in this case) 'has a locus poenitentiae and can change
his mind at any time', thus 'no question of conscience enters into the matter'.[27]
Perhaps such an approach leaves the shorn lamb out in the cold, but the shorn
lamb should have noticed earlier that the promise had been made for past consideration (and had not been made by deed and had not given rise to an estoppel)
and therefore could not be made binding except by subversion of the law. Ada
Crampton, had she lived, could have deflected any charge of unconscionability
by raising in her defence the customary norm, confirmed by law, that a person
intending to make a donation has a right to change her mind. It may in some
sense be morally wrong to raise such a defence (given the great range of possible
moral perspectives it very probably was wrong according to one of them), but
that, to paraphrase Evershed MR in *Re McArdle*, would be 'a matter for her
conscience and not for the court'.

In *Pennington v Waine*, Arden LJ appeared to give express approval to an intuitive
approach when in the process of by-passing the principle 'equity will not assist a
volunteer' she observed that 'historically' the principle may have been accountable to 'the need for equity to follow the law rather than an intuitive development

---

[26] ibid at 676.
[27] ibid at 677.

of equity'.[28] This apparent preference for an intuitive idea of unconscionability was so radical that Margaret Halliwell, a committed supporter of the independent remedial application of the idea of unconscionability, is forced to disown *Pennington v Waine*. Halliwell is honest enough to write that '[a]s a proponent of the principle of unconscionability, I have to admit that this case does do great damage to my cause'.[29] She criticizes the decision on three grounds. First, that the decision disregarded precedent; second, that the decision was not based on 'principled reasoning'; and third, that the decision overlooked the fact that equitable maxims are useful only when they are applied with precision and according to precedent. This writer would agree with every one of Halliwell's criticisms of the case, but, with respect, cannot help but think that Halliwell's own brand of unconscionability is likely to encourage judicial creativity of the sort witnessed in *Pennington v Waine*, since the essence of Halliwell's idea of unconscionability is that it should promote an anti-legal idea of good conscience, whereas this writer's idea of unconscionability is that it should be limited to restraining the peculiarly legal wrong of abusing legitimate rights and powers. Halliwell's idea of unconscionability is really an idea of 'conscionability', for which there is no place in the dictionary or in the law. Unless the legal definition of unconscionability is inherently constrained it will be like an uncaged wolf; one can hardly complain that it does not come to heel or that it runs wild as it did in *Pennington v Waine*. Of course, it is very useful to our story to have a case like *Pennington v Waine* to play the part of the big bad wolf, but such cases are aberrant. It is only fair to note that when Arden LJ reiterated her desire to 'temper the harsh wind to the shorn lamb' in the recent case of *Murad v Al-Saraj*,[30] she rightly preferred to leave the lamb in the cold than to question the strict rule of fiduciary accountability for unauthorized profits. 'That sort of question,' her ladyship said, 'must be left to another court.'[31] If Arden LJ's approach in *Pennington v Waine* was postmodern, her approach in *Murad v Al-Saraj* more closely corresponds to the modern (that is, post-reformation) idea of equity as 'a reasonable measure, containing in it selfe a fit proportion of rigor . . . a ruled kind of Justice'.[32]

Let us return to Halliwell's idea of unconscionability. She is right to assert that 'conscience, as represented by the body of law we all know as equity, contributes a key "morality" to the legal system in general',[33] but the quote marks are a necessary qualification, for they remind us that equity, as with all law, is capable

---

[28] [2002] 1 WLR 2075 at 2088.
[29] N 4 above at 21.
[30] [2005] EWCA Civ 959, Court of Appeal, para 81.
[31] ibid para 82.
[32] William West, *The Second Part of Symboleography* (1593).
[33] N 4 above pp 1–2.

only of advancing its own highly attenuated brand of morality. The morality of equity is especially idiosyncratic in the context of land law, since if 99 per cent of all land were owned by 1 per cent of all people, there can be no doubt that equity would follow the law in defending the rights of the owners against the rest. This would be the case even if a great many of 'the rest' were without the basic necessities of life. This represents a serious qualification to Halliwell's claim that equity 'operates as an anti-legal element via the judicial modification of existing rules of law by reference to current conditions and circumstances'[34] (or 'matches established principle to the demands of social change,'[35] as one senior judge put it). Equity is an anti-legal element, but it is an element intrinsic to, and limited by, the nature of law. It is the law's internalized check upon itself. Furthermore, if judges are to modify existing rules of law by reference to current conditions and circumstances, they should do so (and this is a significant departure from Halliwell) only so far as such reference is made in *defence* of the defendant. Judicial perception of social trends is a sound basis for establishing a defence to the charge of unconscionability, but it is a very dangerous basis on which to impute unconscionability as the ground of a claim. Thus Halliwell oversteps the mark when she suggests that equity '*prescribes* optimum standards of behaviour in social relationships of trust'.[36] There would be no problem if the 'prescription' was a symbolic one intended to perpetuate respect for established relationships, but it appears that Halliwell's concern is more progressive. Her desire is to ensure that the development of the law remains responsive to social change. That is a laudable aim no doubt, but it is not one that we should encourage judges to attain with the tools of equity. Social mores have changed more rapidly since the Second World War than at any other time in English history. In such circumstances, judges should be slow to respond to social change where property rights are concerned. We cannot deny that laws change over time in response to changing social conditions, but parliament is the proper authority to respond to fundamental changes and if a judicial response is called for, respect for the rule of law requires that it be left to the judicial committee of the House of Lords, and no inferior court, to depart from precedent on the ground only that 'it appears right to do so'.[37] Even with that licence, their lordships have determined that they 'will bear in mind the danger of disturbing retrospectively the basis on which contracts, settlements of property and fiscal arrangements have been entered into'.[38]

---

[34] ibid p 5.
[35] L J Waite in *Midland Bank v Cooke* [1995] 2 FLR 915 at 927D.
[36] N 4 above at 153 (emphasis added).
[37] Practice Statement (Judicial Precedent) [1966] 1 WLR 1234.
[38] ibid.

It is respect for history and precedent which cautions against the outright eradication of the language of unconscionability from equitable jurisprudence. Unconscionability *is* equity's jurisprudence, since the word identifies that very species of wrongdoing which it is the peculiar function of equity to remedy, that wrongdoing being any conduct which, having no substantial justification, turns the common law into an instrument of harm by taking advantage of a general provision or general omission of the common law to oppress a party in the particular case. The language of unconscionability may seem quaint but it is not unscientific, in fact, when defined as the illegitimate abuse of legitimacy, and when further refined according to the legal contexts in which 'legitimacy' is itself defined, the term 'unconscionability' is actually more scientific than more general candidate terms such as 'unfair', 'prejudicial', and 'unjust', which from time to time have been advanced with scientific credentials. The language of unconscionability arises from the long saga of law's relationship to morality and in this sense it borders on fiction and has the potential to engage with extra-legal notions of moral or ecclesiastic conscience, but in most jurists long familiarity has bred healthy caution. Judges and academic commentators have, for the most part, acquired a handle on unconscionability which ensures it does not get out of hand in ways that more novel language might. However, two things are required to ensure that we do not lose our grip. First, no resort should be made to the language of unconscionability in any legal context without some attempt being made to define unconscionability according to the terms of the particular legal context. Second, defendants should be afforded a robust defence to any finding of unconscionability. In particular, no finding of unconscionable conduct should be made against a defendant where the conduct in question is consistent with a norm of conduct recognized, by customary practice or by the parties' contractual intent, to be appropriate to the particular context in which it occurred.

B. The Leaping Match

In Hans Christian Andersen's fairy-tale *The Leaping Match*, the flea, the grass-hopper, and the frog compete to see which of them can leap the highest. The flea jumps out of sight and the grasshopper jumps as high as the King's head, but the frog wins when he jumps into the lap of the princess, for as the King says, 'there is nothing higher than my daughter'. The aim of this section is to show that conduct which may appear inferior by certain abstract moral standards should not be considered unconscionable in law if it matches an observable objective standard of acceptable conduct. To be precise, a defendant cannot be said to have conducted himself unconscionably if his conduct was in accordance with the substance of the parties' contractual intentions or was normal according to custom governing the particular context in which the conduct occurred. Indeed, it will suffice for the defendant to demonstrate that his conduct is customary in the context, even if his conduct does not accord with universal practice in that context and even though others acting in the same context may disapprove of the defendant's approach.

In this respect the defence is similar to the defence that is available to medics accused of professional negligence, where it has been held that a doctor has a defence to a claim in negligence if he or she acted in accordance with a practice accepted (at the time) as proper by a responsible body of medical opinion skilled in the particular form of treatment in question, even though a body of competent professional opinion might adopt a different technique.[39] As in the medical negligence context, the defence of normal conduct will not succeed if the defendant's conduct is ratified as normal *ex post facto*; the defendant must demonstrate that during the relevant period he conducted himself in a manner already accepted as normal in the particular context. If he does that, there should be a very strong presumption against finding unconscionability. It is not suggested that the court is required to accept that a particular species of customary conduct inevitably obviates a finding of unconscionability (since it may be that the court takes the view that certain forms of conduct are unconscionable even if they are customary), only that compliance with such norms ought to raise a very strong presumption against liability.[40] The essential point is that there is no room for a finding of unconscionability if the defendant's conduct is consistent with an innocent state of mind. Conduct cannot be sufficiently wrong when it is sufficiently right. Appreciation that the defence of normal or customary conduct operates as a defence to a finding of unconscionability, and that it sets a much needed upper limit or 'ceiling' on the scope of unconscionability, will elucidate, amongst other things, the relationship between the doctrine of unconscionability and the doctrine of notice as they apply to the purchase of property subject to a trust. This is crucial, since the doctrine of notice 'lies at the heart of equity'.[41] Peter Prescott QC has recently emphasized the centrality of the doctrine of notice when sitting as a deputy judge of the High Court in *R Griggs Group Ltd v Evans*.[42] He noted that:

> If equity had tried to make the third party purchaser liable, irrespective of any notice, it would not have been acting *in personam*. It would have been creating a title in the

---

[39] *Bolam v Friern Hospital Management Committee* [1957] 1 WLR 582.
[40] This echoes the gloss made on the *Bolam* test in *Bolitho v City and Hackney Health Authority* [1998] AC 232, House of Lords.
[41] *Barclays Bank plc v O'Brien* [1994] AC 180 per Lord Browne-Wilkinson at 195.
[42] [2005] ch 153.

original purchaser good as against the whole world. Thus it would have been acting *in rem*. It would have been ousting the common law, not supplementing it.[43]

However, it is respectfully submitted that his lordship did not accurately represent the doctrine insofar as he characterized notice as a basis of liability and overlooked the essentially defensive nature of the doctrine:

> I . . . believe that it has been established for at least 250 years that a purchaser who takes a legal estate with actual notice of facts which have created a prior equitable interest, or who deliberately refrains from pursuing obvious enquiries for fear of learning the truth about same, is guilty of equitable fraud or, if one prefers to say so, conduct which is unconscionable.[44]

There is truth in the observation that a purchaser who purchases assets with notice that they are subject to a trust, but without overreaching the trust, is conscience-bound by the trust, but it is not the whole truth. It obscures the fact that the purchaser is liable only if he cannot establish his lack of notice. Notice supplies a basis for finding unconscionability, but it simultaneously supplies the defence. Indeed the primary significance of the doctrine of notice lies in the fact that the bona fide purchaser for value of a legal estate without notice of the trust has an unanswerable defence to the claims of the trust beneficiaries.[45] It is this defensive operation of the doctrine in the hands of the innocent purchaser which denies the universality of equitable property and ensures that the recognition of equitable property does not undermine the system of common law title. It may be that equity considers otherwise innocent conduct to be unconscionable if it is carried out in the face of notice, but it is more significant that equity considers innocent conduct to be unimpeachable if it is carried out without notice. The absence of notice establishes the purchaser with unimpeachable title in law and, since equity follows the law, the question of conscience does not arise at all. Conscience leaps, but it does not leap higher than the law.

The purchaser's defence that he lacked notice is established not only by lack of actual notice but also by the absence of constructive notice, and he can establish the absence of constructive notice only by demonstrating compliance with norms of investigation acknowledged to be appropriate to the purchase of land. If the purchaser made the sorts of enquiries that purchasers are normally expected to make when buying property of the type in question, his conscience is not affected by facts which his enquiries failed to reveal.[46] If the courts were to accept (by analogy to the doctrine of notice) that a finding of unconscionability cannot

---

[43] ibid at 164.
[44] ibid at 168.
[45] *Pilcher v Rawlins* (1872) LR 7 Ch App 259, 268–9.
[46] *Kingsnorth Finance Co Ltd v Tizard* [1986] 1 WLR 783, Chancery Division.

be sustained where the defendant has followed norms of conduct accepted in the particular context, we shall have less to fear from high-flying notions of unconscionability. It has been said that unconscionability 'will commonly involve the use of or insistence upon legal entitlement to take advantage of another's special vulnerability or misadventure . . . in a way that is unreasonable or oppressive to an extent that affronts ordinary minimum standards of fair dealing'.[47] This is as good a general statement on unconscionability as one can find in the cases, but in order to supply unimpeachable conduct with the necessary defence this author would add the rider that 'conduct is presumed not to be unconscionable when it is consistent with ordinary normal standards of fair dealing in the particular context in which unconscionability is alleged'.

We will now turn to consider briefly how the 'normal conduct' defence might operate to set a ceiling on unconscionability in the context of pre-contractual agreements to purchase land, contracts to purchase land, completion of purchase of land, and personal liability for voluntary receipt of misapplied trust property.

1. Pre-contract agreement to purchase land

It is well known that a vendor is permitted to withdraw from the sale provided there is no formal contract to sell. This is despite the vendor giving the customary assurance that he will enter into a formal contract and despite any detrimental reliance the purchaser might have suffered in reliance on that assurance. As Martin Dixon has observed:

> It simply is not unconscionable for the seller to behave in this way. This tells us two things. First, that the 'unconscionability' required to trigger an estoppel does not exist simply because the representor behaves 'badly'. . . Secondly, that . . . the simple proof of an assurance withdrawn after detriment does not equate to unconscionability. The reason is that in these types of case, the *normal* expectation of 'buyer' and 'seller' is that there must be compliance with formality rules . . . before they are bound.[48]

This writer cannot improve upon this analysis, but he does not agree with the phrasing of Dixon's conclusion. Dixon concludes that the vendor will be estopped from withdrawing from the sale only where he gives an express or implied assurance that he will not insist upon the normal contractual formalities.[49] It is, it is submitted, preferable to say that the vendor will be estopped from

---

[47] *The Commonwealth v Verwayen* [1990] 170 CLR 394, per Deane J at 441.
[48] M Dixon, 'Proprietary Estoppel and Formalities in Land Law and the Land Registration Act 2002: A Theory of Unconscionability' in E Cooke (ed) *Modern Studies in Property Law*, Vol 2 (Oxford: Hart, 2003) 165, 179 (emphasis added).
[49] ibid pp 180–1.

withdrawing from the sale only where he gives an express or implied assurance that he will not rely upon his normal right to withdraw. It is important to emphasise that the norm with which we are concerned is the factual norm of withdrawal before contractual formality, and not the legal norm of compliance with contractual formality. The vendor is presumed free to withdraw from the sale prior to contract because his conduct in withdrawing at that stage is normal and therefore cannot be unconscionable. In short, the withdrawing vendor has a defence based on the customary nature of his conduct. This is not mere semantics, for a significant advantage of formulating customary conduct as a defence in this context is that it closely corresponds to the orthodox doctrine that compliance with investigation norms in land purchase, if it does not produce notice, supplies the purchaser with an unanswerable defence.

2. Contract to purchase land

The contract stage of a typical land purchase illustrates perfectly the contextual nature of unconscionability as well as the operation of the 'customary conduct' defence. From the moment the vendor enters into a formal contract to sell to the purchaser it would be unconscionable, in light of the unique nature of the subject matter of the contract, for the vendor to rely upon his usual common law right to break the contract and (to express it as an act) to *offer* damages by way of compensation for breach or (to express it as an omission) to *leave* the claimant to his inadequate common law remedy of damages. Equity's remedial response to the threat of such an unconscionable breach of contract is to insist upon specific performance of the contract. Not only that, equity sees as done that which ought to be done, with the result that equity considers the benefit of the land to pass to the purchaser the moment the contract is made. The inevitable consequence is that the vendor holds the benefit of the land on bare trust for the purchaser from the moment of contract. All this is very familiar to property lawyers, but the implications for the doctrine of unconscionability are perhaps less clearly understood. It is this author's contention that, unconscionability having been defined in this context as the conduct of breaching the contract and leaving the purchaser to his inadequate common law remedy of damages, there is no room for conduct to be labelled unconscionable so long as it is substantially consistent with the contract. Thus if a purchaser pays money to the vendor pursuant to a contract, there is no room for the purchaser to claim that it would be unconscionable for the vendor to deny the purchaser a share in the land under a trust arising independently of the contract. This analysis formed part of the ratio of the decision of the Court of Appeal in *Lloyds Bank plc v Carrick*.[50]

---

[50] *Lloyds Bank plc v Carrick* (1997) 73 P & CR 314, Court of Appeal.

3. Completion of purchase of land

We noted earlier that the bona fide purchaser for value of a legal estate without notice of a trust binding on the vendor has an unanswerable defence to the claims of the trust beneficiaries and that the purchaser can establish the absence of constructive notice only by demonstrating compliance with norms of investigation. This exemplifies how 'normal conduct' supplies a defence to a claim based upon alleged unconscionable conduct. We can now add that even if the purchaser of legal title to unregistered land has actual notice of another person's equitable interest in the land, it will not bind the purchaser's conscience if normal conduct for the context requires the holder of the equitable interest to protect it by registration as a land charge and requires the purchaser to do no more (as regards that interest) than to conduct a proper search of the land charges register and purchase legal title in good faith for money or money's worth.[51] Thus the proposition that unconscionability is contextual and the proposition that normal conduct supplies a defence to a finding of unconscionability hold good at the stage of purchase as well as at the earlier contract and pre-contract stages. In support of the argument that unconscionability is contextual, we can observe that the purchaser's actual notice (that a person other than the vendor has an equitable interest in the purchased land) does not, of itself, justify a finding of unconscionability. Even if actual notice of a trust interest can be said to affect the conscience (subject to overreaching), actual notice of an unprotected contractual interest clearly does not. An estate contract must be registered as a land charge or it will not bind the good-faith purchaser for money or money's worth of a legal estate *with* notice of the estate contract,[52] and, crucially, actual notice of the unprotected interest does not mean that the purchaser lacked 'good faith'.[53] In support of the argument that there is no room for an allegation of unconscionability where the purchaser's conduct was consistent with conduct established, by law or custom, to be normal in the circumstances, we can say that the purchaser who makes a proper search of the land charges register is not bound by any registrable interest that is not revealed by the search and the issue of whether he had notice of the interest or knowledge of the interest or might otherwise have been bound to acknowledge the unregistered interest does not arise. *Lloyds Bank plc v Carrick*[54] confirms that the vendor can rely in his defence upon the normal nature of his acts and omissions. The judge observed that '[i]t cannot be unconscionable for the bank to rely on the non-registration of the contract. I do not see how it could be right

---

[51] ibid. See, also, *Midland Bank v Green* [1981] AC 513, House of Lords.
[52] Land Charges Act 1972, s 4(6).
[53] *Midland Bank v Green* [1981] AC 513.
[54] (1997) 73 P & CR 314, Court of Appeal.

to confer on Mrs Carrick indirectly, and by means of a proprietary estoppel binding on the bank, that which Parliament prevented her from obtaining directly by the contract it has declared to be void'.[55] Thus a defendant in such a case will say: 'When one enters into a formal contract to sell land with unregistered title, the normal practice is for the purchaser to protect himself by registering the contract as a land charge. If he fails to take advantage of the normal procedure and I meanwhile have done nothing out of the ordinary, there is no room to label my acts or omissions unconscionable. There is no scope, therefore, to say that I hold the purchase money on constructive trust for the purchaser.'

Unconscionability can be an issue only where the defendant's conduct is out of the ordinary. One example of abnormal conduct which would give rise to a finding of unconscionability in the present context is a statement by the vendor to the purchaser assuring the latter that 'there is no need to protect this contract by registration, because I consider myself bound in any event'. Such a statement is unconscionable because, like all unconscionable conduct, it employs the law itself, or rights and powers conferred by law, as the very means of abusing the other party.

4. Personal liability for knowing receipt of misapplied trust property

In the context of land purchase, constructive notice is established by failure to make such enquiries as are normal for the context. It has been said that personal liability for knowing receipt of misapplied trust property is established on the same basis, that it 'flows from the breach of a legally recognized duty of inquiry'.[56] In contrast, Sir Robert Megarry V-C has observed in the context of personal liability for knowing receipt of misapplied trust property that:

> The cold calculus of constructive and imputed notice does not seem to me to be an appropriate instrument for deciding whether a [person's] conscience is sufficiently affected for it to be right to bind him by the obligations of a constructive trustee.[57]

Sir Robert Megarry V-C's approach is, with respect, the correct one. In this context, as elsewhere, unconscionable conduct should not be discovered in a failure to comply with 'normal conduct'. Rather, compliance with norms of conduct should supply a defence to a finding of unconscionability, in the same way that the doctrine of notice supplies a defence. The proposition that liability 'flows

---

[55] ibid at 325.
[56] *Citadel General Assurance Co v Lloyds Bank Canada* [1997] 3 SCR 805, per La Forest J para 49.
[57] *Re Montagu's Settlement Trusts* [1987] Ch 264, 273.

from the breach of a legally recognized duty of enquiry' should therefore be reversed. Having said that, one is assuming of course that unconscionability is the proper basis of liability for knowing receipt of trust property. This author doubts that assumption, since it is hard to see what legal right or power the recipient abuses at the moment of receipt. Wrongful receipt seems to be more akin to a general common law tort than a particular instance of unconscionability. Despite this reservation, the decision in *Bank of Credit and Commerce International (Overseas) Ltd (BCCI) v Akindele* establishes that unconscionability is, for the time being at least, the Court of Appeal's preferred basis for this species of personal equitable liability.

The case concerned an attempt by the liquidators of BCCI to recover US$6.79 million from Chief Akindele on the basis of his assistance in a breach of trust or wrongful receipt of trust property. In 1985, Akindele had advanced US$10 million to a company controlled by the bank under a false loan agreement. In 1988 he received US$16.79 million under the agreement. The claimants argued that Akindele's dishonesty could be inferred from his knowledge of the artificial character of the loan and from his receipt of the unusually high return of 15 per cent compound interest. At first instance, the court dismissed the claim on the ground that the claimant had failed to prove that the defendant had been dishonest. The Court of Appeal held that it is not necessary to prove that a defendant was dishonest in order to fix him with liability for knowing receipt, but dismissed the appeal on the ground that the state of the defendant's knowledge in 1985 was not such as to make it 'unconscionable' for him to enter into the transaction and, crucially, did not render it unconscionable for him to retain the benefits of the transaction in 1988, notwithstanding the rumours that were then circulating about the integrity of the bank's management. The test their Lordships adopted was 'unconscionability' pure and simple. The problem, as we have seen, is that unconscionability is never pure and simple. Indeed, the more simple the notion of unconscionability, the more impure the law. It is fair to say that the Court of Appeal was not mindful of the advice of Lord Nicholls of Birkenhead, who in the seminal case in the broadly comparable context of dishonest assistance in a breach of trust, observed that:

> Unconscionable is a word of immediate appeal to an equity lawyer. Equity is rooted historically in the concept of the Lord Chancellor, as the keeper of the royal conscience, concerning himself with conduct which was contrary to good conscience. It must be recognised, however, that unconscionable is not a word in everyday use by non-lawyers. If it is to be used in this context, and if it is to be the touchstone for liability as an accessory, it is essential to be clear on what, *in this context*, unconscionable *means*. If unconscionable means no more than dishonesty, then dishonesty is the preferable label. If unconscionable means something different, it

must be said that it is not clear what that something different is. Either way, therefore, the term is better avoided in this context.[58]

This author has argued elsewhere that if (and for the reasons stated earlier, it is a big 'if') unconscionability 'is to be the touchstone for liability' for knowing receipt of misapplied trust property, it should be taken to mean 'the conscious taking of commercially unacceptable risks to the prejudice of another'.[59] In the same place it was argued (and this is crucial to the present argument) that however one cares to define unconscionability, there should be no liability where the defendant can demonstrate compliance with an industry-recognized norm of enquiry. It might, of course, be difficult for a defendant to establish compliance with normal practice where the transaction, like the one in *Akindele*, is peculiar. Nevertheless, even if he cannot demonstrate that his conscience was cleared by compliance with normal practice, the defendant can establish a clear conscience if he can show that his conduct was consistent with the substance of a contractual agreement between plaintiff and defendant. As we observed in the previous section, facts which establish conscientious compliance with the substance of a contract cannot be relied upon to establish unconscionability. Indeed, Chief Akindele was successful on precisely this basis.

We will conclude this section by considering the recent case of *Martin v Myers*.[60] It did not concern personal liability for voluntary receipt of misapplied trust property, but it usefully demonstrates how a volunteer can rely upon the normality of her conduct to defend an allegation that she has unconscionably retained another person's wealth. It concerned a couple who had lived as husband and wife for many years without it being certain to anyone outside the relationship that they were married. The man died and the woman remained in the 'matrimonial' home for 24 years. When she died she left the house to one son by her will. This action was brought by her four daughters, who claimed that their mother had never been married and must therefore have been conscience-bound to hold the house on constructive trust for all her 'husband's' children after his death, with the result that she could not have acquired title to the land by 12 years' adverse possession against her children under the Limitation Act 1980. It was held that even though the couple were not married, the mother never became a constructive trustee for her children because her conscience was never affected by knowledge of any entitlement her children might have in the house. Her conduct in staying living in the quasi-matrimonial home was perfectly normal

---

[58] *Royal Brunei Airlines Sdn Bhd v Philip Tan Kok Ming* [1995] 2 AC 378, Privy Council at 392.

[59] G Watt, 'Personal Liability for Receipt of Trust Property: Allocating the Risks' in Elizabeth Cooke (ed) *Modern Studies in Property Law – Volume II*, (Oxford: Hart, 2005) 91 at 104.

[60] [2004] EWHC 1947 (Chancery).

and acceptable for a surviving 'spouse' and there was therefore no room for holding her conduct to be unconscionable. As the judge, Mr Strauss QC, observed:

> The basic principle underlying the imposition of a constructive trust is that the owner of the legal interest should not be entitled to hold property, where the circumstances are such as to make it inequitable or unconscionable for him to do so. There must be factors which 'affect his conscience'.[61] It seems to me quite artificial to suggest that any such factors affected Amy Myers' conscience immediately on Edward Myers's death. She simply remained in her home, as no doubt all her children wished her to do whatever suspicions they might have held as to whether or not there had been a marriage.[62]

C. Conclusion

Some jurists attempt to tell the tale of property law without the language of unconscionability. That choice appears to be motivated by a positive desire for a scientific and 'rational' system of allocating property rights, but it implies the negative conviction that unconscionability is in some sense irrational. This chapter has demonstrated that the language of unconscionability is capable of sensible application but that it will play a useful role in the story of property law only if it is defined as the particular wrong of illegitimately abusing legitimacy and provided it is kept distinct from infractions of moral conscience and social mores. It is also necessary to refine the definition of unconscionability according to the legal context in which it is alleged. These suggestions are hopefully uncontroversial; indeed, in one form or another they are already widely accepted. The new twist in the tale is that unconscionability will retain a capacity for dangerously unbounded application until judges acknowledge that the defendant's conduct cannot be unconscionable when it complies with the substance of the parties' contract or with a norm of conduct accepted in the particular context. With such defences in place there is no reason why property law and unconscionability should not live happily ever after.

---

61 See per Lord Browne-Wilkinson in *Westdeutsche Landesbank v Islington LBC* [1996] AC 669, [1996] 2 All ER 961 at 705, 709.
62 [2004] EWHC 1947 (Chancery) para [43].

8

CHANGING CONCEPTS OF OWNERSHIP IN ENGLISH LAW DURING THE NINETEENTH AND TWENTIETH CENTURIES

The changing idea of beneficial ownership under the English trust

Thomas Glyn Watkin

A. Conceptions of Ownership in Modern Law

Writing at the start of the 1960s, the future Regius Professor of Civil Law in the University of Oxford, A M Honoré, described ownership as the 'greatest possible interest in a thing which a mature system of law recognizes'.[1] Although the jurists of ancient Rome never ventured to give a definition of the concept, it was widely believed throughout the nineteenth century that Roman law allowed owners virtually unlimited powers over their property, a concept of ownership which has come to be regarded as absolute.[2] Roman owners are sometimes said to have enjoyed the *ius utendi, fruendi, abutendi* over their property, that is the right to use it, to take its fruits, but also to abuse or even destroy it.

This absolute concept of ownership is regarded by many as having reached its modern zenith in the view of ownership taken by the French *Code civil* of 1804, a legal compilation which draws much of its inspiration from the classical

---

[1] A M Honoré, 'Ownership' in A G Guest (ed) *Oxford Essays in Jurisprudence* (Oxford: Oxford University Press, 1961), 107 at 108.
[2] One of the best discussions of the genesis of this view of ownership is that in Alan Rodger, *Owners and Neighbours in Roman Law* (Oxford: Oxford University Press, 1972), especially ch 1.

philosophy of the preceding, eighteenth century with its emphasis upon individual autonomy and individual rights. The law of property was therefore primarily concerned with ensuring that the principles of liberty and equality governed the enjoyment of things and was therefore essentially individualistic. Those who wished to see property law protect social interests as well, even if unlike later thinkers such as Karl Marx they had no wish to see social interests dominate, somewhat inevitably reacted critically to the *Code civil*'s perspective upon ownership.

One of the clearest and most cogent critiques of the *Code civil*'s view of property was delivered by Alexander Alvarez during the first decade of the twentieth century.[3] He considered that this essentially individualistic view of property law 'protected the individual interests of persons, especially of those who were property owners, and neglected the societary interests', the legislator approaching his task with, before his eyes, 'a type of individual actuated by selfish motives and not restrained by the surroundings in which he lived'. In Alvarez's view, two schools of thought then co-existed, that of the eighteenth-century philosophers and that of Christian morality, and the *Code civil* had not opted for the Christian perspective. Liberty and equality had triumphed at the expense of fraternity.[4] Alvarez passed judgement, or perhaps more accurately his condemnation, upon the *Code civil*'s view of ownership as follows:

> The right of ownership was proclaimed as absolute, exclusive, and perpetual. The legislator thought so little of the interests of society that he imposed neither limits nor conditions upon the acquisition of land. Any person might acquire land without having to prove aptitude or special capacity. He was absolute owner, that is, he could partition the land at will, and work it or not at his pleasure. He was the exclusive owner; none could acquire his title against his will, or effect a dismemberment of it, no matter how great the advantage that might accrue thereby to society. The Code provided, no doubt, for certain cases where general interest was to be preferred to private interests. Thus it established eminent domain, legal servitudes, compulsory partition, and so it prohibited trust-entails. But these were isolated cases. In general the Code drew its inspiration for the regulation of the right of ownership and the dismemberment of that right from private interest alone and not from public interest.[5]

In Germany also, the Pandectists based their view of ownership upon the same individualistic perspective. Windscheid, who was to become the principal influence upon the drafting of article 903 of the BGB, regarded ownership as being

3 A Alvarez, *Une nouvelle conception des études juridiques et de la codification du droit civil* (Paris, 1904); English version published as 'Dominant Legal Ideas in the First Half of the Century following the French Revolution' in A Alvarez et al, *The Progress of Continental Law in the Nineteenth Century* (Boston, 1918; reprinted New York, 1969).

4 ibid (English version) pp 18–19.
5 ibid pp 20–1.

of its own nature, that is of its essence, free of limitations. Limitations might be placed upon it, but these were extraneous safeguards limiting what was of itself unlimited.[6] It was this aspect of the draft which in particular provoked the criticism, probably the anger, of Otto von Gierke.[7] Gierke saw the restrictions which societies placed upon ownership as being necessary to social well-being and not therefore alien to ownership itself but as part of its essence. As Alan Rodger has stated, he saw them as defining the nature of ownership, not detracting from it.[8] During the twentieth century, it has been noted that much of this individualistic element was read anachronistically into the Roman texts by the Pandectists themselves. This for instance has been the viewpoint of scholars such as Fritz Schulz and Franz Wieacker, to name but two.[9]

The uncompromising individualism of the Pandectists and of the French jurists who compiled the *Code civil* was undoubtedly in large measure in itself a reaction against the restrictions which had been imposed upon owners and indeed upon ownership itself during the centuries of feudal government and social organization. According to the feudal viewpoint, all land was held ultimately of the king, so that every other owner was directly or indirectly merely a tenant of the king. However secure the tenant's title, however secure the expectation of his heirs to succeed to that title, no landowner could assert that he and he alone was master of the land. The ruler always had a superior title upon which that of the tenant was based. Likewise, access to the courts of a territorial ruler to defend one's rights to other forms of property was ultimately based upon the feudal conception of being under the protection of the ruler, within his peace, and thereby entitled to justice as a return for loyalty and service. There was nothing fundamental about such property rights; they were essentially a by-product of social relationships. With the arrival of classical ideas regarding individual rights, including individual rights to property, and the catapulting of those ideas into the bills of rights and constitutional declarations which followed the revolutions in the US against British colonial rule and in France against absolute monarchical government, the idea of ownership as an adjunct of liberty and equality, to be protected by the State but not by any means its gift, can be understood as a doctrine which sought to liberate individuals from centuries of subservience and not merely as a means to allow free enjoyment of property rights. Individual ownership

---

[6] B Windscheid, T Kipp, *Lehrbuch des Pandektenrechts* I (9th edn, Frankfurt, 1906), § 167 at 857 ff.

[7] O von Gierke, *Der Entwurf eines burgerlichen Gesetzbuchs und das deutsche Recht* (revised edn, Leipzig, 1889), 103.

[8] Rodger, *Owners and Neighbours*, pp 1–2.

[9] See, for instance, F Schulz, *Classical Roman Law* (Oxford: Oxford University Press, 1951), 338; F Wieacker, *Vom Römischen Recht* (2nd edn, Stuttgart: Koehler, 1961), 187–90, 220.

was an outward and visible legal sign of a new social order, of a brave new world in which liberty and equality, not earthly kings, reigned supreme.

B. Ownership in Modern English Law

Depending upon one's point of view, one might say either that Britain has not experienced a revolution of the sort which so dramatically changed the histories of so many nations on the European mainland during the eighteenth and nineteenth centuries, or else that Britain's revolution had already taken place in the middle decades of the seventeenth century when Parliament fought a civil war against the reigning monarch, Charles I, which ended in its victory over the king and his trial and execution in 1649. However, the period of republican government which followed was of relatively short duration and ended in 1660 with the restoration of the monarchy and the return to England of Charles II.

Although the republic was short-lived, nevertheless the restored monarchy had to agree to certain key changes in the country's legal order. One of these in effect brought to an end true feudal landholding in England and Wales. This was accomplished in the year of the Restoration itself by means of the Tenures (Abolition) Act 1660. Under the terms of this act, chivalric tenures were abolished so that holding land in return for knight service and the like has not existed in England since that time. All military tenures were changed by statute into socage tenures, previously thought to be the tenures most typical of farmers and the agricultural middle classes. Virtually all the services and incidents of socage tenure had been commuted into money payments.

Despite the fact that true feudalism was therefore abolished in England and Wales by the 1660 statute, one aspect of it remained, namely that all socage land was held either directly or indirectly of the Crown.[10] The landowner was always in law a tenant of someone else. Only Crown lands were not held of a superior lord. Despite this fact, a person who held the greatest possible interest in land, what is in English law referred to as the tenant in fee simple, was in all important respects the land's owner. A tenant in fee simple is one who holds the land for himself and his heirs, and is permitted to alienate the land and dispose of parts of it or rights over it exactly as he wishes. On his death, the land passes either under his will to the persons of his choice or to his lawful successors in title. Only if he dies without an heir, and without having made a will, will the land revert – or to use

---

[10] Already, as early as 1290, feudalism in England had been in decline as a result of Edward I's statute, *Quia emptores*, which had forbidden grants of the fee simple by subinfeudation rather than by substitution, so that thereafter the feudal ladder could only shrink, not expand.

the technical legal term escheat – to the Crown. While the tenant, his heirs, and assigns are in possession, the Crown has no more interest than would the State in a civil law jurisdiction. While in control, the tenant in fee simple is, for instance, entitled to commit what is called in English law waste, that is he is entitled to abuse the land as well as use it and take its fruits. He can, therefore, as far as the law of property is concerned, chop down trees, open quarries, remove the soil, mine for minerals, and do all the other things which a person with a lesser interest, such as a tenant for life or a leaseholder – one with only a limited interest in the land – would be debarred from doing.

This is not to say that restrictions could not be placed upon legal owners in English law. As well as giving the legal owner of land, for instance, an interest in it which was less than that of the fee simple – in effect full ownership – for instance by giving only a life interest or a term of years, it was also possible to prevent the legal owner from enjoying full ownership by obligating him to manage the property for the benefit of others. By far the most widespread method of achieving this aim under the law of England and Wales during the last four centuries has been by means of the trust.

C. The Trust in English Law

The trust is often claimed to be the most significant contribution which English law has made to the world of jurisprudence, and such a view is perfectly respectable. In its most obvious form, it involves an owner, whether of land or other forms of property, transferring the legal ownership of that property to one or more other persons who are to act as trustees.[11] The trustees are from that point on the legal owners, and there are no restrictions upon their ownership at common law. In equity, however, they are required to exercise their rights as owners for the benefit of others, usually called the beneficiaries. Often, these beneficiaries are other persons, but they can be, for instance, purposes, such as providing education, facilities for health care, or for promoting religion. In either case, the common factor is that the trustees, although legal owners, are not free to use the property as they wish, but must manage and control it for the benefit of the beneficiaries. The trustees are most certainly not free to abuse the property in any way.

The reason why they may not, in equity, dispose of the property as they wish is that they are, either as a result of their own agreement or of their conduct or of the circumstances in which the property came to them, obligated in conscience to

---

[11] The settlor may also declare himself to be a trustee for the beneficiaries, making a grant of the property to other trustees unnecessary.

utilize it for the benefit of the beneficiaries. The fact that it is an obligation binding the trustees' conscience which stands at the heart of the trust has recently been
emphasized anew by one of England's most senior judges, Lord Browne-Wilkinson,
in the case of *Westdeutsche Landesbank Girozentrale v Islington London Borough
Council*, a case which is now generally referred to as *Westdeutsche* for the sake of
economy.[12] Delivering his speech as senior Law Lord of Appeal in Ordinary in
the final court of appeal in England and Wales, the House of Lords, Lord Browne-
Wilkinson said:

> The equitable jurisdiction to enforce trusts depends upon the conscience of the
> holder of the legal interest being affected …
>
> Equity operates on the conscience of the owner of the legal interest. In the case of a
> trust, the conscience of the legal owner requires him to carry out the purposes for
> which the property was vested in him … or which the law imposes on him by reason
> of his unconscionable conduct … [13]

This equitable obligation, however, obliging the legal owner to exercise his legal
ownership for the benefit of others or to achieve particular purposes, can exist
only if there is some person who can enforce it by going to a court of equity and
drawing to the court's attention the fact that the legal owner in question is subject
to such an obligation. This fact has been recognized for centuries, and is usually
referred to as the beneficiary principle or, from a famous case in which it was
applied, the rule in *Morice v Bishop of Durham*.[14] For there to be a trust, it was
necessary according to the judge in that case, the Master of the Rolls, Sir William
Grant, for it to be possible for the court to assume control of it. If there were no
power of control, the legal owner of the property would have an uncontrollable
power to do as he wished with the property, which Sir William equated with
ownership free from the obligations of trusteeship. He concluded therefore that
for a valid trust to exist, 'there must be somebody, in whose favour the Court can
decree performance'.[15]

In relation to the vast majority of trusts, the person, the 'somebody', in whose
favour the Court can decree performance is a beneficiary, someone who expects
to benefit or is entitled to benefit from the trust's existence. However, during the
first decade of the nineteenth century, when *Morice v Bishop of Durham* was
decided, as now, there were valid trusts in which there are no persons who can be
termed beneficiaries in that manner. The most important category of such trusts

---

[12] *Westdeutsche Landesbank Girozentrale v Islington London Borough Council* [1996] AC 669;
[1996] 2 All ER 961.
[13] ibid at 988.
[14] (1804) 9 Ves 399.
[15] ibid.

by far are charitable trusts, those which are established for what the law deems to be charitable purposes. In English law, such purposes were categorized for over a century as falling under four headings: trusts for the relief of poverty, trusts for the advancement of education, trusts for the advancement of religion, and trusts for other purposes which are beneficial to the community in a manner which the law deems charitable, for instance trusts for the promotion of public health.[16] Such trusts are established for purposes and not for specific individuals. One could not, at the time of their inception, necessarily identify any person who would benefit from their existence. There are therefore no ascertainable human beneficiaries who could enforce the trusts in question by approaching a court of equity to control them by acting upon the conscience of the trustees. However, because such charitable trusts are deemed in law all to be for the benefit of the public – public benefit being an indispensable element in the attainment of charitable status – the Attorney-General enforces such trusts on behalf of the public. Therefore, although there are no direct human beneficiaries to enforce such trusts, there is nevertheless, in Sir William Grant's words in *Morice v Bishop of Durham*, 'somebody, in whose favour the Court can decree performance', that somebody being the Attorney-General.

An important question arises at this point. It is this: How should one describe the interest of this person, the 'somebody', in whose favour the Court can decree performance? Clearly, if one takes into account the similarity of the role of that person in private, that is non-charitable trusts, to that of the Attorney-General in the case of charitable trusts, it would be inappropriate to describe the person as a beneficiary, still less as a beneficial owner, for that would immediately undermine the essential similarity between such persons in the case of private trusts and the Attorney-General in the case of charitable trusts. They both clearly have an interest, and it might be justifiable to call that interest a beneficial interest, in that, in the case of private trusts, the beneficiaries most obviously have that, and in the case of charitable trusts, as they are all for the public benefit, the public has by definition a beneficial interest in their control which the Attorney-General exercises on the public's behalf, literally as its attorney. Hence, it appears justifiable to characterize the required interest as a beneficial interest but not to describe it as beneficial ownership. Nevertheless, until very recently, in the case of private trusts, it has been the rule rather than the exception to require that there should be beneficiaries in the sense of beneficial owners for them to be valid, thus

---

16 The four heads of charity were set out by Lord MacNaghten in the case of *Commissioners for Special Income Tax v Pemsel* [1891] AC 531, a decision of the House of Lords. The four heads were based upon a list of charitable purposes contained in the Preamble to the Statute of Charitable Uses, 1601, on the basis of which other purposes had been deemed to be charitable by analogy in the intervening centuries on the basis that they were 'within the spirit and intendment of the preamble'. They have recently been increased in number by the Charities Act 2006.

concealing the essential similarity in this regard between private and charitable trusts. It will be the purpose of this chapter to attempt to identify the reasons why, in the case of private trusts, beneficial interest came to be equated with beneficial ownership, and also to trace the route by which during recent years it is gradually becoming accepted that the two concepts are not identical, so that at the beginning of the twenty-first century the English law of trusts appears to be regaining the perspective of Sir William Grant at the start of the nineteenth century, having lost that perspective during the intervening two centuries, albeit that it has been gradually regained slowly during the past 30–40 years.

D. The Rise of the Concept of Beneficial Ownership

It was during the course of the nineteenth century that the concept of beneficial ownership grew in importance. This importance manifested itself in two ways. First, the beneficiaries were seen to be collectively the owners of the trust property in equity, and second they came to be seen as individually the owners in equity of that portion or fraction of the trust property which produced the income to which they were entitled under the terms of the trust. These two facets of beneficial ownership will now be examined in turn.

1. The beneficiaries as owners collectively in equity

In 1841, in the case of *Saunders v Vautier*,[17] property had been given to trustees by a deceased settlor with a direction to invest it and accumulate the income until the beneficiary reached the age of 25. When the beneficiary reached the age of 21, he demanded that the trustees hand over the capital and the accumulated income to him immediately, thus bringing the trust to an end. In this case, the beneficiary was the person in whose favour the court could decree performance. The question therefore was, as no one else was entitled to enforce the continuation of the trust, the settlor being dead, should the court require the trustees to obey the settlor's direction or those of the sole, adult beneficiary? The Master of the Rolls, Lord Langdale, ordered that the whole trust fund should be handed over to the beneficiary, thereby recognizing that he was entitled to become full owner of the property. Not surprisingly, this was taken to mean that in equity, that is beneficially, a sole adult beneficiary was already the beneficial or equitable owner of the property. Thereafter this approach was extended to situations in which there was more than one beneficiary, provided they were all of full age and of sound mind, that is *sui iuris*, and unanimous in their wish to terminate the trust. This was so even if their interests were held for them not concurrently but in succession.

---

[17] (1841) 4 Beav 115.

These further propositions were gradually established during the later nineteenth century and during the first half of the twentieth century.[18]

There can be no doubt that two different principles of English law have affected the development of this rule, commonly called the rule in *Saunders v Vautier*. These are, first, that where a beneficiary instigates what is technically a breach of trust, he cannot then complain of it. In other words, the trustees are safe from future action by him. However, the rule goes further than that in that it places the trustees under a duty to conform to the beneficiary's as opposed to the settlor's wishes where the beneficiary is *sui iuris*, or where there is more than one beneficiary, all are *sui iuris* and unanimous. This is the second principle, namely that the wishes of those currently entitled to enjoy the property are to be preferred to those of a settlor who was once the property's owner, particularly where the settlor is no longer alive. The settlor has parted with his ownership; he is not therefore allowed to dictate what will happen to the property where there are others who are now collectively solely entitled to it. It is this second point which converts the beneficiaries collectively from persons who may call upon the court to enforce the trustees' obligations into persons who may collectively dispose of the property itself, that is beneficial owners.

2. The beneficiaries as individual owners in equity

At much the same time as these principles were becoming established, a development in the law of taxation also affected the manner in which beneficiaries' interests were viewed. In 1796, the requirement that stamp duty be paid on receipts of legacies was changed into a requirement that a tax should instead be paid upon the legacy itself. In 1805, proceeds of sale of land given by testamentary gift also became liable to this legacy duty, and in 1853, succession duty became payable on all testamentary gifts of land or other settled property. In 1881, a new tax called account duty was placed upon forms of property which escaped the other taxes. The end result of these developments was finally recognized in the Finance Act of 1894, which introduced estate duty, a tax which was payable on all property passing on the death of its owner and the percentage rate of which increased with the value of the deceased's patrimony.

For the purposes of the current discussion, the key question is how these taxes, and in particular estate duty, affected the estates of those with beneficial interests under a trust. As far as the revenue was concerned, where a person had a right to income under a trust, that portion of the trust capital which produced the beneficiary's income should be taxable as part of his estate. In other words, the

---

[18] See *Brown v Pringle* (1845) 4 Hare 124; *Anson v Potter* (1879) 13 Ch D 141; *Re White* [1901] 1 Ch 570; *Re Sandeman's Will Trusts* [1937] 1 All ER 368; *Re Smith* [1928] Ch 915.

beneficiary was to be treated for tax purposes as the owner of that portion of the trust property to which his or her beneficial interest related. If he received half the income, half of the capital was liable to estate duty on his death; if a third, then a third, and so on. The revenue in other words recognized the beneficiary as a sort of owner of the trust property according to his share of the benefit and despite the fact that legal ownership was clearly vested in the trustees. The trust property was not subject to tax on the death of the trustees as they did not have this sort of beneficial ownership.

It has perhaps not been properly recognized how far these developments in the taxation of trusts affected the manner in which the interests of beneficiaries were considered. As the twentieth century progressed, estate duty became an increasingly confiscatory tax, so that much effort and legal learning was directed to reducing the impact of estate duty upon family property.[19] Increasingly, therefore, the taxman's view of the beneficiaries' interests came to predominate, and that view was that they were, as individuals, the beneficial owners. This individual beneficial ownership was not recognized only by the taxman. In 1914, in the case of *Re Marshall*,[20] it was held that a beneficiary with a share of the beneficial interest under a trust could ask for his beneficial interest to be capitalized and handed over to him, even without the other beneficiaries wanting to have the trust terminated. While this is permitted only where it does not prejudice the interests of the other beneficiaries,[21] it nevertheless recognized individual beneficiaries as beneficial owners of their fraction of the trust property. This was not without its consequences for other kinds of trust.

E. Some Consequences of the Concept of Beneficial Ownership

Charitable trusts, as has been seen, do not have beneficiaries who can enforce them in the same manner as private trusts. Nevertheless, as has also been seen, there is somebody in whose favour the court can decree performance, namely the Attorney-General. Nevertheless, the capital forming the trust property of a charitable trust is not beneficially owned by anyone. Therefore, no estate duty can arise on the capital of a charitable trust. This poses no problems however, because, in English law, charities are exempt from most forms of taxation. They pay no income tax on their income, nor capital gains on the increases in the value

---

[19] In 1975, estate duty was replaced by capital transfer tax, and in 1984 capital transfer tax was abolished and in effect estate duty was reintroduced under the name of inheritance tax.

[20] [1914] 1 Ch 192.

[21] See, for instance, *Re Sandeman's Will Trusts* [1937] 1 All ER 368.

of their capital. Gifts to charity are exempt from inheritance tax when made in the will of the donor. Charities must however pay value added tax on property and services which they purchase.

There are, nevertheless, some trusts which are neither charitable nor for the benefit of specific persons. Such trusts are often described as private purpose trusts, so as to distinguish them from charitable trusts which are for public purposes. The types of private purpose trusts which are valid in England and Wales are few in number, and the reason why they are so few is not unconnected with the concept of beneficial ownership which has prevailed over the last two centuries.

Under the current law of England and Wales, only two kinds of trusts fall into this category.[22] These are those for the care and maintenance of specific pet animals and those for the upkeep of specific graves, tombs, or monuments. It is important to stress that the animals and the memorials have to be specific, for a trust for animals generally or for a whole cemetery or burial ground would both be charitable under English law.

Both categories, first of all, were recognized before the concept of individual beneficial ownership had made significant headway. Thus, trusts for pet animals were treated as valid as early as 1842 in Pettingall v Pettingall.[23] This decision was affirmed and followed by North J in Re Dean in 1889.[24] Trusts for the upkeep of specific graves or monuments were recognized as valid in 1856 in Trimmer v Danby,[25] which was followed 20 years later in Musset v Bingle,[26] 20 years after that in Pirbright v Salwey,[27] and affirmed in 1932 in the case of Re Hooper.[28] In both lines of authority, the question was raised as to whether the lack of a human beneficiary who could enforce the trust was fatal to its validity. North J rejected this view in the light of the existing authorities in Re Dean, and in Re Hooper, Maugham J – later to be Lord Chancellor – confessed to feeling that he would have had difficulties with the case were it not for the earlier authority of Pirbright v Salwey, which he noted had been argued by eminent counsel and had not been the subject of any adverse comment.

---

[22] There used to be five such categories, the other three being trusts for the saying of Requiem masses (now charitable), trusts for unincorporated associations (now seen as being arrangements for the benefit of the members and thus enforceable), and trusts for other miscellaneous purposes (now probably enforceable as discretionary trusts following the decisions in Re Denley's Trust Deed and McPhail v Doulton, of which see further below).

[23] (1842) 11 LJ Ch 176.

[24] (1889) 41 Ch D 552.

[25] (1856) 25 LJ Ch 424.

[26] [1876] WN 170.

[27] [1896] WN 86.

[28] [1932] 1 Ch 38.

Adverse comment was to come however. In 1952, Roxburgh J was required to decide upon the validity of a trust for a variety of non-charitable purposes, including the maintenance of good understanding among nations and the independence and integrity of the press.[29] He relied heavily upon *dicta* of Lord Parker in the case of *Bowman v Secular Society* in 1917.[30] The *dictum* which impressed him was that 'a trust to be valid must be for the benefit of individuals ... or must be ... charitable ...'. Speaking of trusts for individuals, Roxburgh J said:

> The typical case of a trust is one in which the legal owner of property is constrained by a court of equity so to deal with it as to give effect to the equitable rights of another. These equitable rights have been hammered out in the process of litigation in which a claimant on equitable grounds has successfully asserted rights against a legal owner or other person in control of property. Prima facie, therefore, a trustee would not be expected to be subject to an equitable obligation unless there was somebody who could enforce a correlative equitable right.

Roxburgh J accepted that in the case of charitable purpose trusts, although there was no individual who could enforce them as having a correlative equitable right, enforcement remained possible through the role of the Attorney-General. He could not, however, 'contemplate with equanimity the creation of large funds devoted to non-charitable purposes which no court and no department of state can control, or in the case of maladministration reform'. Moreover, he rejected the view that the settlor if living, and one supposes his personal representatives or next of kin if dead, could enforce the arrangement because 'if the purposes are valid trusts, the settlors have retained no beneficial interest'. In other words, for Roxburgh J, a beneficial interest requires ownership of some sort, not just an interest in the general sense of the term. He regarded the authorities relating to pets and tombs as 'anomalous and exceptional' and agreed with the author of a leading textbook that they were best regarded as 'concessions to human weakness and sentiment'.[31] He concluded his judgment by saying:

> A court of equity does not recognize as valid a trust which it cannot both enforce and control. This seems to me to be good equity and good sense.

And who would disagree?

However, the question really is whether either equity or good sense equates the enforceability or control of a trust with the need for a beneficial owner of the trust property. Charitable trusts illustrate that that equation is unnecessary. A later decision relating to private purpose trusts raises pertinent questions concerning it.

---

[29] *Re Astor's Settlement Trusts* [1952] Ch 534.
[30] [1917] AC 406, at 437 and 441.
[31] See Sir Arthur Underhill, *Law of Trusts* (8th edn, London: Butterworths, 1926), 79.

Eight years after Roxburgh J decided the case of *Re Astor's Settlement Trusts*, the Court of Appeal was confronted, in *Re Endacott*,[32] with a will in which the testator had left his residuary estate, valued at around £20,000, for the purpose of providing some useful memorial to himself. The Master of the Rolls, Lord Evershed, refused to accept that the non-charitable gift could be valid because there were persons, the next of kin, who could come to court and complain if the trust were not carried out. Instead, he stated categorically that 'a trust by English law, not being a charitable trust, in order to be effective, must have ascertained or ascertainable beneficiaries'. The animal and tomb cases he considered exceptions. Harman LJ, who applauded Roxburgh J's verdict in the earlier case, went further. He described them as 'troublesome, anomalous and aberrant' and even suggested that their validity might at some time be reconsidered. *Re Endacott* refused to accept that anyone other than a beneficiary with a proprietary interest under the trust could have an equitable right to enforce it. To that extent, it goes much further than the beneficiary principle in *Morice v Bishop of Durham*, and to that extent it also goes further, it is submitted, than either equity or good sense requires.

F. The Decline of the Concept of Beneficial Ownership

Within ten years of the decision in *Re Endacott*, the first signs of a retreat from the extreme doctrine of beneficial ownership which it contains can be discerned in the authorities. The last 40 years, it can be argued, have seen a gradual reinstatement of the purity of the beneficiary principle as it was understood at the start of the nineteenth century, purged of its unnecessary connection with the need for a beneficial owner. The process has been gradual, and probably as unintended as was the development of the connection in the preceding century.

1. Discretionary trusts and individual beneficial ownership

A discretionary trust, sometimes called a trust power or a trust in the nature of a power, is one where the settlor gives property to trustees on trust for named beneficiaries or a class of beneficiaries, but does not give the beneficiaries fixed interests under the trust. In other words, when the time comes for the income of the trust fund to be distributed, instead of the trustees being under a duty to give each beneficiary a fixed amount of the income, the trustees have a discretion, hence the name, to distribute according to their assessment of each beneficiary's needs at that time. Thus, the distributions can vary from time to time to take

---

[32] [1960] Ch 232.

account of the changing needs and circumstances of the beneficiaries. None of this, of course, affects the beneficiaries' equitable rights to compel the trustees to carry out the terms of the trust, to control their management of the trust property, or to reform any maladministration. However, it does mean that no beneficiary can regard himself or herself as owner in any sense of any portion of the capital in the trust fund, for they have no right to a fixed portion of the income.

This is one of the great advantages and attractions of the discretionary over fixed-interest trusts. In that the beneficiaries have no right to any particular portion of the income, they cannot be regarded individually as beneficial owners of any quantifiable portion of the capital. Thus, when a beneficiary under a discretionary trust dies, there is no portion of the capital of the trust fund which can be regarded as belonging to the deceased beneficiary's estate and therefore no portion of the trust fund which is assessable for the purposes of estate duty or, as it is now called, inheritance tax. This means that the death of a beneficiary does not result in the depletion of the trust fund for the surviving beneficiaries. The Revenue has, however, responded to this challenge. On the death of a beneficiary under a discretionary trust, the Revenue enquires as to what fraction of the total income of the trust the deceased beneficiary received during the last seven years of his or her life. The Revenue then treats that fraction of the trust capital as having been during that period the property of the deceased beneficiary and therefore part of his estate. That fraction of the trust property is therefore assessable for the purposes of estate duty.

While for estate duty purposes a fraction of the trust property can be quantified as being the beneficiary's after the beneficiary has died, it remains the case that under a discretionary trust while a beneficiary is living, it is not possible to calculate what is his or her beneficial entitlement as a portion of the trust fund.[33] The beneficiaries under a discretionary trust cannot therefore be regarded as individually the beneficial owners of distinct portions of the trust property even though they are undoubtedly persons with an equitable right to approach the court to enforce the trustees' obligations.

2. Discretionary trusts and collective beneficial ownership

It may be objected that, despite the fact that the beneficiaries are not individually entitled to distinct portions of the trust property under a discretionary trust, nevertheless collectively they are the beneficial owners in that they could, if they

---

[33] Indeed, the trustees may be able to avoid paying estate duty altogether. A frequently used solution is to give a beneficiary a lump sum on the attainment of a particular age, and thereafter make no more income payments to him. If the beneficiary then survives for seven years, no estate duty will be payable. The trustees may even be able to insure against the beneficiary dying before seven years have elapsed, or could require the beneficiary to do so in return for the lump sum being given.

were all of full age, sound mind, and in agreement, terminate the trust under the rule in *Saunders v Vautier* discussed earlier and have the capital distributed amongst themselves. This is true, provided that they are all *sui iuris* and that it is possible to determine that they are in agreement.

Until the decision of the House of Lords in the case of *McPhail v Doulton* in 1970, this was definitely true.[34] It is no longer true as a result of that decision for all manner of discretionary trusts. Until that decision, for a private trust to be valid, it was essential that the identity of all of the beneficiaries should be ascertained. This was the requirement of certainty of beneficiaries, which had been most recently spelt out in the case of the *Inland Revenue Commissioners v Broadway Cottages Trust*.[35] The *Broadway Cottages* test as it came to be known was often described by saying that it was necessary that the trustees should be able to draw up a complete list of all the beneficiaries. Clearly, if that is possible, it is also possible to determine whether the beneficiaries are unanimous in wishing to end the trust or not.

In the case of *McPhail v Doulton*, however, the House of Lords, by a bare majority of three to two, Lords Hodson and Guest dissenting, held that the *Broadway Cottages* test was not appropriate at least for discretionary trusts. Instead, the majority affirmed that for discretionary trusts it was sufficient if the beneficial class was conceptually certain in the sense that it was possible for the trustees to say for any given individual that he or she either was or was not a member of the class. Accordingly, discretionary trusts could validly be created and operate even though the trustees were not aware of the identity of all of the beneficiaries.

This change of approach meant that where, as in *McPhail v Doulton* itself, a discretionary trust was created for a large beneficial class, such as the employees and ex-employees of a large, multi-national corporation, the fact that all of the beneficiaries could not be ascertained would not cause the trust to fail so as to deprive those who could be found of their chance to benefit, provided that the class was defined with sufficient conceptual certainty to allow the trustees to say for any given individual that either they were or were not within the class. The consequence of this change, however, for the application of the rule in *Saunders v Vautier* is that, as it is no longer necessary to have a complete list of all the beneficiaries, there will be some discretionary trusts, namely those with large beneficial classes, in which it will in reality be impossible to say that all of the beneficiaries are agreed that the trust should terminate. In other words, there is no longer an ascertained group of beneficiaries who can as a collectivity be regarded as owners of the trust property.

---

34 *McPhail v Doulton* (also referred to as *Re Baden's Deed Trusts*) [1971] AC 424.
35 [1955] Ch 20.

3. Purpose trusts which benefit an ascertainable person, persons, or a class

At roughly the same time as the litigation which culminated in the decision in *McPhail v Doulton* was progressing through the courts, another significant case for the current theme came before the Chancery Division of the High Court. This was the case of *Re Denley's Trust Deed*.[36] It concerned a gift of land for use as a recreation ground mainly for the benefit of the employees of a particular company but with the possibility that the trustees could allow other persons to use the facilities with their permission. The gift was phrased as though it were for an abstract, private purpose – to provide a sports ground. However, Goff J recognized that although it was expressed as being for a purpose, there were actually ascertainable human beneficiaries who would enjoy the facilities. He refused to accept that the beneficiary principle operated to invalidate a trust which had beneficiaries who could enforce it.

> The beneficiary principle of *Re Astor's Settlement Trusts*, which was approved in *Re Endacott (deceased)* . . . is confined to purpose or object trusts which are abstract or impersonal. The objection is not that the trust is for a purpose or object *per se*, but that there is no beneficiary . . .

> Where, then, the trust, though expressed as a purpose, is directly or indirectly for the benefit of an individual or individuals, it seems to me that it is in general outside the mischief of the beneficiary principle.

Some have taken this decision to mean that, provided there are human beneficiaries who can enforce the trust, in other words, somebody in whose favour the court can decree performance – to return to Sir William Grant's language in *Morice v Bishop of Durham* – a trust set up for a purpose rather than to confer direct benefits upon human beneficiaries will nevertheless be valid. This was the opinion, for instance, of Megarry V-C in *Re Northern Developments (Holdings) Ltd*.[37] Others, however, disagree, insisting that the decision instead holds the trust to be one for the human beneficiaries, the method of conferring the benefit being a secondary issue. This second perspective, presented forcefully in an article by Mr Peter Millett QC, later Lord Millett, a Lord of Appeal in Ordinary,[38] in effect regards the beneficiaries as beneficial owners of the facilities who could collectively, if they so wished, all being *sui iuris* and in agreement, terminate the trust and claim the capital for themselves.[39]

---

[36] [1969] 1 Ch 373.

[37] Unreported, 6 October 1978, but considered and discussed in *Carreras Rothmans v Freeman Mathews Treasure Ltd* [1985] Ch 207.

[38] See P J Millett QC, 'The *Quistclose* Trust: Who can enforce it?' (1985) 101 *Law Quarterly Review* 269, especially 280–2.

[39] Clearly, in this case, it would not be permissible for individual beneficiaries to claim their respective shares while the trust was ongoing, as this would have a detrimental effect upon the interests of the remaining beneficiaries.

Lord Millett's viewpoint is crucial to the answering of one particular question, namely what would happen to the trust property if the purpose was not capable of being achieved. Suppose in *Re Denley*, for instance, that the trustees could no longer afford to maintain the sports ground. Should the property be sold and the proceeds divided amongst the beneficiaries, or should it be returned to the settlor or his estate, because the trust was no longer capable of achieving what he wished? On analogy with private trusts for human beneficiaries, the Millett solution would prevail. With charitable trusts, however, where a particular purpose cannot be achieved there is either a cy-près scheme, which devotes the property to the nearest equivalent charitable purpose, or else – in the case of an initial failure where the settlor has no paramount charitable intention – the property is returned to the settlor. This question brings to the fore the vexed issue of whether the purpose of a trust is at all relevant to its establishment or survival. This issue has been highlighted in the cases dealing with so-called *Quistclose* trusts.

4. *Quistclose* trusts and the concept of beneficial ownership

Quistclose trusts are so called from a leading decision of the House of Lords concerning them, *Barclays Bank Ltd v Quistclose Investments Ltd*,[40] a decision from the same productive period of adjudication as *McPhail v Doulton* and *Re Denley's Trust Deed*. The facts were that Rolls Razor Ltd was in financial difficulties. It had considerably exceeded its overdraft with Barclays Bank. It had also declared a dividend on its ordinary shares which it was unable to pay the shareholders. Quistclose Investments, which was hoping to do business with Rolls Razor, if it continued trading, lent Rolls Razor £210,000 specifically in order to pay the dividends to the shareholders. The loan was paid into a special bank account at Barclays Bank, the bank knowing the purpose of the loan. Before the dividends were paid, Rolls Razor went into liquidation. Barclays wanted to set off the money in the special account against what it was owed on the overdraft. This was refused. Instead, it was held that the money had to be returned to Quistclose. In the Court of Appeal, Harman LJ was clear as to why. He said:

> The money was deposited with the respondent bank, and accepted on the footing that it should only be used for payment of the dividend. That purpose was, however, frustrated by the liquidation of Rolls Razor . . . before the dividend had been paid.

Lord Wilberforce agreed with this analysis in the House of Lords. In his speech, he said:

> The essence of the bargain, was that the sum advanced should not become part of the assets of Rolls Razor Ltd, but should be used exclusively for payment of a

---

[40] [1970] AC 567. The House of Lords upheld the decision of the Court of Appeal, which is reported as *Quistclose Investments Ltd v Rolls Razor Ltd* [1968] 1 Ch 540.

> particular class of creditors, namely, those entitled to the dividend. A necessary consequence of this . . . must be that, if for any reason, the dividend could not be paid, the money was to be returned to the respondents.

Despite the fact that the shareholders were still in existence and that the money was still available, the decision was that the frustration of the purpose ended the primary trust, to pay the dividends, and activated a secondary trust, under which the property was destined to return to the lenders. The question therefore arises of who has the beneficial interest, in the sense of beneficial ownership, while the primary trust is still in existence. This question did not require to be answered in the *Quistclose* case itself, but it did arise in the later case of *Carreras Rothmans v Freeman Mathews Treasure Ltd* in 1985.[41]

In that case, the plaintiff, Carreras Rothmans, was a cigarette manufacturer which had engaged the defendant, an advertising agency, to arrange an advertising campaign for its products. The defendant entered into contracts with the advertising media as principal and not as the plaintiff's agent. The defendant got into financial difficulties, so the plaintiff paid sums of money in advance to the defendant in a vain attempt to keep it solvent. When the defendant went into liquidation, the question was raised whether these funds were available to pay the defendant's general creditors or whether on the *Quistclose* principle, they had to be returned to the plaintiff. Peter Gibson J upheld the latter view.

It was his judgment which excited the response of Mr Peter Millett QC, as he then was, in the *Law Quarterly Review*.[42] Peter Gibson J, following Megarry V-C's judgment in *Re Northern Developments (Holdings) Ltd*, thought that while neither the defendant's creditors nor Carreras Rothmans had a beneficial interest in the property in the sense of being beneficial owners of it, nevertheless they had sufficient interest in the due management of the fund by the defendant to be entitled to approach the court if necessary to require it to control the manner in which the defendant managed it. They were persons in whose favour the court could decree performance of the defendant's obligation in conscience to utilize the property not for their own purposes but for the purposes which had been directed by the settlors. In other words, despite the fact that there might be, as Peter Gibson J recognized, a situation in which the beneficial interest, in the sense of ownership, was in suspense, the trust could still exist because there were those

---

[41] [1985] Ch 207.

[42] See note 38 above. It is fascinating to note that Mr Peter Millett was leading counsel for the plaintiff in the *Carreras Rothmans* case, and that the plaintiff won. Nevertheless he disagreed with the reasoning in the judgment which secured his side the victory. The clue to understanding this enigma probably lies in Peter Gibson J's closing words, when he congratulated junior counsel for the plaintiff for his presentation and argument in the absence of his learned leader. One may suspect that had Mr Millett been present, the plaintiff's case might have been dealt with differently.

with *locus standi* to enforce it according to the beneficiary principle as set out in *Morice v Bishop of Durham*.

G. The Future of the Beneficiary Principle

In the *Westdeutsche* case, as has been seen, Lord Browne-Wilkinson emphasized that the essential prerequisite for a trust was that the trustee had received property in circumstances in which it was inequitable for him to dispose of it as he wished but was, instead, in conscience bound to use it in some other manner. According to the beneficiary principle in *Morice v Bishop of Durham*, such a trust to be perfect, that is capable of being enforced by the court, must have somebody in whose favour the court can decree performance. As the recent development of discretionary trusts since *McPhail v Doulton* shows, such persons need not be beneficial owners of the trust property either individually or collectively. As *Re Denley* and the development of *Quistclose* trusts suggest, such persons need not have beneficial interests in the sense of beneficial ownership at all.

What is required therefore, as Professor David J Hayton of King's College, London, has argued,[43] is that there must be someone who is capable of enforcing the trust, what he calls an 'enforcer'. This is reflected in the language and conception of the *Principles of European Trust Law* developed by an international working group of the Hague Conference on Private International Law.[44] Article I of those principles describes the obligation of the trustee as that of managing the trust property 'for the benefit of another person called the "beneficiary" or for the furtherance of a purpose', and article IV, which is entitled 'Trusts for Beneficiaries or for Enforceable Purposes', states in its first subparagraph that:

> (1) Upon creating a trust, the settlor must designate ascertained persons as beneficiaries to whom the trustee's obligations in respect of the trust fund are owed or will be owed, or must designate purposes in respect of which there is an enforcer.

Clearly, if English law were to allow settlors to appoint 'enforcers' of this kind, the difficulties attending so-called private purpose trusts for pet animals, the maintenance of tombs, and the like would be removed at a stroke. Likewise, the remaining controversy concerning who can enforce the *Quistclose* trust would vanish, for the settlor could nominate himself or some other person to act as 'enforcer'. The same method might even be employed to regulate large discretionary trusts

---

[43] D J Hayton, 'Developing the Obligation Characteristic of the Trust' (2001) 117 *Law Quarterly Review* 96.

[44] These may be found in the Appendix to D J Hayton, *The Law of Trusts* (3rd edn, London: Sweet & Maxwell, 1998) 193 ff.

effectively and to safeguard the interests of younger beneficiaries under any kind
of trust. It is interesting to speculate whether such a development would impinge
upon the rule in *Saunders v Vautier*, for if the settlor nominated himself as enforcer,
it might well be asked why even adult beneficiaries acting unanimously should be
allowed to override his wishes.[45]

It is worth noting in passing that the concept of an 'enforcer' has already emerged
in the English law of contract, where under the terms of the Contracts (Rights of
Third Parties) Act 1999, third-party beneficiaries are now able to enforce contracts in their favour if the contracting parties so intended, as may any third party
if the contract expressly provides that he may.[46] Such non-beneficiary third
parties are in effect nominated enforcers. If trusts are to compete against such
contractual arrangements, it is submitted that it is only a matter of time before a
similar development is undertaken. Given that the beneficiary principle already
requires only 'somebody, in whose favour the Court can decree performance', it
is not obvious why such a development should require the authority of a statute
as opposed to the exercise of ingenuity on the part of the draftsman of a trust deed
or will. There seems no reason why a lawyer called upon to create a trust for pet
animals, the maintenance of a tomb, or even a *Quistclose* arrangement should not
attempt to do so, as the inclusion of an enforcer in the draft could only benefit
and in no way damage his client's interests. The courts could then either approve
or disapprove of the device if and when it was challenged before them.

H. Conclusion: the Future of the Trust

It has been the purpose of this chapter to demonstrate that the English law relating to the interest of a beneficiary under a trust has passed through a whole circle
of development during the last two centuries and is now arriving close to the
point from which it started, namely that there must be someone who can approach
the court to enforce the trust. During the nineteenth century, when it was felt
in England as in Europe that there must be someone who could dispose of the
greatest possible interest which the law allowed, that person's beneficial interest
crystallized into the concept of beneficial ownership of the trust property. In this
regard, it is important to note that the legal history of England and those of its
nearest European neighbours were not as different at this time as many have

---

[45] Particularly as no private trust can last in perpetuity. One might well ask why the settlor's
wishes should not prevail for as long as the law allows if an interested party wishes them to do so.
That is, of course, the current law, only settlors are not included among those classified as interested
parties – only beneficiaries are so included.

[46] Contracts (Rights of Third Parties) Act 1999, s 1 (1) (a).

believed and some would continue to have us believe. Part of the price of this development was to cast doubt upon the validity of private purpose trusts, even where there were persons who had sufficient interest to enforce them despite being in no sense owners.

As on the European mainland, however, ownership in its unrestricted, absolute sense has been in retreat while the nineteenth and twentieth centuries advanced. Public-law restrictions have restored to owners the need for responsibility in the way they manage their own property. Thus, owners of land are no freer in England than in Germany or France to build upon it as they wish without obtaining permission from public bodies, or to change the use of their land from, for instance, the agricultural to the industrial. In England, it is also possible for an owner to discover that his property is of such historical or architectural value to the community that it is classified as a listed building and that accordingly he may not develop or maintain it as he wishes, but must conform to standards imposed to reflect the public's interest in it. If an owner lives in a conservation area, he will face similar restrictions on how he develops and maintains his property in order to protect the character of the neighbourhood. Certain trees may not be felled by their owners by reason of the public interest in them.

By and large, such restrictions are imposed by public law and regulated by public authorities. However, when an owner seeks planning permission from a public authority to develop his land or buildings, the authority is required to give his neighbours an opportunity to make their views known concerning the proposed development. Failure to do so will invalidate the permission granted, as natural justice requires that those with an interest in the development, albeit they have no rights let alone ownership in the property, must be given the opportunity to be heard. In other words, as with the trust, those with an interest less than ownership are recognized as having sufficient *locus standi* to approach the court and enforce the rules. In some countries, most notably Italy, this interest has come to be described in the legal doctrine as a legitimate interest. Thus, for instance, although I cannot own the air which I breathe, I have a legitimate interest in its quality sufficient to give me the right to object if another threatens to pollute it, even if the pollution does not threaten to harm me in a way which the law would deem unlawful.

In the US, developments such as these have gone further and given rise to what is termed 'the public trust doctrine', and in Canada to the 'trusteed' environmental fund.[47] Under the former, things which in civil law jurisdictions are deemed to

---

[47] See, for instance, Parker and Mellows, *The Modern Law of Trusts* (7th edn, by A J Oakley, London: Sweet & Maxwell, 1998), 9–10.

be *extra commercium*, not susceptible to private ownership, are held by the State subject to a fiduciary obligation to manage them in the public interest. Such things include the coastline, tidal rivers, and so forth. Thus, public authorities are made accountable for their management and control of public property in the same manner as trustees. Again, while this may recognize a beneficial interest in any member of the public sufficient to allow them recourse to the court to enforce the public right, there can hardly be said to be a beneficial owner. Under the latter, the Canadian 'trusteed' environmental fund, private concerns which are engaged in activities which have a harmful effect upon the environment, such as mining or quarrying, are required to pay sums to trustees while their activities are ongoing, which accumulated fund, having been invested and managed according to the usual obligations placed upon trustees in that regard, becomes available when the activity ceases for restoration and reclamation of the land affected.

Both developments involve a recognition that ownership – the former in public law, the latter in private law – no longer necessarily embraces the *ius abutendi*. Owners are required to respect the things they own and show a due sense of social responsibility with regard to the manner in which they use, enjoy, and exploit their property. This raises the question of how the observance of such an obligation can be ensured. In the past, when for instance things which according to Roman law had been outside of private ownership – such as the seashore, rivers, forests, and so on – came to be under the protection of feudal rulers, it was but a short step for their duty to protect the general interest in such things to transform itself into a peculiar privilege of being alone allowed to exploit the property in question, which is how the rights of regality and other seigneurial privileges emerged in mediaeval Europe. The public trust doctrine in the United States is, in effect, a rectification of this process, as a result of which the general public interest has reasserted itself. However, if such a reassertion of the general interest can be allowed against public law owners, there is no reason why it cannot also be employed to allow those with legitimate interests in the property of others, but who have no rights therein, to prevent exploitation which is detrimental to the common good. The standards have already been determined in the law of England and Wales when applications are made for planning permission or permission is given or withheld for work to be done on listed buildings or properties situated within a conservation or heritage area. In effect, every owner would have some trustee obligations with regard to the manner in which he managed his property. In other words, certain restrictions would be, as Otto von Gierke argued, of the essence of ownership itself.

Allowing private individuals the right to challenge the activities of owners according to common standards of responsible management would help democratize this area of the law and move control of owners' activities in part from the domain of public law to that of private law. The demise of the need to establish beneficial ownership in order to enforce trustee obligations against the legal owners of property opens up the possibility for such a development in English law. In reality, it is a return to the situation which prevailed before the absolute conception of ownership gained sway at the start of the nineteenth century. At that time, only another form of ownership, beneficial ownership, was thought sufficient to limit the legal owner's rights. Previously, the rights of a superior lord would have been asserted in a feudal context. Since then, public authorities have sought to impose limitations in the name of the people. The process of democratization will be complete when the people themselves are able to assert their interests. The waning of the importance of the concept of beneficial ownership paves the way for that possibility to become a reality. The outcome may well be a further fascinating chapter in the history of the English law of trusts, and this time one it is likely to be sharing in a wider jurisprudential world.

9

THE REGULATION OF TRUSTEES

Alastair Hudson[1]

A. The Argument

1. Differentiation in the law of trusts

To understand the modern law of trusts properly it is important to be aware both
that there are a number of very different types of trust and that there are qualitatively different types of obligation imposed on the different types of trustee.
One particularly significant development in the differentiation between types of
trust has been the introduction of formal regulation to deal with some trustees
but not others: principally pension fund trusts regulated under the Pensions
Acts,[2] unit trusts regulated under the UCITS Directive[3] and the Financial Services
and Markets Act 2000,[4] and trustees who are 'authorized persons' regulated
by the Financial Services Authority (FSA) under the Financial Services and
Markets Act 2000.[5] There are also other forms of trust which are described in
detail by primary legislation, such as trusts of land under the Trusts of Land and
Appointment of Trustees Act[6] and strict settlements under the Settled Land Act
1925,[7] with the result that the obligations of the trustees are different from those

---

[1] Professor of Equity & Law, Queen Mary, University of London.

[2] Pensions Act 1995, Pensions Act 2004. See G W Thomas and A S Hudson, *The Law of Trusts*
(Oxford: Oxford University Press, 2004), Ch 43–6.

[3] Directive 85/611 on Undertakings for Collective Investment in Transferable Securities
(UCITS) ([1985] OJ L375/3).

[4] Financial Services and Markets Act 2000, s 237. See G W Thomas and A S Hudson, n 2 above,
51.10 et seq.

[5] Financial Services and Markets Act 2000, Schedule 2. See G W Thomas and A S Hudson, n 2
above, 47.18 et seq.

[6] [1996], s 1.

[7] The strict settlement code under the Settled Land Act 1925 has now been repealed in relation
to trusts created after 1 January 1997 by the Trusts of Land and Appointment of Trustees Act 1996,
s 2(1).

of an ordinary trustee whose obligations are controlled by the terms of any trust instrument and the general law of trusts.

As we shall see, trustees regulated under these codes occupy a very different position in many senses from trustees under ordinary, traditional trusts whose obligations are described solely by the general law of trusts. Indeed, as we shall explore, the scope of the 'traditional trust', whether express, resulting, or constructive, is becoming more limited in the modern world of increasingly regulated trusteeship. Nevertheless, despite this differentiation between types of trusteeship, this chapter will endeavour to show that all trusts are predicated on traditional principles of equity and of trusts law and so remain a coherent intellectual whole. The purpose of this chapter is to survey this differentiation in the law of trusts, to consider the way in which some forms of trustee are subject to formal regulation, and to identify the central principles from which these otherwise very different forms of trusteeship flow.

2. The traditional conceptualization of the trust

Traditional trusts theory always posits the trustee as the defendant. From the outset the trust is predicated on the conscience of the legal owner of property being affected:[8] thus we can understand express trusts, constructive trusts, and resulting trusts as being imposed on any defendant who acquires legal title in property in circumstances in which his conscience obliges him to hold that property for the benefit of some other person. While we may talk of the *powers* of trustees[9] – to seek a variation of the trust, to advance property, and so forth – we do not tend to talk about the *rights* of trustees.

The only aspects of trusteeship which might be said to equate to rights are in fact limitations placed by a trust instrument on the trustees' obligations. Thus exclusions or limitations of liability set out in a trust instrument do not equate to general rights properly so called. Instead they are immunities from liability or merely narrow rights specifically to receive payment under a particular trust instrument. A general right would give the right holder complete freedom to act, whereas any rights held by a fiduciary, for example to receive payment, give only a legal entitlement to demand such a payment and not a general liberty to act outwith the terms of that right. In this sense, it is more common to talk of trustees having 'powers': that is, powers which will be void if the trustee seeks to act outwith the terms of that power. When we consider the rights of beneficiaries below we shall

---

[8] A concept explicitly at the heart of the trustees' responsibilities in cases spanning the centuries from *Gresley v Saunders* (1522) Spelman Rep 22–23 through to *Westdeutsche Landesbank v Islington* [1996] AC 669. See A S Hudson, *Equity & Trusts* (5th edn, Routledge Cavendish, 2007), s 1.1.

[9] See G W Thomas and A S Hudson, n 2 above, ch 13 and 14; and A S Hudson, n 8, ch 10.

see that these are general rights because the beneficiary may exercise them in any way that she sees fit in a qualitatively different sense from the trustee. Thus, the ability of a trustee to seek an indemnity for expenses or to take a fee for work done are not rights in the fullest sense of that term because the trustees' entitlement is specified only by the terms of any particular trust instrument but does not attach to trustees in general terms. Seeking to advance capital or to vary the trust, for example, are really just extensions of the means by which trustees may seek to carry out their fiduciary duties, as opposed to being general rights or freedoms to act.

By analogy the *rights* of beneficiaries are focused primarily on rights to the trust property under the principle in *Saunders v Vautier*[10] and to force the trustees to account, inter alia to account for any breach of trust. There are other rights for the beneficiaries, however, such as the right to set aside exercises of the trustees' discretions on grounds of taking into account irrelevant considerations or for failing to take into account relevant considerations,[11] qualified rights to obtain information from the trustees,[12] and exceptionally under the Trusts of Land and Appointment of Trustees Act 1996 rights to be consulted as to the use of the trust land.

The general law of trusts conceives of the rights of beneficiaries in two principal senses: one positive and one negative. The negative conceptualization of the rights of beneficiaries is bound up with the right of beneficiaries to petition the court in the event of any perceived wrongdoing by the trustees. This is a negative form of right in that it only gives the beneficiaries the right to complain, the right to prevent malfeasance or the right to recover compensation for loss. By contrast, the principle in *Saunders v Vautier*[13] grants the beneficiaries – provided that they are acting in unison, that they constitute the entirety of the equitable interest in the trust property, and that they are all *sui juris* – the right to terminate the trust and to call for delivery of the trust property to them as absolute owners inter se. This is a positive right in that the beneficiaries are able to deal with the property in whatever way they wish as a result. The principle in *Saunders v Vautier* has a stronger metaphorical force, however, in English law beyond a right to terminate the trust because, even if the claimants do not constitute the entirety of the equitable interest, this principle expresses the ideology in English trusts law that the beneficiaries ultimately have *proprietary* rights in the trust fund as opposed to merely *personal* rights in equity against the trustees. The roots of the beneficiaries'

---

[10] (1841) 4 Beav 115.
[11] *Re Hastings-Bass* [1975] Ch 25.
[12] *Schmidt v Rosewood Trust Ltd* [2003] 2 WLR 1442.
[13] (1841) 4 Beav 115.

rights are therefore in their equitable proprietary rights in the trust fund, whatever that fund may be from time to time and however those rights may be circumscribed. Thus, the law of trusts must be thought of as being a part of the law of property as opposed to the law of obligations.[14] The beneficiaries have rights in the trust property itself and furthermore the trust property is required to be separately identifiable from all other property before the trust itself will even be valid.

Lord Grant gave us the basis of the beneficiary principle and of the rules relating to certainty of objects when he required that there be some person in whose favour the court can decree performance before there will be a valid trust.[15] Thus, the basis of traditional trust theory is that there must be at least one beneficiary who can sue the trustees in the event of any wrongdoing.[16] In this way, a form of regulation is achieved by the courts ultimately, or at least by legal advisors applying case-law principles to individual circumstances. As this brief survey of the land shows, the beneficiaries' principal rights rest in the control of the trustees through the courts. Again, the main focus of trusts law is on the duties of the trustee. To consider the differentiation in trusts law, however, it is important to consider how the statutory codes dealing with some trusts have expanded the obligations of trustees.

3. Trends in the differentiation of trusts

The first point, then, is to understand how differentiated trust practice has become: that pension trust schemes differ markedly from trusts of land from unit trusts and so on. The coverage offered by traditional trusts law is no longer absolute: that is, the decisions of the Courts of Chancery are no longer the whole of the law of trusts. So, for example, trustees in unit trusts and occupational pension fund schemes are regulated by the Financial Services Authority[17] and the Pensions Regulator respectively.[18] The presence of these regulators constitutes a very different form of oversight from the traditional trusts law model which is based on beneficiaries bringing trustees' misfeasance before the courts, as expressed in the words of Lord Grant MR in *Morice v Bishop of Durham*[19] to the effect that 'there must be someone in whose favour the court can decree performance'. Successive incursions by public policy, in the form of statutory regulators (as in unit trusts

---

[14] Cf Penner, 'Exemptions', in Birks and Pretto (eds) *Breach of Trust* (Hart, 2002), 241.

[15] *Morice v Bishop of Durham* (1804) 9 Ves 399, (1805) 10 Ves 522.

[16] *Morice v Bishop of Durham* (1804) 9 Ves 399, (1805) 10 Ves 522; *Bowman v Secular Society Ltd* [1917] AC 406.

[17] Financial Services and Markets Act 2000, ss 1, 247.

[18] Pensions Act 2004, s 5.

[19] (1804) 9 Ves 399, (1805) 10 Ves 522.

and pension funds) and statutory codes on particular uses of trusts (such as the Trusts of Land and Appointment of Trustees Act 1996 and the Trustee Act 2000), are contributing to these marked differences between various forms of trust. Consequently, it is tempting to see trusts law as breaking apart in the way that Lord Browne-Wilkinson predicted that it might in *Target Holdings v Redferns*[20] when his Lordship suggested:

> In the modern world the trust has become a valuable device in commercial and financial dealings. The fundamental principles of equity apply as much to such trusts as they do to the traditional trusts in relation to which those principles were originally formulated. But in my judgment it is important, if the trust is not to be rendered commercially useless, to distinguish between the basic principles of trust law and those specialist rules developed in relation to traditional trusts which are applicable only to such trusts and the rationale of which has no application to trusts of quite a different kind.

Thus the possibility of a differentiation in trusts law has been latent in the case law. The regulation of trustees is one key aspect in this development, as considered next.

B. The Regulation of Trustees

1. The significance of trustees being subject to regulation

Briefly put, the significance of trustees being subject to regulation is this: once trusts are subject to formal regulation, we must accept that the thin patina of confidence in the beneficiary principle as the foundation stone of the general law of trusts has been broken. The principal aim of the law of trusts has always been to secure the protection of the beneficiaries against any breach of trust. It is unsurprising that the judiciary should have sprung so enthusiastically to the defence of the beneficiaries. As any reader of Jane Austen knows, the settlements which governed the lives of the upper middle classes and the aristocracy in England cut to the very core of their beings. Young women who stood to lose the shelter of their childhood homes as the result of a fee tail spent their lives seeking suitable husbands.[21] It was a truth universally acknowledged that any patriarch in possession of a large fortune was in need of a trusts lawyer and a settlement to provide for generations as yet unborn. If beneficiaries under trusts were to lose their trust funds, the result would be penury and chaos. In consequence, stringent principles as to the liabilities of trustees for breach of trust were developed so that those

---

20 [1996] AC 421.
21 See, for example, Austen's novels *Pride and Prejudice* and *Sense and Sensibility*.

trustees would be liable to make specific restitution of any property taken in breach of trust or to account more generally for any loss suffered by the beneficiaries.[22] More generally the strict principles dealing with trustees making secret profits[23] (even where no bad faith was present[24]) or permitting any possibility of a conflict of interest through the self-dealing[25] or fair-dealing[26] principles ensured that beneficiaries were protected in so far as equity could allow. Further principles were developed to trace after the proceeds of any breach of trust regardless of the good faith of the recipient of that property,[27] or to hold personally liable to account to the beneficiaries for any loss suffered by a breach of trust any person who had knowingly received the trust property into his possession or control at any time[28] or who had dishonestly assisted in the breach of trust.[29] All of these species of claim, most of them unique to equitable jurisdictions, were developed precisely so that the proprietary rights of the beneficiary would be protected no matter what.

Consequently, the law of trusts has developed an understanding that the trustee is always a defendant who is required to justify the conscionability of his actions and frequently to account in circumstances in which he was not even acting in bad faith.[30] Thus, the central, underpinning ideology of the law of trusts was that the interests of the beneficiaries were to be protected by means of the beneficiary bringing the trustees to court. Thus the beneficiary principle has developed its pivotal place in English trusts law jurisprudence. No other principle has greater sanction or authority, we have been told.[31]

If we fast forward from the world of Jane Austen to the present day, we can see a much broader range of trusts in existence. In particular pension fund trusts, mutual investment funds, and unit trusts have acquired an enormous economic importance, both in the sense that they constitute some of the largest institutional

---

[22] *Clough v Bond* (1838) 3 My & Cr 490; *Nocton v Lord Ashburton* [1914] AC 932; *Target Holdings v Redferns* [1996] AC 421.
[23] *Boardman v Phipps* [1967] 2 AC 46.
[24] See, for example, *Keech v Sandford* (1726) Sel Cas Ch 61; *Bray v Ford* [1896] AC 44.
[25] *Ex p Lacey* (1802) 6 Ves 625; *Ex p James* (1803) 8 Ves 337, 345, per Lord Eldon.
[26] *Tito v Waddell (No 2)* [1977] 3 All ER 129.
[27] See, for example, *Re Diplock* [1948] Ch 465 where a charity received property under a void charitable purpose clause and was nevertheless required to restore the property under an equitable tracing claim.
[28] *Barnes v Addy* (1874) 9 Ch App 244; *Re Montagu's Settlement Trust* [1987] Ch 264; *Polly Peck International v Nadir* (No 2) [1992] 4 All ER 769.
[29] *Barnes v Addy* (1874) 9 Ch App 244; *Royal Brunei Airlines v Tan* [1995] 2 AC 378; *Barlow Clowes v Eurotrust* [2005] UKPC 37, [2006] 1 All ER 333.
[30] *Keech v Sandford* (1726) Sel Cas Ch 61.
[31] *Re Endacott* [1960] Ch 232.

investors in the UK's financial markets and that many more ordinary citizens than ever before are reliant on these institutional investors for their well-being in old age as the state pension is allowed to wither away. Consequently, the social significance of these forms of trust has led successive governments to introduce and progressively to enhance the level of regulatory scrutiny of forms of trust such as unit trusts and occupational pension funds. For trusts law the important factor here is that confidence in the ability of the beneficiary principle – by virtue of which the beneficiaries could sue malfeasant trustees in the courts – has deteriorated both in significance and in practical effect. It is no longer enough to expect beneficiaries to bring an action against the trustees. In some cases this process will simply be too expensive or too lengthy to offer a practical recourse to ordinary investors. In other cases it will be impracticable to expect that the beneficiaries would be able to contact one another so that they could begin an action against their trustees, or that the courts would be able to weigh the respective interests of different groups of beneficiaries, or that the beneficiaries would be able to acquire or evaluate the complex decisions bound up with the investment of large trust funds. Consequently, prudent regulation of the providers of financial services (whether through trusts or otherwise) is expected to maintain integrity in financial markets, and similarly ombudsmen are considered to be a more approachable conduit for beneficiaries' complaints than lawyers and litigation. Traditional trusts law has therefore been usurped in many contexts by statutory regulation.

Nevertheless, while there are some trusts which require regulation to reassure the investing public that their rights are capable of enforcement and that the market can be expected to act with integrity, the shortcoming in formal regulation is that in truth it may offer only limited protection. The presence of a regulator is a palliative in that the investor is lulled into thinking that there is some sentinel who can be called into action on her behalf. That sentinel will require authorized firms to comply with its formal requirements as to maintenance of capital, oversight and training of individual employees, and so forth. This may indeed restrict a large amount of abuse and sharp practice but it has not expunged all such abuses. Thus, indirectly, the regulator will inculcate a culture of integrity into all regulated entities and most of their employees. What the regulator cannot do is to *prevent* a rogue trader from falsifying his accounts or fleecing his customers. Once there has been a breach of regulatory principles, the investor's principal mode of redress will be through lawyers and litigation: it will generally be little consolation to learn that the firm has been fined by the regulator or that the trader has been banned from trading in the future. For traditional trusts law, however, the point remains that confidence in the traditional beneficiary principle model has waned – even if it may in practice be the beneficiaries' principal means of compensation for loss.

2. The meaning of 'regulation'

A definition of what is meant by regulation in this context would be as follows:

> Oversight by some statutory, public body, by reference to formal principles which do
> not carry the sanction of law effected by a court. This may include two limited forms
> of power: (a) the power to impose penalties, but not sanctions under the criminal
> law; and (b) the power to deny authorization to act in a given market, but not the
> power to award damages (except in an arbitral sense) nor rights in property under the
> general law.

The term 'oversight' in this context refers to the power to provide for the behaviour of authorized persons as to (i) capital requirements and so forth, as to the standing of the regulated entity; (ii) rules as to the manner in which that regulated entity conducts its business and deals with its customers; (iii) principles against which the integrity of the regulated entity may be measured (even possibly by the general law);[32] (iv) high-level objectives, such as protection of the British economy, which will guide the regulator itself as to the exercise of its own actions and powers.

The expression 'by reference to formal principles' includes both statutory principles and regulations created by the regulator itself further to powers which have been delegated to it under such a statute. These regulations typically take the form both of guidance and of prescriptive rules which impose both positive and negative obligations on regulated persons. It is generally in the nature of these regulations that they are created on the basis of the shared perception of the regulator and of the regulated entities of the market in which those regulated entities are operating.

That these regulations do not carry the sanction of law means that it is not a court which imposes penalties for transgressions of the regulatory code nor which makes awards of damages under the private law in the way that courts do so under the general law. Rather, it is the regulator which imposes penalties in the manner set out in the statute or in the regulations. By contrast, any principle in a statute which, for example, creates a criminal offence for carrying on regulated activities without formal authorization from the regulator, will be enforceable only by a court of law and so constitutes a part of the general criminal law as opposed to a part of the regulatory code. Regulation is, in effect, a public-law activity exercised so as to oversee the private-law activities of an identified class of regulated persons.

---

[32] See generally Hudson, 'The liabilities of trustees under international finance law' in Glasson and Thomas (eds) *The International Trust* (2nd edn, Jordans, 2006), 639.

3. The dissonance in principle between formal regulation and the general law of trusts

What is most significant about those types of trust which are regulated by statutorily appointed regulators is that the regulation is much more stringent than the ordinary law of trusts, in that regulation imposes positive obligations on regulated persons and not simply negative obligations to refrain from certain types of action.[33] Public policy demands that the integrity of the investment market be protected by regulating the sellers' conduct of business. So, whereas an ordinary trustee under a traditional trust may limit her liability for any infraction except dishonesty, trustees of regulated trusts are frequently not permitted to exclude their liabilities. For example, a trustee of a pension trust under section 33 of the Pensions Act 1995 bears 'liability for breach of an obligation under any rule of law to take care or exercise skill in the performance of any investment functions' and it is further provided that this liability 'cannot be excluded or restricted by any instrument or agreement'. There is also a statutory restriction placed on the ability of the manager of a unit trust to seek to restrict its own liability in the following terms:

> Any provision of the trust deed of an authorized unit trust scheme is void in so far as it would have the effect of exempting the manager or trustee from liability for any failure to exercise due care and diligence in the discharge of his functions in respect of the scheme.[34]

So, any provision of the trust deed of an authorized unit trust scheme will be void if it has the effect of exempting the manager or trustee from liability for any failure in due care and diligence.

It is an interesting feature of the law of trusts that the courts are frequently eager to advance the commercial attractiveness of the trust concept in a manner which is directly contrary to the regulation imposed on commercial people by the law of finance and statutory regulation. So, in relation to the ability of trustees to limit or exclude their liability in a trust instrument, it is clear that trustees are permitted to exclude their liability for gross negligence in the performance of their fiduciary duties.[35] However, a trustee of a pension fund is not permitted to exclude its liability in general terms,[36] nor is a trustee of a unit trust.[37]

---

[33] See the discussion to follow of the obligations imposed by the FSA *Conduct of Business* rulebook especially para 2.1.2R restricting exclusion of liability.

[34] Financial Services and Markets Act 2000, s 253.

[35] *Armitage v Nurse* [1998] Ch 241.

[36] Pensions Act 1995, s 33.

[37] Financial Services and Markets Act 2000, s 253.

A second context in which this phenomenon is significant can be illustrated by the law on knowing receipt. Where a financial institution receives trust property into its control or possession further to a breach of trust, its liability for knowing receipt will depend upon whether or not it had knowledge (imputed to it from the knowledge of its agents) of the breach of trust or, seemingly on recent authority, whether or not it had acted unconscionably in so doing.[38] Scott LJ has held that an institution will be deemed to have had the requisite knowledge if there was something about the context which ought to have made its employees suspicious.[39] The precise issue in that case was said to be whether or not a reasonable central bank should have realized that the money transferred to it had been acquired by means of a breach of fiduciary duty. Millett J has held, similarly, that there is no obligation on account officers employed by banks to investigate the source of payments made to the bank by its customers or counterparties.[40] As his Lordship put it: 'Account officers are not detectives.' That is, there is no obligation under the case law on such people to be on the front foot when receiving deposits or channelling payments between accounts under their control. Importantly, however, the financial regulation dealing with bankers *does* impose positive obligations on regulated persons to investigate their clients on opening accounts and to be observant of any payments which come from suspicious sources.[41] Therefore, there is a mismatch between the law on knowing receipt and the law of finance, whereby in relation to the same context each imposes radically different obligations on banks and on their employees.

4. Paradoxes in the exclusion of trustees' liability

There are two paradoxes relating to the professionalism which trustees of ordinary trusts claim for themselves while, using their professional knowledge, they protect themselves against the possibility that their professionalism is not capable of protecting the beneficiaries from loss. The first point is this: an ordinary trustee without any experience of such matters may accept the office of trustee without insisting on an exclusion of liability clause in the trust instrument and so expose herself to liability for breach of trust, whereas a professional trustee with sufficient nous to have such an exclusion of liability provision included in the trust instrument, and who will have attracted the settlor's custom ironically by emphasizing her expertise, is entitled to have her liability excluded. The second point is this: many commentators on trusts law celebrate the ability of professional

---

[38] *Bank of Credit and Commerce International v Akindele* [2001] Ch 437.

[39] *Polly Peck v Nadir (No 2)* [1992] 4 All ER 769.

[40] *Macmillan v Bishopsgate* (No 3) [1996] 1 WLR 387.

[41] See, for example, Criminal Justice Act 1993, s 93A, the Money Laundering Regulations 2003, art 3 et seq, and the FSA Conduct of Business Sourcebook further to the Markets in Financial Instruments Directive (2004/39/EC), art 19.

trustees to exclude or limit their liabilities for losses caused by their management of a trust and accord it the status of a natural part of commercial practice necessary to encourage professionals to continue to act as trustees,[42] whereas the statutes underpinning formal investment trust structures (such as pensions and unit trusts) prohibit any such exclusion of liability.

Investment trusts which are marketed to the public in the UK are regulated by the FSA in accordance with the *Conduct of Business* rulebook[43] and the other provisions of the FSA Handbook. Under those regulations investment professionals are held to a rigorous set of duties when dealing with thier clients. The law of trusts, by comparison, looks Neanderthal with its unsophisticated insistence on the total exclusion of the trustees' liability even if the trustees had originally been touting their expertise to act as trustees.[44] Contrariwise, it would make more sense for the general law of trusts to limit the liability of inexpert trustees who could not have known better, as opposed to protecting the position of professional trustees. Consequently, the provision in the Trustee Act 2000 which requires that the trustees must take proper advice[45] before making investment decisions is a sensible equalization of the implicitly different treatment of professional and non-professional trustees in that it recognizes the limits on the inexpert trustees' capabilities. Nevertheless, it still does not match the development of FSA regulation in this context. Thus, if the principles governing regulated investment trusts do not permit limitation of liability, then it cannot be said to be a necessary part of ensuring that professionals continue to act as trustees when advocating the rights of trustees to have their liabilities excluded by provision to that effect in the trust instrument.

The question in this context must therefore be: what is the irreducible core of trusteeship in relation to trust investment? The focus of the traditional law of trusts is on the conscience of the trustee. Consequently, it could be said that the trustee ought properly to account to the beneficiaries for any loss resulting from her breach of trust, regardless of the presence of an exclusion of liability clause. The approach we can extrapolate from cases such as *Armitage v Nurse*[46] is that a trustee is not acting unconscionably if she refuses to bear a liability for breach of trust which she did not agree to face at the outset, and this is particularly so if that trustee was sufficiently prudent to have the settlor exclude this form of

---

[42] *Armitage v Nurse* [1998] Ch 241.
[43] Referred to as the 'FSA, *Conduct of Business Rulebook*', implementing the Markets in Financial Instruments Directive (2004/39/EC) in a new version as from 1 November 2007. References here are to that version.
[44] *Armitage v Nurse* [1998] Ch 241.
[45] Trustee Act 2000, s 5.
[46] [1998] Ch 241.

liability in the trust instrument. So, the Court of Appeal was prepared to absolve a trustee from liability for gross negligence because that was the exemption granted to him by the trust instrument. By contrast, *Walker v Stones*[47] seemed to reinstate much of the traditional approach by finding that an exclusion clause which purported to exclude liability for loss caused by dishonesty would be of no effect. We can of course reconcile *Armitage v Nurse* with *Walker v Stones* at a technical level (as to the distinction between negligent and dishonest acts), but this does not answer the more general question as to the rationale for excluding the liability of professional trustees in circumstances in which statutory regulation would not have permitted such an exclusion of liability.

This distinction does not explain why private trustees should be permitted to exclude their liabilities when regulated trusts such as pension funds or unit trusts do not permit their trustees to do so. In relation to private trustees, however, it should be remembered that professional trustees selling their services to the public as part of a business may be regulated under the Financial Services and Markets Act 2000. Under the FSA's *Conduct of Business* rulebook, such a person will be obliged to treat the settlor-client in accordance with its level of expertise.[48] Consequently, exclusion of liability will not be possible under these regulations if the products sold to the client are unsuitable.[49] The terms of business must include mention of the commencement of the terms of business, the applicable regulator, the client's investment objectives, any restrictions on the relevant designated business, which services will be provided, how payment for services will be effected, disclosure of any polarization, whether the seller is to act as investment manager, any conflicts of interest, and whether or not the client has a right to withdraw.[50]

The case law on the exclusion of trustees' liability is an example of the law of trusts wishing to make itself amenable to commercial people and so to combat the notion that there is something unattractive about the discretionary jurisdiction of courts of equity.[51] Whereas by contrast, commercial law and financial regulation are equally concerned with the integrity of those markets in terms of the proper behaviour of its participants with the certainty of contracts and so forth: in consequence these areas of law are less concerned to appease the commercial community and more concerned to regulate the integrity of the market. In short, there is no reason for trusts law to seek to protect commercial activity above and beyond the manner in which financial regulation prohibits exclusion of liability

---

[47] [2001] QB 902.
[48] FSA, *Conduct of Business Rulebook*, ch 3 generally.
[49] ibid, 2.1.2R.
[50] ibid, 8.1.2R, 8.1.3R, et seq.
[51] See A S Hudson, *Equity & Trusts* (5th edn, Routledge Cavendish, 2007), para 21.2.

and in which contract law precludes unfair contract terms. The general law of trusts in this context is beginning to seem antique.

C. Differentiation in Trusts Law

1. The extensive differentiation of trusts

Professor Hayton has suggested that trustees of pension funds should be considered to be different from trustees of other trusts.[52] This argument appears to be unobjectionable on the face of it: there is something different in the quality of acting as trustee of a large pension fund when compared with a trustee of, say, a will trust of an individual of limited means. However, I would suggest that this analysis is scratching at the topsoil of a much deeper phenomenon. In truth, there have long been great differences between various forms of trust and the various uses to which trusts are put in practice. At the simplest level there were distinctions between strict settlements and other settlements at the very least from the enactment of the Settled Land Act in 1925, as with trusts of land in 1996 with the Trusts of Land and Appointment of Trustees Act, pension fund trusts with the Pensions Act 1995, unit trusts most recently with the Financial Services and Markets Act 2000, and so on, as considered below.

Professor Hayton's suggestion is thus a perfectly sensible one. However, the ramifications of this argument more generally require consideration. The real issue is what flows from the observation that there is something different about being the trustee of a pension fund when compared with other forms of trustee. If what is meant by this observation is that those trustees must be subject to principles of fiduciary law which are modified to account for their particular context, then the argument seems sensible. If what is suggested is that pension fund trustees should be subjected to none of the ordinary principles of fiduciary law which apply to trustees generally, then the argument is problematic. My preferred approach is to think of the many forms of trusteeship as being differentiated one from another, but that does not require that we should dispense with the basic notion of trusteeship and instead develop new, 'commercially relevant' principles which will be appealing to different sections of the financial services industry. Instead, recognizing differentiation between types of trusteeship is merely to recognize, as Lord Browne-Wilkinson has reminded us, that there is not one narrow set of obligations imposed on fiduciaries in general (nor on trustees in general), but it is rather to recognize that the general principles underpinning those

---

[52] D Hayton, 'Pension Trusts and Traditional Trusts: Drastically Different Species of Trusts' [2005] *Conveyancer* 229.

obligations will have to be analysed closely in their particular context.[53] However, those obligations are nevertheless to be understood in *Armitage v Nurse* as arising on the basis of some 'irreducible core',[54] an expression which Millett LJ must have borrowed from Professor Hayton.[55]

2. The nature of the differentiation in the law of trusts

If the reader will permit me a short digression into autobiography, I want to try to illustrate the point that differentiation is necessarily a part of trusts law (whether we like it or not) but also to demonstrate that recognizing this development does not mean that we should now ignore the traditional principles of trusteeship and of fiduciary law. When Professor Geraint Thomas and I sat down to plan our book *The Law of Trusts*,[56] we were faced with one obvious dilemma: did we simply ape the achievements of Snell, Lewin, Underhill, and their successive editors in terms of structure and content, or did we plough a furrow of our own? Indeed, our impetus in writing that book flowed from a shared view that the legal profession needed a more modern but equally scholarly treatment of the law of trusts. It was clear to us that our purpose in writing that book was to plough a new furrow which we thought needed to be ploughed; it was not simply to replicate the work of those who had gone before. We had already come severally to the view that there needed to be a book which reflected the work of trusts law practitioners in different areas but which nevertheless linked those different contexts into the pool of equitable concepts which are common to all trusts. Thus we broke the project into two sections (each section a little shy of 1,000 pages): first, the *General Principles* of trusts law and, second, detailed examinations of *Specific Trusts*. We had identified that there was a deeply ingrained differentiation of the various types of trust which drew on fundamental, conceptual principles which were being adapted in practice from context to context. So, unlike Professor Hayton's limited suggestion that there is something different about pension trusts from other trusts, our assertion is that there are *many* different types of trust, each of which has its own esoteric features and sub-principles.

The different types of trust which we identified at this conceptual level were:

- Traditional trusts (impliedly dealt with in the *General Principles* section)
  - express trusts

---

[53] *Henderson v Merrett Syndicates* [1995] 2 AC 145, 206.

[54] *Armitage v Nurse* [1998] Ch 241.

[55] D Hayton, 'The irreducible core content of trusteeship' in A Oakley (ed) *Trends in Contemporary Trusts Law* (Oxford: Oxford University Press, 1996) 47.

[56] G W Thomas and A S Hudson, *The Law of Trusts* (Oxford: Oxford University Press, 2004) 1907.

- resulting trusts
- constructive trusts
- Private client trusts, including
  - interest in possession trusts
  - accumulation and maintenance trusts
  - discretionary trusts and disabled trusts
  - testamentary trusts
- International trusts, including
  - asset protection trusts
  - offshore purpose trusts
- Pension trusts, especially
  - occupational pension scheme trusts
- Trusts in financial transactions, including
  - investment trusts and
  - unit trusts
- Trusts used in commercial contexts, including
  - trading trusts and
  - trusts implied by law in the operation and termination of transactions
- Trusts of land and of the home, including
  - trusts of land under the 1996 Act and
  - trusts implied by law over the home.

This list emerged because it seemed to us that these various forms of trust operated on different statutory or other, practical bases from traditional trusts. Thus, it is suggested that the differentiation in trusts law as a combined matter of practice and deployment of principle is much more variegated than Professor Hayton's analysis permits.[57] The recognition that there is such a broad differentiation in the law of trusts suggests to me that it is not so serious a matter as to indicate a crisis in the law of trusts. Rather, it suggests that we are simply bound up in the process (which is long understood in the law relating to fiduciaries) of deciding how general principles are to apply to particular contexts and at what point we must stop qualifying those general principles before what is left in the context cannot properly be called a fiduciary office at all. This is the heart of the debate as to the extent of the 'irreducible core content of trusteeship'. To consider the nature of that core content, it is necessary to outline the core duties of trustees (albeit briefly, given the constraints of space imposed here).

---

[57] D Hayton, 'Pension Trusts and Traditional Trusts: Drastically Different Species of Trusts' [2005] *Conveyancer* 229.

D. The Core Duties of Trustees

1. The glorious 13

There is no comprehensive list of the duties of trustees either in general terms or in particular contexts. In relation to the general duties of trustees there are, it is suggested, 13 principal duties incumbent on all forms of trustee:[58]

(1) The duties on acceptance of office relating to the need to familiarize oneself with the terms, conditions, and history of the management of the trust.[59]
(2) The duty to obey the terms of the trust unless directed to do otherwise by the court.[60]
(3) The duty to safeguard the trust assets,[61] including duties to maintain the trust property, as well as to ensure that it is applied in accordance with the directions set out in the trust instrument.
(4) The duty to act even-handedly between beneficiaries,[62] which means that the trustees are required to act impartially between beneficiaries and to avoid conflicts of interest.
(5) The duty to act with reasonable care,[63] meaning generally a duty to act as though a prudent person of business acting on behalf of someone for whom one feels morally bound to provide; or under Trustee Act 2000 to act reasonably.[64]
(6) Duties in relation to trust expenses.
(7) The duties of investment, requiring prudence and that the trustees act in the best interests of the beneficiaries.[65]
(8) The duty to distribute the trust property correctly.[66]
(9) The duty to avoid conflicts of interest,[67] not to earn unauthorized profits from the fiduciary office,[68] not to deal on one's own behalf with trust property on pain of such transactions being voidable,[69] and the obligation to deal fairly with the trust property.

---

[58] See A S Hudson, *Equity & Trusts* (5th edn, Routledge Cavendish, 2007), para 8.1.
[59] *Clough v Bond* (1838) 3 My & Cr 490.
[60] ibid.
[61] For example, *Moyle v Moyle* (1831) 2 Russ & M 710.
[62] *Stephenson v Barclays Bank Trust Co Ltd* [1975] 1 WLR 882.
[63] *Speight v Gaunt* (1883) 9 App Cas 1.
[64] Trustee Act 2000, s 1.
[65] *Speight v Gaunt* (1883) 9 App Cas 1; *Cowan v Scargill* [1985] Ch 270. See Trustee Act 2000 generally.
[66] *Clough v Bond* (1838) 3 My & Cr 490.
[67] *Bray v Ford* [1896] AC 44; *Boardman v Phipps* [1967] 2 AC 46.
[68] *Keech v Sandford* (1726) Sel Cas Ch 61; *Boardman v Phipps* [1967] 2 AC 46.
[69] *Ex p James* (1803) 8 Ves 337; *Tito v Waddell (No 2)* [1977] 3 All ER 129.

(10) The duty to preserve the confidence of the beneficiaries,[70] especially in relation to Chinese wall arrangements.[71]

(11) The duty to act gratuitously, without any right to payment not permitted by the trust instrument or by the general law.[72]

(12) The duty to account and to provide information.[73]

(13) The duty to take into account relevant considerations and to overlook irrelevant considerations in exercising a fiduciary power or a power under a discretionary trust, where failure to do so may lead to the court setting aside an exercise of the trustees' powers.[74]

There is no space in this chapter to explore the detail of these obligations. Of particular significance is the difficult seventh obligation in relation to the investment of the trust property which, it is suggested, may take on a radically different form in practice depending on the precise nature of the trust.[75] For present purposes, the most important point to note is that these 13 principles give a sense of the obligations of trustees rather than legislating for them in detail. That is how equity operates in the round: rather than seeking to provide in detail for each possible future circumstance, equity operates by means of establishing general principles which must be adapted or applied to suit such circumstances.[76] This opens up equity to the complaint that it is not possible to know with certainty in advance exactly how each principle will apply to each case, in the manner that the Parliamentary draftspersons and judges in common law courts hope that their principles will function. But that is the very purpose of equity: to permit the court to fit the solution to the problem. The law of trusts is a good example of how general principles have been synthesized from the authorities and married to later authorities which have hardened equity's more lyrical principles – such as the requirement to come to equity with clean hands[77] or that equity will not permit statute to be used as an engine of fraud[78] – into predictable rules, such as the requirements of certainty of subject matter and certainty of objects. Indeed in the law of finance , for example, the development of high-level principles to be adapted to each circumstance has been identified by the EU and the FSA

---

[70] *Tito v Waddell (No 2)* [1977] 3 All ER 129.

[71] *Bolkiah v KPMG* [1999] 2 AC 222.

[72] See *Robinson v Pett* (1734) 3 P Wms 249.

[73] *O'Rourke v Darbishire* [1920] AC 581; *Schmidt v Rosewood Trust Ltd* [2003] 2 WLR 1442.

[74] *Re Hastings-Bass* [1975] Ch 25; *Abacus Trust Company (Isle of Man) v Barr* [2003] 2 WLR 1362.

[75] See generally G W Thomas and A S Hudson, *The Law of Trusts* (Oxford: Oxford University Press, 2004) ch 52; and A S Hudson, *Equity & Trusts* (5th edn, Routledge Cavendish, 2007), ch 9.

[76] A S Hudson, *Equity & Trusts*, s 1.1.

[77] *Jones v Lenthal* (1669) 1 Ch Cas 154; *Guinness v Saunders* [1990] 2 WLR 324; *Quadrant Visual Communications v Hutchison Telephone* [1993] BCLC 442.

[78] *Rochefoucauld v Boustead* [1897] 1 Ch 196.

as the way forward.[79] The law of finance, however, lacks equity's subtle understanding as to how these principles operate at present, lacking as it does equity's centuries of precedent.

2. How the 13 core duties retain their significance

It is important to remember that, even though there is now a range of trusts which exists outside the exclusive control of the law of trusts, nevertheless these core equitable principles still govern the liabilities of trustees. It is true that the prudential principle in cases like *Learoyd v Whiteley*[80] is of reduced significance in the light both of the ability of settlors to exclude that principle in the trust instrument and of the Trustee Act 2000 which prioritizes 'reasonableness' over 'caution'. This is an important alteration in a central plank of trusts law: the shift from prudence to reasonable, professional risk-taking; from the protection of the Jane Austen family members to the modern aspirations of a twenty-first-century beneficiary with dreams of wealth in a rising housing market. This suggests shifts in the cultural appreciation of such principles, rather than that they are being discarded in a newly fragmented world of differentiation between trustees' duties. Rather, the complete set of core trustees' duties remains important. A trustee, of whatever stripe, may not permit conflicts of interest, nor favour one class of beneficiary over another, nor breach the confidence of their beneficiaries, and so on. The point being that the obligations of trustees respond to an underlying core of principles still, even if the detail may differ from context to context. A new differentiation between forms of trusteeship may therefore be a feature of modern trusts law, but, if you will permit me a closing metaphor, repapering the wall does not alter the brickwork beneath.

---

[79] See AS Hudson, *Securities Law* (London Sweet & Maxwell), chs 2, 3.
[80] (1887) 12 App Cas 727.

10

PUBLIC BENEFIT AND CHARITIES: THE IMPACT OF THE CHARITIES ACT 2006 ON INDEPENDENT SCHOOLS AND PRIVATE HOSPITALS

Peter Luxton

The Charities Act 2006, when brought fully into force,[1] will make many changes to the law of charities. Among the most important of these will be some modification to the meaning of charity, including the introduction of a statutory list of charitable purposes and alterations to the public-benefit requirement;[2] the creation of a new form of charitable corporation, the Charitable Incorporated Organization;[3] the setting up of a Charity Tribunal to hear appeals from the Charity Commission;[4] changes to the administration of charities, including registration[5] and accounting and auditing requirements,[6] cy-près, and schemes;[7] a new unified regime for public charitable collections;[8] and an overhaul of the constitution of the Charity Commission.[9] Most of these changes are uncontroversial and received broad support both from the charity sector and in Parliament.

---

[1] The Act received the Royal Assent on 8 November 2006 and is being brought into force in stages from early 2007. The provisions relating to the legal meaning of charity, charitable purposes, and public benefit, which are contained in Part I of the Act, are expected to be brought into force early in 2008. The delay is intended to enable the Charity Tribunal to be established and to give the Charity Commission time to consult and to develop its guidance on the operation of the public-benefit requirement.

[2] Charities Act 2006, ss 1–5.

[3] ibid, s 34 and Schedule 7.

[4] ibid, s 8 and Schedule 3.

[5] ibid, ss 9–14.

[6] ibid, ss 28–30, 32–3.

[7] ibid, ss 15–18.

[8] ibid, ss 45–66.

[9] ibid, ss 6–7 and Schedules 1 and 2.

This cannot be said, however, of the changes to the legal meaning of charity, which are contained in Part I of the Act. Whilst there was little objection to the introduction of a statutory list of charitable purposes, the provisions relating to public benefit proved highly contentious.

It is the aim of this chapter to examine the likely impact of the new Act on the public-benefit requirement, with particular reference to the independent schools (as the Government's concern seems to be primarily with them) and private hospitals, whose charitable status might also be affected. The chapter seeks to identify the Government's aims relating to public benefit, and to determine the extent to which the new Act is likely to achieve those aims. It should be emphasized that the argument in this chapter is a legal analysis; it is not intended to be a polemic. It seeks neither to defend nor to attack the charitable status of the independent schools or private hospitals, and it offers no opinion on whether such institutions might be considered to be for the public benefit using that expression in a popular sense. That is an issue going beyond the realms of legal analysis into the forum of political debate.[10]

A. Charitable Status and the Charging of Fees

Under the law before Part I of the new Act comes into force, there is no statutory definition of charitable purposes.[11] The legal concept of a charitable purpose has been developed over the centuries by the courts, which have used as a guide the list of purposes set out in the Preamble to the Statute of Charitable Uses 1601. This list was not intended to be exhaustive (religious purposes, for instance, are barely mentioned), but in the centuries after its enactment reference was frequently made to the Preamble as a touchstone to what is in law charitable. It was not until the early nineteenth century,[12] however, that it was established that a purpose could not be charitable unless it fell within either the letter or the spirit and intendment of the purposes mentioned therein. The modern law is generally regarded as dating from *Pemsel*'s case in 1891, where Lord Macnaghten set out his famous four heads:[13] the relief of poverty, the advancement of

---

[10] It was the view of the Goodman Committee that any decision to phase out or to curtail independent education 'would be a political one' and that 'any such policy should be implemented directly by political decision': Goodman Committee Report, *Charity Law and Voluntary Organisations* (London: Bedford Square Press, 1976) para 60 p 25. See also the observation of Lord Bingham, albeit in a different context, in *A v Secretary of State for the Home Department* [2005] 2 AC 68, 102: 'The more purely political (in a broad or narrow sense) a question is, the more appropriate it will be for political resolution and the less likely it is to be an appropriate matter for judicial decision.'

[11] Apart from the limited definition in Recreational Charities Act 1958.

[12] In *Morice v Bishop of Durham* (1805) 10 Ves Jun 522.

[13] [1891] AC 531, 583.

education, the advancement of religion, and other purposes beneficial to the community. In determining what falls within the fourth head, the courts require the purpose not merely to be beneficial to the community but also to fall within the letter or the spirit of the Preamble.[14] There is nevertheless an unresolved tension between the Preamble and the *Pemsel* classification, which, as will be explained, illustrates the difference in the categorization of charitable purposes in the period between 1601 and 1891, and indirectly throws light on the public-benefit requirement.

In the modern law, however, it is not enough that a gift, trust, or other institution has purposes that are prima facie (and wholly and exclusively) charitable; it must also satisfy the requirement of public benefit. The modern law therefore treats charitable purpose as the primary ingredient for charitable status, and public benefit as a distinct secondary ingredient. On closer analysis, the term 'public benefit' appears to have two separate aspects. First, it can mean that the purpose itself must be one which is for the public benefit. Second, it can mean that the community or class of persons to benefit must be a sufficient section of the community. What is a sufficient section of the community varies from one head of *Pemsel* to another; but, at least under the second head (the advancement of education) and the fourth (other purposes beneficial to the community), it has been established that the persons to benefit must not be negligible in number, and the quality which distinguishes them from other members of the community must not depend on any personal or contractual nexus.[15]

Most of the estimated 2,400 independent fee-paying schools in the United Kingdom are charities.[16] A few, mostly small preparatory schools, are run as private profit-making institutions and are therefore not charities,[17] but generally the loss of tax relief afforded to charities makes it difficult for independent

---

[14] *Re Macduff* [1896] 2 Ch 451.

[15] *Oppenheim v Tobacco Securities Trust Co Ltd* [1951] AC 297.

[16] The Charity Commission's register of charities is of limited assistance in calculating the number of independent schools that are charities because it does not classify such schools separately, but only under the more general category of Education/Training and Children/Young People: see Charity Commission, *Briefing Paper for the Joint Committee on the Draft Charities Bill: Fee-Charging Charities* (September 2004). In any event, some of the well-known independent schools are exempt charities, so do not appear on the register. The figure of 2,400 independent fee-paying schools mentioned in the text was estimated by the Independent Schools Council (ISC), and was quoted by the Charity Commission in its *Briefing Paper* (above). About half of the independent schools are members of the ISC: see *Briefing Paper* (above). The ISC estimated that 83 per cent of the schools that were its members were charities. The Charity Commission considers it likely that schools that are not members of the ISC 'are less likely to be charitable because most are privately owned' (*Briefing Paper*, above).

[17] See *The Abbey Malvern Wells Ltd v Ministry of Local Government and Planning* [1951] Ch 728, 737, where J Danckwerts mentioned, as not being charities, those schools of learning that 'exist purely as profit-making ventures such as certain preparatory schools'.

schools to exist other than as charities.[18] For many independent schools, the most important fiscal benefits are rate relief, the exemption from tax on investment income, and tax relief on gifts through gift aid, although other exemptions (including those relating to stamp duty land tax, inheritance tax, and capital gains tax) can be significant in appropriate circumstances.[19] The reason why most independent schools currently enjoy charitable status under English law is that they have purposes that satisfy the above-mentioned requirements: they have wholly and exclusively charitable purposes (the advancement of education) and satisfy both aspects of public benefit.

There are judicial statements to the effect that a charity cannot exclude the poor, notably Lord Camden's comment from the mid-eighteenth century that a charitable gift is 'a gift to a general public use, which extends to the poor as well as to the rich'.[20] In similar vein, Lindley LJ once declared: 'I doubt very much whether a trust would be declared to be charitable which excluded the poor.'[21] More recently, the court has opined that a home of rest for millionaires could not be a charity.[22] However, the charitable fee-paying schools do not *in terms* exclude the poor. Although the objects of some restrict admission to the children of certain classes of persons, such as the children of those following a particular calling,[23] or to the sons of gentlemen[24] or noblemen,[25] these restrictions do not in terms exclude the poor – even the sons of gentlemen and noblemen can be poor.

Although the effect of fee-charging is no doubt to reduce the number of persons capable of benefiting, charitable status is denied only if the class of persons who can benefit is numerically negligible. This is a matter of evidence, and the numbers may vary (as Goodman pointed out) 'with fluctuating economic circumstances and government policies'.[26] The threshold is, however, low. Many independent schools provide bursaries and free or assisted places, and some make their facilities available to the community; but, at least under the law before Part I of the new Act comes into force, their charitable status does not depend

---

[18] The ISC (see n 16 above) had estimated the annual fiscal benefit through tax relief for charitable status enjoyed by schools that were its members to be some £88 million in 2004: see ISC's *Further Written Evidence to the Joint Committee on the Draft Charities Bill*, DCH 277 (2004).

[19] See ISC's *Further Written Evidence to the Joint Committee on the Draft Charities Bill*, DCH 277 (2004).

[20] *Jones v Williams* (1767) Amb 651, 652.

[21] *Re Macduff* [1896] 2 Ch 451, 464.

[22] *Re White's Will Trusts* [1951] 1 All ER 528, 530 (Harman J).

[23] *Hall v Derby Urban Sanitary Authority* (1885) 16 QB D 163 (DC) (orphanage for boarding, lodging, clothing, and educating the children of deceased railway servants held to be a public charity and so exempt from rates).

[24] *AG v Earl of Lonsdale* (1827) 1 Sim 105 (school for the sons of gentlemen).

[25] *Brighton College v Marriott* [1926] AC 192 (school for the sons of noblemen and gentlemen).

[26] Goodman Committee Report, para 47 p 21.

upon such things. There is, of course, a contract between the school and the fee-payer, but this does not fall foul of the nexus test because the selection for places is not made from amongst those who have already entered into a contract – rather the contract is entered into in order to enjoy the benefit that has been conferred (ie the offer of a place). Thus in *Joseph Rowntree Memorial Trust Housing Association Ltd v A-G*,[27] Peter Gibson J held charitable the building of homes for sale to the elderly on long leases for a capital sum. He rejected the argument that the existence of a contract between the housing association and the elderly persons was repugnant to charitable status: the beneficiaries were merely being required to contribute to the cost of the benefits they received, and there were numerous cases where beneficiaries had received benefits from a charity only by way of bargain.[28]

The charitable status of private hospitals derives from the fourth head of *Pemsel*. Public benefit in these instances is satisfied because they promote a purpose that has been held to fall within the fourth head, the relief of the sick, which is of course a purpose within the letter of the Preamble (the relief of the impotent) and so for the public benefit in the first sense. Public benefit in the second sense is satisfied because, although the charging of fees restricts the numbers who can take advantage of such hospitals, the number remaining is more than negligible. There is no contractual nexus, for the same reasons as already mentioned in connection with the independent schools. This is sufficient to explain the charitable status of private hospitals under the existing law. Additionally, in *Re Resch's Will Trusts*,[29] Lord Wilberforce indicated that public benefit in private hospitals is to be found in the *indirect* benefit that they provide in relieving the pressure on the State sector.

B. The Background to the Legislative Changes to the Meaning of Charity

The provisions in the Charities Act 2006 relating to the meaning of charity are derived from a report of the Cabinet Office's Strategy Unit published in 2002.[30] The report's recommendations in this area were two-fold.

---

[27] [1983] Ch 159.

[28] For example, *Re Estlin* (1903) 89 LT 88 (home of rest for lady teachers at a rent); *Re Cottam* [1955] 1 WLR 1299 (flats to be let to aged persons at economic rents); *Re Resch's Will Trusts* [1969] 1 AC 514 (gift to a private hospital).

[29] [1969] 1 AC 514, 544 (PC).

[30] Strategy Unit Report, *Private Action, Public Benefit: a Review of Charities and the Wider Not-for Profit Sector*, September 2002.

First, it suggested that a new statutory list of charitable purposes was desirable both explicitly to recognize the range of modern charitable purposes and to extend them. As a result, section 2(2) of the new Act sets out a list of 13 'descriptions' of charitable purposes. The first three (in paragraphs (a) to (c)) are essentially the first three heads of *Pemsel*, although the first head includes the prevention, as well as the relief, of poverty.[31] The next nine purposes (in paragraphs (d) to (l)) are mostly, though not entirely, purposes that are currently recognized as chari-table, either by the courts or by the Charity Commission. Some of these were added during the passage of the Charities Bill as a result of lobbying by particular groups.[32] The final paragraph, (m), refers to any other purpose within subsection (4). That subsection is equivalent to (though not precisely the same as) the fourth head of *Pemsel*, which enables new purposes to be held charitable by analogy with the foregoing purposes, and it also includes purposes charitable under the Recreational Charities Act 1958.

Second, the Strategy Unit Report recommended the tightening up of the public-benefit requirement, so that, under the new statutory categories of charity, 'all charities will have to demonstrate public benefit'.[33] This proposal appears to derive from a recommendation of the National Council for Voluntary Organisations (NCVO) in 2001 that 'all charitable purposes should pass the same test for public benefit, this being the "strong test" currently applicable to charities falling under the fourth head, "other purposes beneficial to the com-munity" '.[34] Under the new Act, every purpose, to be charitable, must be for the public benefit.[35] Furthermore, by section 3(3) public benefit has the same mean-ing as it has under the law relating to charities applicable immediately before the coming into force of the new Act. The problem is with section 3(2), which states that, in determining whether the public-benefit requirement is satisfied, 'it is not to be presumed that a purpose of a particular description is for the public benefit'. This is intended to implement the Strategy Unit's proposal that '[t]here would not . . . be a presumption that certain categories are for the public benefit'.[36]

---

[31] This had been recommended in the Goodman Committee Report, paras 58–9 p 25 and para 93(4) p 38, but what will rank as the prevention of poverty is uncertain.

[32] Examples are the addition of the saving of lives (now included in para (d), which is intended to recognize the charitable status of the provision of lifeboats) and the advancement of animal welfare (para (k)). These purposes, which were charitable even before the new Act, would otherwise have remained charitable under the residual category in para (m).

[33] Strategy Unit Report, *Private Action, Public Benefit*, 2002, para 4.18 p 40.

[34] NCVO, *For the Public Benefit? A consultation document on charity law reform*, (London: NCVO, 2001) para 4.2.1 p 30; see also para 3.5.1 p 23, which refers to oral evidence of the charity barrister Francesca Quint: 'Legislation on charitable status should merely require positive proof of public benefit for all charities, removing the present anomalies and disparities'.

[35] Charities Act 2006, s 2(1)(b).

[36] Strategy Unit Report, *Private Action, Public Benefit*, 2002, para 4.18 p 40.

From the Strategy Unit Report, it seems that the aim of section 3(2) is to ensure that a body will satisfy the public-benefit requirement only if it can show that it provides sufficient open access, or in some other way reaches out, to the community. The report says that the requirement will not be met if a body charges high fees which thereby effectively exclude the majority of the public from being able to use it. According to the report,[37]

> those charities that charge have to ensure that they have a public character, that is, that they provide access for those who would be excluded because of the fees. For example, to maintain their charitable status, independent schools which charge high fees have to make significant provision for those who cannot pay full fees and the majority probably do so already.

The report treats this as an existing requirement, and it identifies the absence of any systematic programme to check what it calls 'the public character of charities',[38] which it states is considered only at registration. It proposes 'that the Charity Commission would identify charities likely to charge high fees and undertake a rolling programme to check that provision was made for wider access'.[39] To this extent, it appears that section 3(2) is designed to enable the Commission to examine the public character of charities on an ongoing basis. The Strategy Unit Report does not, however, clarify what constitutes 'high fees' or what type or level of open access suffices. It is therefore unclear whether it is enough, for instance, for fee-paying schools to make their sports fields available periodically to local state schools, or whether they would have to provide a reasonable number of free, or assisted, places.

A draft Charities Bill had been subjected to pre-legislative scrutiny in 2004 by a Committee of both Houses. In its report, the Joint Committee noted that the interpretation of the public-benefit provisions put forward in evidence by the Charity Commission and by a number of lawyers who adopted a similar approach 'left the draft Bill in the ludicrous position of promising to bite on the public benefit bullet without having any teeth to do so'.[40] The Home Office, on the other hand was confident that the Bill was effectively tightening up on public benefit, so that, after its enactment, the independent schools would have to show

---

[37] ibid, para 4.26 p 41.

[38] This phrase appears very frequently in the Strategy Unit Report, eg pp 4, 35, 38 (para 4.10), 40 (para 4.18), 41 (paras 4.26 and 4.27), and 42 (para 4.30). The Charity Commission had previously published a document with this very title: Charity Commission, RR8: *The Public Character of Charities* (February 2001). Hubert Picarda QC takes the view (correctly in my opinion) that the term 'public character' 'is no more than a recently assembled patchwork criterion for which there is no precedent or rationale in the cases': Hubert Picarda QC, Written Evidence to the Joint Committee on the Draft Charities Bill, DCH 297, 2004, HL Papers 167–2; HC 660–2, para 10.

[39] Strategy Unit Report, *Private Action, Public Benefit*, 2002, para 4.28 p 41.

[40] Joint Committee Report, 2004, HL Paper 167–1; HC 660–1, para 76 p 22.

that they were for the public benefit. The Joint Committee, which did not mince its words, described this divergence of opinion between the Charity Commission and the Home Office as 'ludicrous', 'deeply unsatisfactory', and 'nothing short of farcical'.[41] In the event, a joint position (called a concordat) was agreed between the Home Office and the Charity Commission on how the public-benefit test would be applied,[42] although one might speculate whether the Commission felt itself under indirect political pressure to modify its previous stance.[43] The Joint Committee recommended that the basic principles for a definition of public benefit should be those set out in the concordat, either in non-exclusive criteria included in the Bill or in non-binding statutory guidance issued by the Secretary of State.[44] In its response, the Government rejected the suggestion that non-exhaustive criteria should be included in the Bill, because it saw that there was a risk that such criteria might, over time, be viewed as exhaustive.[45] It did accept the merit of issuing guidance, although it considered that the guidance-making function should lie with the Charity Commission, as an independent regulator, rather than with the Secretary of State. It indicated that the Charity Commission would be required to prepare such guidance, and provision for this is made in the Charities Act 2006.[46]

In the concordat between the Charity Commission and the Home Office, it was agreed that in considering the impact of fee-charging on public benefit the Commission would apply the principles in *Re Resch*.[47] The concordat set out those principles as follows:[48]

(a) both direct and indirect benefits to the public or a sufficient section of the public may be taken into account in deciding whether an organisation does, or can, operate for the public benefit;

(b) the fact that charitable facilities or services will be charged for and will be provided mainly to people who can afford to pay the charges does not

[41] ibid.

[42] ibid, para 78 pp 23–5.

[43] Cf, in the context of the Review of the Register, the comments of C Mitchell, 'Reviewing the Register', ch 7 in C Mitchell and S Moody, *Foundations of Charity* (Oxford: Hart Publishing, 2000) ch 1, p 190: 'It may be said that the Review is obliquely the product of political pressure, insofar as the Commissioners felt obliged to justify their Parliamentary grant by undertaking to perform their quasi-judicial functions in a new way'.

[44] Joint Committee Report, 2004, HL Paper 167–1; HC 660–1, para 102 p 33.

[45] The Charities Bill: The Government Reply to the Report from the Joint Committee on the Draft Charities Bill Session 2003–04, HL Paper 167/ HC 660, Cm 64406 (December 2004), pp 6–7.

[46] Charities Act 2006, s 4.

[47] [1969] 1 AC 514.

[48] The concordat is set out in the Joint Committee Report, 2004, HL Papers 167–1; HC 660–1, para 78 p 23.

necessarily mean that the organisation does not operate for the public benefit; and

(c) an organisation which wholly excluded poor people from any benefits, direct or indirect, would not be established and operate for the public benefit and therefore would not be a charity.

Following the concordat, and during the passage of the Bill, the Charity Commission published illustrative material explaining (at greater length) what is meant by the public-benefit requirement [49] and how the Commission will ensure that charities satisfy it.[50] The Commission's paper detailing the legal principles mentions, amongst other things, tangible and intangible benefits, direct and indirect benefits, and incidental private benefits. Since the Charities Act 2006 passed onto the statute book, the Commission has issued draft guidance on public benefit.[51]

C. Purposes and Activities

It is to be noted from the outset that the Strategy Unit Report's concern is with the way in which fee-paying charities conduct their activities. The report makes it clear that failure to satisfy the Charity Commission that provision is made for sufficiently wide access could result in loss of charitable status.[52] Fear that the new provisions relating to public benefit threaten their charitable status has led some independent schools to reconsider their admissions' policies.[53]

The Government has approached the public-benefit issue on the assumption that charitable status can be lost by virtue of the trustees' policy on admissions. This assumption must, however, be challenged. In English law, if an institution's funds are dedicated to wholly and exclusively charitable purposes, its charitable

---

[49] Charity Commission, *Public Benefit – the legal principles* (January 2005).
[50] Charity Commission, *Public Benefit – the Charity Commission's approach* (January 2005).
[51] Charity Commission, *Consultation on Draft Public Benefit Guidance* (March 2007); see also Charity Commission, *Analysis of the Law Underpinning Charities and Public Benefit* (March 2007).
[52] Strategy Unit Report, *Private Action, Public Benefit*, 2002, para 4.26 p 40.
[53] See *The Times*, 21 October 2006 (pp 1, 38–9), reporting that the public-benefit provisions in what was then the Charities Bill were causing a number of the country's leading independent schools, including Dulwich College and Roedean, to consider a 'needs blind' policy on admissions, whereby places would be offered solely on merit. At present, the only 'needs blind' independent school is Christ's Hospital, which has an endowment fund of some £350 million. The article also reported that the governors at another such prominent independent school, St Paul's (founded in 1509), had voted that the school should become 'needs blind' within 25 years, during which period efforts would be made to encourage alumni and philanthropists to contribute to an endowment fund sufficient to provide an income to be applied in subsidizing the places of fully funded pupils.

status cannot be lost merely because of the activities of its trustees.[54] Were this otherwise, the power of the Attorney-General and the Charity Commission to intervene to protect charity funds would effectively be lost by the trustees' very act of applying such funds in breach of trust to non-charitable purposes. If charity trustees commit breaches of trust, there are various sanctions available against them, including making them personally liable to repair the breach, and removing them from the trusteeship, but the breaches do not threaten the charitable status of the institution itself.

There is therefore a startling mismatch between the Government's concern with a charity's activities and the way in which the Government intends to deal with this, namely through section 3(2) of the new Act. This subsection, like the whole of Part 1 of the new Act, is dealing not with activities but with charitable purposes. If the purposes of a fee-paying school or private hospital are wholly and exclusively charitable, the trustees are not in breach of trust in carrying out those purposes. If the institution is registered as a charity, the Charity Commission has already accepted that its purposes, as stated in its governing instrument, are charitable. The charitable nature of those purposes cannot vary according to whether the Commission is satisfied that the trustees have an adequate policy of open access. To threaten the removal of such a body from the register of charities unless the trustees change the way the charity is run is to threaten what the Commission has no power to do. As there will have been no change in the institution's purposes as stated in its governing instrument, its removal from the register would have to be on the ground that the initial registration was a mistake. In these circumstances, it is not clear whether the assets would be applicable cy-près.[55] The Joint Committee recommended that the Charities Bill should clarify the effect of loss of charitable status on the assets of a charity,[56] but the Government declined the opportunity to amend the Bill in this way.[57]

---

[54] There are exceptional circumstances in which purposes can be inferred from activities: first, where the institution's purposes are ambiguous: *Southwood v AG, The Times*, 26 October 1998 (Carnwath J), affirmed by the Court of Appeal, 28 June 2000; and second, where the institution has no governing instrument, or where such instrument has been lost, or where it is clearly not intended to be comprehensive: *AG v St Cross Hospital* (1853) 17 Beav 435, 464. More controversially, the Charity Commission will decline to register as a charity even a body with unambiguously charitable objects if it considers that it is likely that the trustees will apply the property to non-charitable purposes; but the Commission's power to do this lacks either statutory or judicial authority: see J Fryer, 'The Charity Commission: determination of charitable status on the sole basis of the stated objects' [1985] NLJ Christmas Appeals Supp 10 (29 November).

[55] See the discussion in P Luxton, *The Law of Charities*, Oxford: Oxford University Press, 2001) paras 15.77–15.79 pp 572–3.

[56] Joint Committee Report, 2004, HL Papers 167–1; HC 660–1, paras 103–5 p 33.

[57] Draft Charities Bill: Government Reply to the Joint Committee (Cm 6440), 2004, pp 7–8.

It might have been open to the Government to seek to legislate specifically to regulate the activities of charity trustees in order to procure compliance with its open-access policy, but section 3(2) is not directed towards this. In marked contrast is the recent legislation requiring universities in receipt of funds from the Higher Education Funding Council which decide to charge tuition fees above the standard level to ensure that their admissions policies provide for sufficiently wide access.[58] Such legislation is specifically geared to activities, and the consequences of non-compliance are clear. A similar approach might have been adopted in relation to independent schools and private hospitals, perhaps with tax reliefs through charitable status being made dependent on satisfying criteria for widening access to the community. A somewhat different activities-based approach was suggested by the Joint Committee. Faced with the problem of public benefit, it put forward a radical proposal that the Government 'should consider reviewing the charitable status of independent schools and hospitals with a view to considering whether the best long term solution might lie in those organisations ceasing to be charities but receiving favourable tax treatment in exchange for clear demonstration of quantified public benefits'.[59] The Government did not accept this suggestion.[60]

In any event, the Government has not taken the activities route. Whilst expressing its concern about the activities of some fee-paying charities, the Government has nevertheless put all its eggs into the basket marked 'purposes'. Any impact that the Charities Act 2006 has on independent schools and private hospitals, therefore, can only be on the basis that their purposes might no longer be charitable, and as public benefit will retain its present meaning, any change can result only from section 3(2). It therefore becomes vital to determine the circumstances in which public benefit under the pre-2006 Act law is presumed.

D. The Presumption of Public Benefit

The most promising starting point is in what appears to be the first clear judicial enunciation of a presumption of public benefit. This is in a dictum of Lord Wright in *National Anti-Vivisection Society v IRC*:[61] 'The test of benefit to the community goes through the whole of Lord Macnaghten's classification, though,

---

[58] Higher Education Act 2004, Part 3; s 31 establishes the Director of Fair Access to Higher Education.

[59] Report of the Joint Committee on the Draft Charities Bill, 2004, HL Papers 167–1; HC 660–1, para 95 p 31.

[60] Draft Charities Bill: Government Reply to the Joint Committee (Cm 6440), 2004, p 7.

[61] [1948] AC 31, 42.

as regards the first three heads, it may be prima facie assumed unless the contrary appears.' It might be surmised that it was this dictum that provided the basis for the recommendation by the National Council for Voluntary Organisations,[62] later adopted by the Strategy Unit Report, and eventually emerging as section 3(2) of the Charities Act 2006, that the presumption of public benefit in the first three heads should be reversed.

Unfortunately, further perusal of the case law reveals what seems, at least at first blush, to be a startling absence of judicial comity. There is, for instance, the observation of Russell J in *Re Hummeltenberg*[63] that 'no matter under which of the four classes a gift may prima facie fall, it is still, in my opinion, necessary (in order to establish that it is charitable in the legal sense) to show . . . that the gift will or may be operative for the public benefit'. As if this were not enough, we must consider the following statement by that great charity judge, Lord Simonds, who, speaking in *Oppenheim v Tobacco Securities Trust Co Ltd,*[64] commented:[65]

> We are apt now to classify [charitable trusts] by reference to Lord Macnaghten's division in *Income Tax Commissioners v Pemsel*, and . . . it was at one time suggested that the element of public benefit was not essential except for charities falling within the fourth class, 'other purposes beneficial to the community'. This is certainly wrong except in the anomalous case of trusts for the relief of poverty . . . In the case of trusts for educational purposes the condition of public benefit must be satisfied.

It would therefore appear that whilst Lord Wright is willing to presume public benefit in the first three heads, Russell J requires proof in all four, whereas Lord Simonds does not consider public benefit necessary in the first head. Although it must be admitted that what has been described as the 'wilderness' of legal charity[66] contains illogicalities and inconsistencies, it would be surprising to find such eminent judges of modern times at loggerheads over public benefit if the concept were as simple as its treatment in the Charities Act 2006 would appear to suggest. There is clearly something wrong here, and the explanation is that these dicta are not essentially at variance. Although each of the judges is explaining public benefit by reference to the *Pemsel* classification, each is looking at it from a different perspective. Together, as will be explained, these dicta throw light on the likely impact of section 3(2).

---

[62] See n 34 above.
[63] [1923] 1 Ch 237.
[64] [1951] AC 297.
[65] ibid, at 305.
[66] N Bentwich, 'The wilderness of legal charity' (1933) 49 LQR 520.

1. Public benefit and the concept of a charitable purpose

Lord Wright's dictum is essentially concerned with public benefit in relation to the *Pemsel* heads as considered in the abstract. He is saying that, as concepts, the relief of poverty, the advancement of education, and the advancement of religion are prima facie for the public benefit in the first sense. His reference to the possibility that the contrary might appear recognizes that the purposes of a particular trust instrument might be shown to lack public benefit in the second sense. A trust for the advancement of education will therefore not attain charitable status if it is limited to the testator's children.

In the common law system, concepts tend to emerge from the pattern revealed in piecemeal decision-making on a case-by-case basis, rather than from any *a priori* reasoning. The purposes mentioned in the Preamble comprise merely a list, but they contain a pattern from which a Tudor concept of charitable purposes might be inferred. It is possible to conceptualize the list of purposes in the Preamble into the relief of poverty (where individuals benefit directly) and public works (where there is a benefit to the community at large, not restricted to the poor). The relief of poverty is closer to charity as a moral virtue,[67] but it is easy to appreciate why, as a legal concept, charity was extended to public works, which would assist in economic development and facilitate political control (eg the repair of highways would assist the movement of troops). This two-fold notion of legal charity within the letter of the Preamble seems to run through into the late eighteenth century, and Lord Camden's comment[68] quoted above,[69] that charity cannot exclude the poor, appears to reflect it.

Before *Morice v Bishop of Durham*,[70] there had been no significant attempt to impose a conceptual classification on the diverse list of purposes that had been held to be charitable within either the letter or the spirit of the Preamble. The explanation for Romilly's classification cannot lie merely in the importance (both financially and numerically) of trusts which might now be considered to fall within the first three heads, since trusts for such purposes (broadly interpreted, so as to include, for instance, almshouses) had long been the most important charitable purposes. The explanation seems rather to be that by 1805 the requirements of charity law had been subtly modified according to the nature of the charitable purpose. During the eighteenth century, the courts were beginning to apply slightly different criteria to the relief of poverty, with the emergence of

---

[67] See J Gardner, 'The Virtue of Charity and its Foils' in C Mitchell, and S Moody, *Foundations of Charity*, (Oxford: Hart Publishing, 2000) ch 1.

[68] In *Jones v Williams* (1767) Amb 651, 652.

[69] See text to n 20 above.

[70] (1805) 10 Ves 522, 532 (Samuel Romilly *arguendo*).

the so-called 'poor-relations' cases.[71] The advancement of religion, which had long connoted only the Established Church, had correspondingly received distinctive treatment, and it is not surprising that Romilly accorded it a separate category. The advancement of religion was evidently too sensitive a purpose to be enumerated in the Preamble, and so was beyond the jurisdiction of the commissioners established under the Act of 1601. Although the advancement of religion was later treated as charitable within the equity of the statute, charitable trusts for the purposes of the Roman Catholic[72] or Jewish[73] religions were (until the religious emancipation in the nineteenth century) applied cy-près to the Established Church. Even before Lord Macnaghten's categorization in *Pemsel's* case near the end of the nineteenth century, the advancement of religion had been further developing in its own way, with the emergence of a limited presumption that a trust for the advancement of religion was for the public benefit.[74] The advancement of education had also been developing in the late eighteenth century with judicial acceptance of the charitable status of fee-paying schools.

That those benefiting from a charity might have to pay for their benefits is a relatively recent notion, and it originates from developments that occurred towards the end of the eighteenth century. Many of the independent schools were founded in Tudor times for the free education of local boys. The constitutions of a few schools permitted the admission of fee-paying boarders, and the courts often refused to intervene to stop their admission even when the evidence was that the fee-paying pupils had effectively taken over the school.[75] In other cases, where the schools' constitutions made no provision for the admission of fee-payers, the courts' approval was sought to admit them on the ground that the additional funds were needed to support the foundation. Sometimes the courts sanctioned such admissions, sometimes not,[76] but where approval was given, the boarders were usually permitted to enjoy the benefits of the foundation.[77]

---

[71] *Isaac v Defriez* (1754) Amb 595.

[72] *Cary v Abbot* (1802) 7 Ves 490.

[73] *Da Costa v De Paz* (1754) 1 Dick 258.

[74] *Thornton v Howe* (1862) 31 Beav 14.

[75] See in particular *AG v Clarendon* (1810) 17 Ves 491, where Harrow School had admitted substantial numbers of fee-payers. It was contended that this had made it impossible for the local boys to be educated there. It was alleged that those paying fees were 'chiefly the sons of the nobility and gentry', and that this resulted in the poor children being 'constantly scoffed at and ill-treated . . . and their lives not only rendered uncomfortable, but often in great danger' (ibid at 493–4). Grant MR dismissed the prayer, saying that he could see no benefit in turning 'this distinguished seminary of learning' into 'a mere parish school' (ibid, 502).

[76] *Re Bristol Free Grammar School* (1860) 28 Beav 161 (application refused).

[77] See the protracted litigation concerning the admission of fee-paying pupils to Manchester Grammar School in *AG v Stamford* (1839–42) 1 Ph 737, and in *The Manchester School Case* (1867) LR 2 Ch App 497.

In some instances, the court gave its blessing even to the imposition of fees on the foundationers.[78] The charitable status of such schools was unaffected by this development.[79] This marks a shift away from the Tudor idea of charity that benefits were directly conferred on individuals only where this relieved their financial need. The effect of this change, ultimately enshrined in *Pemsel*, was to isolate the advancement of education as a distinct head of charity. Relieving need ceased to be a pervasive notion and solidified into a distinct category, namely, the relief of poverty. The resulting move away from the view of charity in the Preamble is occasionally revealed when it appears to clash with the classification in *Pemsel*.[80] To this extent, the four-fold division in *Pemsel* recognized the collapse of the Tudor concept of charity that had been under way since at least the late eighteenth century. Although Lord Macnaghten's classification is usually viewed as the beginning of the modern law, it is also a summation of more than 100 years of legal development.

Lord Macnaghten's fourth division is different in character from the others, in that it does not point to any type of charitable purpose: it merely requires that all purposes within it be for the benefit of the community.[81] In reality, Lord Macnaghten identifies only three charitable purposes: the fourth head does not itself designate any charitable purpose, but merely indicates a quality (that of being beneficial to the community) which any purpose must possess in order to fall within it. Unfortunately, it is not clear whether, in using the expression 'beneficial to the community', Lord Macnaghten intended to refer to what in this chapter has been called public benefit in the first sense (namely, that the purpose itself must be beneficial) or to public benefit in the second sense (namely the class of persons capable of benefiting), or perhaps to both.[82] That public benefit in the

---

[78] *Re Trustees of Orchard Street School* [1878] WN 211, although in the *Berkhampstead School Case* (1865) LR 1 Eq 102, such approval was given only on the footing that some free places would be retained.

[79] See further P Luxton, (1987) 51 *NLJ Christmas Appeals Supp* viii.

[80] For example, whether the phrase 'aged impotent and poor people' in the Preamble is to be read conjunctively or disjunctively: *Re Glyn's Will Trusts* [1950] 2 All ER 1150n; *Re Robinson* [1951] Ch 198, 201; *Re Resch's Will Trusts* [1969] 1 AC 514, 542; *Joseph Rowntree Memorial Trust Housing Association Ltd v AG* [1983] Ch 159, 171–4.

[81] Lord Macnaghten's fourth head has been judicially accepted as in substance broadly similar to the fourth category that had been put forward in argument by Samuel Romilly in *Morice v Bishop of Durham* (1805) 10 Ves 522, 532; but Lord Reid noted in *IRC v Baddeley* [1955] AC 572, 607–608, that, in omitting the word 'general' from his fourth head, Lord Macnaghten must have intended a difference. Romilly's fourth category ('the advancement of objects of general public utility') also seems to point more directly to the type of charitable purpose that might be called 'public works', of which there are numerous instances in the Preamble (including the repair of bridges, sea-banks and highways): see the argument of JH Stamp as junior counsel for the appellants in *IRC v Baddeley* [1955] AC 572, 578.

[82] See paragraph in text preceding n 15 above.

second sense may differ in the fourth head of *Pemsel* from the other three heads is evident from the emergence of the class-within-a-class prohibition, which affects the fourth head only.[83] The possibility, however, that Lord Macnaghten was referring to public benefit in the first sense seems to have led to speculation whether it also had to be present in the first three heads. Such heresy was soon scotched: that public benefit is needed in all four divisions was made clear in the dictum of Lord Wright in the *National Anti-Vivisection Society* case already quoted.[84] Thus the emergence of public benefit as a second and separate requirement from charitable purpose is a post-*Pemsel* development.

How are the pre-*Pemsel* decisions to be treated if they did not expressly consider public benefit as a distinct element? One view is that they will have to be reconsidered in the light of section 3(2), so that the fee-paying schools will need to show that they are for the public benefit.[85] There are two objections to this view.

First, merely because the pre-*Pemsel* authorities did not refer to public benefit as a separate ingredient from charitable purpose does not mean that what is now characterized as public benefit (in both senses of the term) is something relatively new. On the contrary, what today goes by the name of public benefit has for centuries been inherent in the legal concept of charity, and indeed explains equity's particular tenderness towards charitable trusts. Gareth Jones has stated that '[p]ublic benefit was the key to the statute [of 1601], and the relief of poverty its principal manifestation'.[86] The explanation for the paucity of explicit references to public benefit before *Pemsel* is that, until the end of the Victorian era, public benefit was implicit in the legal meaning of charity, so that a charitable purpose was necessarily a purpose for the public benefit.[87] Until *Pemsel*, trusts

---

[83] *IRC v Badddeley* [1955] AC 572, 591–592 (Lord Simonds).

[84] See text to n 61 above.

[85] For example, as suggested in the Supplementary Written Evidence presented to the Joint Committee by the Charity Law Association: DCH 175. See also the Written Evidence to the Joint Committee of the Independent Schools Council, DCH 47, which, having referred to *AG v Earl of Lonsdale* (1827) 1 Sim 105, said that that case 'comes from the early 19th Century, before charity law had properly developed to the point at which charitable objects were treated as distinct from public benefit. For that reason alone, the issue of public benefit was not even discussed and accordingly the case is weak'.

[86] G Jones, *History of the Law of Charity*, (Cambridge: Cambridge University Press, 1969) 27.

[87] That the courts before *Pemsel* were concerned with public benefit (in relation to the purpose itself) is evident from the sprinkling of references in the cases to expressions such as 'public purpose' (*AG v Heelis* (1824) 2 Sim & St 67,76; *Trustees of the British Museum v White* (1826) 2 Sim & St 594, 596) and to the 'good' of the public (*AG v Whorwell* (1750) 534, 537); in each instance such reference was made in the context of determining whether the purpose was charitable within the letter or the spirit of the Preamble. See also *Townley v Bedwell* (1801) 6 Ves 94; G Jones, *History of the Law of Charity*, (Cambridge: Cambridge University Press, 1969) 121–2; *Hoare v Osborne* (1866) LR 1 Eq 585 (where Kindersley V-C held a gift inter alia to repair the chancel of a church to be 'for the public benefit' and therefore charitable); and *Re Vaughan* (1886) 33 Ch D 187.

that might nowadays be regarded as failing the public-benefit test in the first sense were often denied charitable status on the ground that their purposes were not within the spirit of the Preamble;[88] and trusts whose benefits were restricted to a very small class (and so might now be characterized as lacking public benefit in the second sense) were (except in the poor-relations cases) treated as being for private purposes, and so not charitable.[89] What occurred after *Pemsel* was not the introduction of a new element of public benefit that had not existed before, but rather a distilling of an ingredient that had been intrinsic to the concept of charitable purpose, and a designating of such distillation as 'public benefit'. This probably occurred because of the ambiguous way in which Lord Macnaghten expressed his fourth head: what had arguably been a purpose in Romilly's classification ('the advancement of objects of general public utility') became, through a subtle change in language, a quality in Lord Macnaghten's (that of being beneficial to the community), and was later treated as a requirement distinct from charitable purpose. This process merely separated out, however, a quality of public benefit that had always been present. It should be noted that Lord Macnaghten described his fourth head as '*other* purposes beneficial to the community, not falling under any of the preceding heads',[90] which can be read as indicating that his first three heads had already satisfied this requirement. The last head of *Pemsel* has been likened to a portmanteau,[91] so that when purposes are held charitable under the fourth head they are necessarily for the benefit of the community. Continuing the analogy, it might be said that the first three heads are merely an enumeration of some purposes that have been unpacked from the portmanteau because they possess the quality of being for the benefit of the community, and so for the public benefit. The advancement of education is therefore charitable for the public benefit. ·

Second, it is necessary to consider the precise wording of section 3(2). This states that it is not to be presumed that 'a purpose of a *particular description*' is for the public benefit. The subsection is therefore not referring to the statutory

---

[88] For example, *Cocks v Manners* (1871) LR 12 Eq 574, 585; there Wickens V-C held that a trust for a Dominican convent was not charitable because it was not within either the letter or the spirit of the Preamble. His judgment does not use the language of public benefit as such, but he said: 'A voluntary association of women for the purpose of working out their own salvation by religious exercises and self-denial seems to me to have none of the requisites of a charitable institution.' *Cocks v Manners* was applied directly in *Gilmour v Coats* [1949] AC 426 as authority for the proposition that a trust for an enclosed order could not be shown to be for the public benefit.

[89] *Ommaney v Butcher* (1823) Turn & R 260 (gift in 'private charity' held not legally charitable).

[90] Italics supplied. It is perhaps significant that in *Morice v Bishop of Durham* (1805) 10 Ves 522, 532, Romilly's fourth category is not prefaced by the word 'other'.

[91] *Scottish Burial Reform and Cremation Society Ltd* v *Glasgow Corporation* [1968] AC 138, 150 (per Lord Upjohn).

categories of charity already listed (the descriptions of charitable purposes set out in section 2(2) and contained in the case law), but rather to the particular form of words used in a will, trust instrument, or an organization's constitution. This indicates that the subsection has an impact, not at the conceptual level indicated by Lord Wright (which would now be the descriptions of purposes set out in section 2(2) and in the case law) but rather at an evidential level. If the subsection were to operate conceptually, it would mean that the courts would have to determine, for instance, whether the advancement of education is for the public benefit. If they were asked to determine this question, their answer could hardly be in doubt.[92] The courts are therefore spared the absurd task of having to enquire whether a charitable purpose set out expressly in section 2(2) is for the public benefit. What this means, however, is that, whilst at first sight it might appear that section 3(2) is intended to reverse Lord Wright's dictum, it cannot have this effect since it does not operate at a conceptual level. It is therefore to the evidential level that the analysis must now turn.

2. Public benefit and evidential presumptions

It can now be appreciated that it was at an evidential level that Russell J was speaking in *Re Hummeltenberg*, in the quotation above.[93] One of the effects of conceptualizing charitable purposes is that it leads to attempts to fit the particular purposes specified in trust instruments within one of the conceptualized categories, namely within one of the first three heads of *Pemsel's* case. The tendency thereafter has been to treat each of the first three heads as if it were the glass slipper in the fairy-tale, into which an endeavour is made to shoehorn the particular purpose specified in the gift. However, the existence of the presumption that, as a concept, the advancement of education, for instance, is for the public benefit, does not mean that it should be presumed that any particular gift is for the public benefit and so falls within that head. It is still necessary to show that the particular objects of that gift are in fact for the advancement of education, and they will be for the advancement of education only if they are found to have merit. At this evidential level, there is no presumption of public benefit: the court has to be satisfied that the gift is for the public benefit, in the sense that it is meritorious.

The foregoing assertion is supported in numerous cases in which it has been sought to bring a particular gift within the category of the advancement of education. In some instances the public benefit is self-evident. As Vaisey J said in

---

[92] The Goodman Committee commented that 'education is . . . widely regarded as one of the main foundations on which civilised life depends': Goodman Committee Report, para 60 p 25.

[93] See text to n 63 above.

Re Shaw's Will Trusts,[94] 'there are many cases . . . where the purpose is so obviously beneficial to the community that to ask for evidence would really be quite absurd'. In other cases the court will form an opinion upon the evidence before it.[95] In *Re Dupree's Deed Trusts*,[96] for instance, the court held that the promotion of a chess tournament for boys and young men in Portsmouth was charitable because it accepted the evidence of a schoolmaster that chess was educational. In *Re Pinion*,[97] a gift by will to establish a museum for the public was held not to be charitable for the advancement of education because expert evidence showed that none of the objects was of any real merit: Harman LJ declined to foist onto the public what he called 'this mass of junk'.[98] Similarly, propaganda masquerading as the advancement of education will not be charitable either because it will lack merit, or (as where the purpose is political) merit cannot be assessed.[99]

The only *Pemsel* head in respect of which Russell J's dictum in *Re Hummeltenberg* needs qualifying is the advancement of religion, where there is an evidential presumption of public benefit, although only to the extent that the court will not enquire into the merits of any particular religion or into the quality of religious writings.[100] This is hardly surprising, since if it had to be proved that a trust for the advancement of a particular religion were for the public benefit, the court might be called upon to determine the merits of the tenets of different religions, or different religious sects, which the courts have consistently shown themselves unwilling to do.[101] Instead, the courts have usually preferred to fall back on dicta in *Thornton v Howe*[102] that, as between religions, equity stands neutral, and that a trust will be denied charitable status only if it is evident that the purpose is immoral or against all religion.[103] Section 3(2) might affect this, although there is likely to be little practical impact as the court is satisfied of public benefit on less

---

[94] [1952] 1 Ch 163, 169.

[95] *Re Hummeltenberg* [1923] 1 Ch 237, 242.

[96] [1945] Ch 16.

[97] [1965] 1 Ch 85.

[98] ibid, 107.

[99] *Re Shaw* [1957] 1 WLR 729 (Harman J); *Southwood v AG* (CA) *The Times*, 18 July 2000.

[100] See, for example, *Re Watson* [1973] 1 WLR 1472; *Holmes v AG*, *The Times* 12 February 1981; *Re Hetherington* [1990] Ch 1; *Re Le Cren Clarke* [1996] 1 WLR 288. The court will need to be satisfied of public benefit in the sense that a sufficient section of the community is capable of benefiting, as is discussed under 3 below.

[101] A similar consideration underlies the courts' unwillingness to become involved in doctrinal disputes where a religious sect has split into rival factions: see *Varsani v Jesani* [1999] Ch 219 (CA), and older decisions of the House of Lords in the Scottish appeals in *Craigdallie v Aikman* (1813) 1 Dow 1 and *General Assembly of Free Church of Scotland v Lord Overtoun* [1904] AC 515. See also R Atkinson, 'Problems with Presbyterians', ch 6 in C Mitchell, and S Moody, *Foundations of Charity*, (Oxford: Hart Publishing, 2000).

[102] (1862) 31 Beav 14.

[103] ibid, 19–20.

stringent evidence in the advancement of religion, and takes into account indirect benefits.[104]

3. Public benefit as a sufficient section of the community

If the poor-relations cases (and the poor-employee and poor-members-of-a-club cases) are explained on the basis that the relief of poverty is charitable without public benefit, section 3(2) may deprive them of charitable status. Lord Simonds explained them in this way in the *Oppenheim* case (in the extract quoted earlier).[105] No assistance on this point is to be found in the leading case of *Dingle v Turner*.[106] It appears that the Government did not intend to deprive this line of cases of their charitable status, however, and the decisions of the courts to treat such cases as charitable might be an implicit recognition that the relief of poverty is always for the public benefit, even if the benefit is indirect, as where the class to benefit is defined by reference to a personal or contractual nexus.

In the advancement of religion there is no presumption of public benefit in the sense that a sufficient section of the community will benefit.[107] This aspect of public benefit may be satisfied directly, if there is some dissemination of religious writings[108] or where religious services are open to the public,[109] or indirectly, as where the members of a religious order mix with their fellow citizens in the world.[110]

There is a final uncertainty in the new Act in respect of the class to benefit. Under the fourth head of *Pemsel*, the class to benefit must not be a class within a class.[111] It is unclear whether this restriction, which does not presently apply to the other three heads of *Pemsel*, is to be treated under the new Act as an aspect of public benefit, with the result that some bodies currently charitable under one of the first three heads will lose their charitable status.

---

[104] As in *Neville Estates Ltd v Madden* [1962] Ch 832.

[105] See text to n 65 above.

[106] [1972] AC 601 (HL). A submission of counsel in *Dingle v Turner* was that the poor-relations cases are charitable because, under the first head, public benefit is presumed. However, whilst as a concept the relief of poverty is for the public benefit (in accordance with Lord Wright's dictum in the *National Anti-Vivisection Society* case), it does not follow that there is a presumption of public benefit, in the sense of the section of the community to benefit, where the trustees can apply the fund only to persons defined by reference to a contractual nexus (in that case, the employees of a specified company). Lord Cross, who gave the only substantial speech, upheld the charitable status of the poor-employee and analogous cases, but did not mention public benefit.

[107] *Gilmour v Coats* [1949] AC 426.

[108] *Thornton v Howe* (1862) 31 Beav 14; *Re Watson* [1973] 1 WLR 1472.

[109] *Re Hetherington* [1990] Ch 1.

[110] *Neville Estates Ltd v Madden* [1962] Ch 832.

[111] *IRC v Baddeley* [1955] AC 572, 591 (Lord Simonds).

E. Conclusion

As the advancement of education is conceptually a charitable purpose, and the purpose of the charitable independent schools is in fact the advancement of education, such schools are both conceptually and evidentially for the public benefit. The indirect benefit recognized in *Re Resch* will continue to apply to private hospitals, and could (if necessary) be similarly applied to the independent schools. Even if no direct provision is made for the poor, the poor will not be excluded from indirect benefits. Section 3(2) of the Charities Act 2006 will therefore have no effect on the charitable status of the independent schools or private hospitals. As Hubert Picarda QC has expressed it most succinctly, the charitable status of the independent schools is based on public benefit established by law, and does not rest on any presumption.[112] As the meaning of public benefit is preserved by section 3(3), it cannot be changed by any guidance which the Charity Commission is required by section 4 to provide. The concordat between the Charity Commission and the Home Office, and the Commission's subsequent expositions of what is meant by public benefit, can be no more than a description of the pre-existing law. The conclusion must be that, in this respect, the Charities Act 2006 will not achieve what the Government intends.

This failure to deal with the public-benefit issue in relation to independent schools and private hospitals was described as 'a central flaw in the Bill',[113] which the Government nevertheless allowed to proceed to legislation. The question remains why, in the face of considerable evidence, the Government persisted in this stance. The minister, Fiona Mactaggart, maintained before the Joint Committee that if the Government had intended the removal of the presumption of public benefit to particular classes of charities to have no impact at all, it would not have bothered to remove it.[114] At Second Reading in the House of Lords, however, Lord Phillips of Sudbury said:[115] 'Some think that that is precisely what the Government intend; that they want the appearance of change without the substance and that they want to satisfy critics of the status quo

---

[112] 'Mere reversal of the "presumption" of public benefit cannot change the declared law on this point': Hubert Picarda QC, Written Evidence to the Joint Committee on the Draft Charities Bill, DCH 297, 2004, HL Papers 167–3; HC 660–3, para 9.
[113] Lord Phillips of Sudbury, House of Lords Debates, Charities Bill 2005, Second Reading, Hansard, 20 January 2005, col 907.
[114] Joint Committee on the Charities Bill, HL-660–2, HC-660–2, Minutes of Evidence, HL-660–2, HC-660–2, 21 July 2004, answer to q 1071.
[115] House of Lords Debates, Charities Bill 2005, Second Reading, Hansard, 20 January 2005, col 907.

without arousing the middle classes. In short, they want the credit without any opprobrium.' It is certainly tempting to view the Government's obstinacy in this light; but, whatever the explanation for its intransigence may be, the contention of this chapter is that the public-benefit provisions in the Charities Act 2006 will miss the Government's main targets, yet may have an unintended impact on other types of charities.

11

THE MALTA TRUSTS PROJECT – THE GENESIS OF A NEW TRUSTS ACT IN A CIVIL LAW JURISDICTION

Max Ganado* and Gerwyn LL H Griffiths**

A. Introduction

In any collection of works dealing with the ways in which principles of trusts, equity, and property law have adapted, changed, and upon occasion re-invented themselves, in order to regulate and facilitate novel and contemporary situations, the continued development and flexibility of the trust offer many areas of investigation. Indeed in the field of commerce alone, the uses of the trust are manifold and often ingenious.[1] This chapter, however, considers a different issue: the impact of the trust on different legal traditions and systems. It does so because of our belief that nowhere is the flexibility and adaptability of the trust and the advantages it can offer better illustrated. It may have traditionally been the guardian angel of the Anglo Saxon,[2] but more recent history and current practice provide numerous examples of the adoption or utilization of the trust by jurisdictions having an essentially civil – or at least not common law – background and tradition. To give but three examples: as early as 1922 Japan, which at that time had a civil code derived from the German, introduced a Trusts Law modelled on US law

* Senior Partner, Ganado and Associates, Advocates, Malta.

** Professor of Equity and the Law of Property, University of Glamorgan.

The authors acknowledge the contributions of Drs Stephen Attard, Paula Vella Scrih, and Rachel Cassar Torregiani. All errors and omissions do of course remain the responsibility of the authors alone.

[1] J Langbein, 'The Secret Life of the Trust – The Trust as an Instrument of Commerce' (1997) 107 Yale LJ 165.

[2] P Lepaulle, *Traite Theoretique et Pratique Des Trusts en Droit Interne, en Droit Fiscal et en Droite International* (1932) 113.

to meet a perceived need to regulate investment activities. Four years later Lichtenstein embraced the concept of the trust in its Persons and Companies Act,[3] while in 1929, the trust was the favoured vehicle by which those nations victorious in the First World War sought to administer German reparation settlements.

This very situation does, in turn, raise a question: if such a phenomenon is clearly established, wherein lies the significance of the approach taken by Malta? How and in what way is it anything more than another, albeit recent, example? Its significance (and therefore its worthiness as a subject for this chapter) we suggest lies in the fact that, unlike some jurisdictions where the adoption of the trust has been achieved by a single piece of legislation, unaccompanied by any level of analysis, not embedded in the domestic law, and often seeking to provide merely a 'product' in the financial services sector, the approach of the Malta legislator was to undertake a far-reaching review (The 'Trusts Project' of the title). Trusts law and the regulation and conduct of trustees was, under-standably, the major focus, but the project also addressed the impact on the Civil Code of Malta, particularly those parts of it relating to the law of property, the law of obligations, securities, and the contract of mandate, on both a practi-cal and theoretical level. Thus it sought to achieve the embedding of the trust in Maltese domestic law and the qualitative upgrading of Malta's law as it relates to the holding of property for others not only under trusts but also under other civil law fiduciary obligations. In order to ascertain whether this aim was fulfilled, we first examine the background to the trust in Maltese law and then identify and evaluate the changes effected by the new reforms to both the substantive law and the regulatory framework.

B. The Evolution of the Law of Trusts in Malta

Maltese law is essentially a civil law system with a civil code based on Roman law and the Code Napoleon. In the fields of public, private, international, and com-mercial law Malta may more accurately be described as a 'mixed' system because, as a result of more than 150 years of British rule, the legal system in these areas was supplemented by a number of statutes and principles derived from English law.[4] However, this influence did not extend to the law of trusts. Neither it nor

---

[3] Personen- und Gesellschaftsrecht *(PGR)*.

[4] J M Ganado, 'Malta: A Microcosm of International Influences' in *Studies in Legal Systems – Mixed and Mixing* (The Hague: Wolters Kluwer, 1989).

equity were statutorily incorporated or absorbed into Maltese law. Indeed, one has to search hard for even a rare mention of the device of the trust, resorting eventually to the Income Tax Act of 1948!

1. The Offshore Trusts Act 1988

The picture changed to an extent in 1988 with the enactment of the Offshore Trusts Act of that year based almost entirely on the model of the Trusts (Jersey) Act of 1984. Coming into force in June 1989, the significance of the Act was that it not only provided for the first time a definition of what would constitute a trust under Maltese law but also in so doing emphasized the specific functions of the settlor, trustee, and beneficiary. Its weakness, in terms of the criteria we adopt above, was that the legal framework provided by the Act did not introduce the concept of the trust into the domestic law of Malta. It did not apply internally. Perhaps driven by a perception that the trust was not a legal institution which fitted naturally into nor was beneficial to the Maltese community, the law was therefore 'ring fenced' in favour of non-residents, with trusts being recognized only when the settlor and the beneficiaries were non-resident and the trust property did not include immovable property in Malta or stocks, shares, or debentures in a Maltese-registered company. Its 'offshore' 'product-orientated' nature was further underscored by the fact that at least one of the trustees had to be a Maltese 'nominee company',[5] which although it had to be registered with the Maltese regulator was able to operate in a way which was open to the allegation that it went beyond confidentiality and bordered on secrecy.

2. Act XX of 1994 and The Recognition of Trusts Act 1994

The adoption of the Jersey model was, we would suggest, a sound and appropriate strategy. The offshore emphasis was less successful. It sometimes sat uneasily with the approach of the Organisation for Economic Cooperation and Development (OECD) in regard to harmful tax practices and the requirements of the Financial Action Task Force (FATF) for the prevention of money laundering that financial institutions should obtain and record information on the identity of their clients.[6] A third issue, we believe, was to be found in Malta's stated ambition to become a member of the European Union (EU)[7] which required that its legal and regulatory structures were fully compliant with EU Directives.

---

[5] This terminology was to prove unfortunate. See below.
[6] Recommendation II of the 'Forty Recommendations' See: Financial Action Task Force on Money Laundering – The Forty Recommendations. Available at <http//www.1.oecd.org/fat40Recs_en.htm>
[7] Malta acceded to the EU in May 2004.

These factors resulted in amendments to the law in 1994. These not only eliminated the word 'offshore' from the very title of the Act itself and limited the tax advantages available, but a provision was also introduced allowing redomiciliation in order to increase Malta's attractiveness to settlors with trusts already established in other jurisdictions. The office of protector was also created and, perhaps most significantly for anyone seeking evidence that the trust was now being viewed less as an offshore product, the equitable principle of tracing was introduced. The amendments still did not, however, introduce the trust into the domestic Maltese legal system.

1994 also saw the passing of Malta's Recognition of Trusts Act, ratifying and giving effect to the Hague Convention on the Law Applicable to Trusts and on their Recognition.[8] Unanimously adopted by delegates from 32 states at the end of the Fifteenth Session of the Hague Conference on Private International Law, the Convention recognized the potential impracticability of civil law states adapting their legal concepts or changing their domestic law to deal with matters such as the status and powers of trustees, the nature of the beneficiaries' interests in the trust property, and the relative positions of settlor, trustees, and beneficiaries. Thus, its intention was not and is not to compel 'non-trust' states which do not already have the trust concept in their law to introduce it. What it does do is set up a situation where the signatory state will recognize the trust as a matter of its private international law. To put it another way, its purpose is not to incorporate the idea of the trust into other jurisdictions, it merely allows the ratifying state to know a trust when it sees one.

So far as Malta was concerned, the major impact in practice was that it opened the doors to the free use of trusts within what might be termed the Maltese 'internal market'. Because, albeit that the proper law of the trust was not Maltese law, a trust and its effects were now recognized, the incentive to use such a trust when it was both needed and appropriate was an obvious one, even when all the major elements of the trust except the proper law were local. Thus, after 1995, there is evidence that many trusts with a foreign, ie non-Maltese, proper law were being used in essentially domestic contexts. In terms of actual occurrence, we accept that this is not an unusual occurrence and one replicated in many other civil law jurisdictions,[9] but would also point out that it is open to the criticisms that not only might it be regarded as jurisprudentially weak to use a foreign law in regulating essentially local or domestic structures but there is also

8 See generally D J Hayton, 'The Hague Convention on the Law Applicable to Trusts and on their Recognition' (1987) 36 LQR 260.
9 For a similar situation in Italy, see the decision of the Court of Bologna in *Landini v Trompetti*, Sezione Prima Civile no 9634/2000 RG.

the perhaps more practical problem of a judiciary having perhaps infrequent experience of such a situation but still needing to apply a foreign law to a local problem.

3. The Trusts Act (Amendment) Act 2004

This Act can be seen as the culmination (or at the very least the continuation) of those strategies begun in 1994 to achieve compliance with international fiscal commitments, redirection from an offshore to a mainstream emphasis, and achievement of a vibrant and attractive financial services industry. Thus, the nominee company has been eliminated, as have certain former rules on confidentiality. The degree of allowable settlor control is low and the rights of the beneficiary to gain information have been safeguarded. The taxation of trusts has been addressed in detail – for example, there can be no allowances for asset protection trusts – and a comprehensive regulatory framework has been introduced for trustee activities. Indeed, this latter feature is underscored by the re-designation of the Trusts Act as the Trusts and Trustees Act (TTA) to reflect the fact that it has as one of its objects the regulation of trustees. Its greatest relevance, however, may lie in the fact that for the first time it effectively introduces trusts into the civil law of Malta itself, providing for the use of trusts in an ordinary domestic context.

One particular and fundamental issue was the treatment of the concept of equity. It would be both misleading and naive to deny that the history of the trust in its common law form is inextricably bound up with the development of equity. It is equally well recognized that a legal system may accommodate the trust without any recourse to equity.[10] One need look no further than Scotland for confirmation of this. Although that country has a mixed or hybrid legal system, its property law is unabashedly civilian in character and content. So much is clear not only from the existence of a *numerus clausus* of real rights but the fact that ownership of real rights is indivisible. Indeed, as Kenneth Reid pithily observed: "It is possible to have the trust and still remain virtuous!"[11]

This approach was not adopted by the drafting team and the Malta legislator. There is no attempt to exclude equity or to create what might be termed the 'equityless trust'. This, we submit, is an entirely correct approach for the following reasons. First, even prior to the 2004 amendments, the provisions of the then

---

[10] A Honore, *Honore's South African Law of Trusts* (4th edn, Capetown: Juta, 1992); D J Hayton, 'The Development of the Trust in Civil Law Jurisdictions' (2000) 8(3) JITCP 159; M Lupoi, 'The Civil Law Trust' (1999) *Vanderbilt Journal of Transnational Law* 967.

[11] Quoted in D J Hayton, B Koortmann, H Verhagen, *Principles of European Trust Law* (The Hague and Derenter: Kluwer Law/Tjeenk Willink, 1999) 3–5.

Trusts Act already incorporated many of the rules of equity as they relate to trusts, perhaps most notably article 33 on tracing. Second, the Civil Code of Malta, the Code of Civil Procedure, and existing jurisprudence address many issues within the province of equity. So much can be seen from an examination of recent judgments of the Malta Civil Court in cases such as *Zammit Tabona v Simlar Ltd*,[12] where the Actio Pauliana was used to recover specific property after a transfer in breach of contract, and *Vella v Vella*,[13] where implied verbal mandate concepts founded a claim in property. Thus, principles of equity as they relate to trusts are an accepted part of Maltese law and when one also comes to realize that in practice they will have a part to play only if there are no express provisions on a principle,[14] an inclusive approach is both logical and acceptable. For the sake of completeness, it should also be noted that no specific directions as to interpretation of such principles were included in the Act. The simple reason for this is that if there is a need to deal with a lacuna in an area of the law having its origins in the law of England and Wales, the general approach of the Malta courts is to refer naturally to that law and sources to interpret or fill it.[15]

In order to achieve these goals, the law amends not only the Trusts Act itself but 18 other laws relating to subjects such as income tax and tax management, companies, arbitration, and notarial procedure. Perhaps most significantly, there are amendments to the Civil Code of Malta itself which for the first time now contains several articles on the legal nature of trusts, trust transactions, and the particular uses and effects of trusts. It is these which we will consider next.

C. The Interrelationship Issue: Trusts, The Civil Code and The Trusts and Trustees Act

An examination of those jurisdictions which have, while already possessing a civil code, then adopted or incorporated trusts into their law quickly reveals no single drafting strategy. In some cases, all matters of trust law have been addressed in 'free standing' trusts legislation, leaving the civil code untouched. Alternatively, trusts issues have been dealt with as necessary throughout the civil code itself.

---

[12] PA 13.02.2003.

[13] PA 28.02.03.

[14] For example, in the Trusts and Trustees Act, the Civil Code or the Code of Civil Procedure.

[15] We admit, however, that some Maltese statutes are more specific in this respect. For example, section 22(2) of the Income Tax Act states: Words and expressions used in this Act which are not known to the Law of Malta but are known to the English law, shall so far as may be necessary to give effect to this Act . . . have the meaning assigned to them in English Law and be construed accordingly.

Examples of still further variations can be seen in the cases of Quebec, where a title on trusts was inserted into the code, and Louisiana, which has a schedule on trusts inserted at the back of the code itself.[16]

Recognizing that many principles relating to trusts were already to be found in two existing specific or special laws on trusts, ie the Trusts Act and the Recognition of Trusts Act, but that many of the proposed changes would, of necessity, impact upon the Civil Code itself, the approach taken in Malta was that if detailed aspects of issues were already addressed in the specific statutes themselves, then the logical way to deal with these was via an appropriate amendment to that statute. If not, then it should be dealt with via a change in the Civil Code in a manner which did not result in scattered, piecemeal changes across the Code. In order to achieve this the two statutes were merged (into the TTA), two new titles were inserted in the Code – one in the law of things and one in the law of obligation – with each new title dealing with fundamental issues arising in that particular area – and it was only in the law of persons that ad hoc amendments to specific sections of the Code were made.[17] This 'locking together' is clear from a reading of Article 958A of the Civil Code, which states: "Property under trusts shall be regulated by the special law on trusts[18] and to the extent applicable, the rules of the Code relating to trusts".

1. The law of persons

Two amendments were created here. The first relates to the obligation to maintain. Such an obligation, based as it is on a recognition by the law that people who are linked together in some way by blood or other legal relationship should support and assist each other, is a feature of many legal systems. The law of Malta recognizes such a duty and, in order that the device of the trust will not be used to circumvent such a fundamental obligation, Article 20[19] now stipulates that any property held in trust for the person obliged to maintain or to be maintained must be taken into account when the court is assessing maintenance.

The second amendment deals with the situation where the beneficiaries of a trust are minors, incapacitated, or absent. As readers may be aware, in civil law, an equivalent role is played by the institutes of tutorship or curatorship. Tutorship is

---

[16] K Venturatos Lorio, "Louisiana Trusts: The Experience of a Civil Law Jurisdiction with the Trust" (1982) 42 *Louisiana Law Review* 1723.

[17] This approach was generally avoided in other parts of the Code where articles were not amended individually.

[18] Although various other pieces of legislation have been amended in order to allow for the concept of the trust to function in Malta's civil law system, they all tend to make reference to the TTA as the Maltese special law on trusts.

[19] Article 20(3); 20(5).

a relationship arising from the inability of non-adults to manage their own affairs, this duty being entrusted to a tutor who is appointed to look after that child's care and best interests. A curator has the same obligations except that he acts in the interests of someone who is incapacitated or absent. Motivated by the aim of creating checks and balances in the functions of the respective offices, Article 163 of the Code prevents trustees of such trusts also being appointed as tutors or curators for those same beneficiaries.

Of particular interest over and above the substantive provision itself is, however, the rationale which underpins it.[20] Frequently, the trust, as a fiduciary relationship, is compared with similar fiduciary structures to be found in the civil law,[21] notably the Roman concept of 'Fiducia' and the German device of 'Treuhand'. It is certainly true that the trust is classified as such an obligation. Indeed Article 1124A of the Malta Civil Code is specific: '(1) Fiduciary obligations arise in virtue of law, contract, quasi contract, *trusts* (emphasis added), assumption of office or behaviour.' What is sometimes forgotten is that while these obligations share some[22] common characteristics, each institute is distinct and the rules applicable to one cannot freely be applied to the other. Article 163 is a manifestation of this need to avoid confusing the various institutes and any potential conflict of interest.

2. The law of things

The amendments in this part of the Code reflect a detailed debate as to whether the law of trusts is part of the law of property or the law of obligations. Following a consensus view that it has roots in both, aspects of the law of property were amended by the insertion of a new title – title IIIA, 'Of Trusts and Their Effects'. The first article in this title, Article 958A,[23] begins by making clear that trust property is to be regulated by the special law relating to trusts and then goes on to list transactions which may relate to property held under a trust. Although it is by no means exhaustive, it establishes that these will include settlement, distribution, and application, the reversion of property to a settlor or his estate if the trust fails or is ended, and the assignment or transfer of trust property from a trustee to another trustee under the same trusts. In view of the fact

---

[20] We admit that in strict terms this might be more properly dealt with under the law of obligation, but it is considered here as an illustration of the civil law approach to the need for institutes to be kept separate.

[21] P LePaulle, 'Civil Law Substitutes for Trusts' (1927) 35 Yale LJ 1126.

[22] But not all. Thus in the present context tutors and curators do not assume ownership of the assets of the minors, incapacitated persons, or absentees, they are responsible only for the administration and protection of those assets and are answerable to the court in this respect.

[23] The article is compendious, having parts A–J with numerous subsections in each part.

that the subject of this chapter is the reception of trusts into a civil law system, we focus, however, on the provisions in the article dealing with the effect on the transfer or disposal of trust property by a trustee to a third party of the concept of 'legitim', or 'forced heirship'.

Although it is axiomatic that trust property is held by or under the control of the trustee who has full powers and duties to administer, employ, or dispose of that property under the terms of the trust, in all civil law systems marriage and parenthood create certain obligations in favour of an individual's spouse and children which restrict his freedom to dispose of his property on either a testamentary or even an inter vivos basis.[24] These rights give certain members of the individual's family fixed minimum shares in his estate and a right to sue to obtain those shares. In Malta, this right is not only provided for by Articles 615–653 of the Civil Code but is also regarded as a major issue of public policy, traditionally even affecting the ability to dispose of inherited property as the right to legitim was considered to be part of the ownership of each asset.[25] A solution which would allow these two apparently competing concepts to co-exist without one or the other being seriously compromised was therefore essential. In order to achieve this, Article 958A(3) of the Civil Code allows a trustee validly to dispose of trust property to third parties despite any claims of legitim, whether these arise out of Articles 615–653 of the Code or any other provision of it. In this way, the amendments sought to prevent a situation where all settlors, beneficiaries, and those claiming legitimary rights would need to be signatories to any disposal. This left the need to provide a safeguard for the person with the legitimary right. In order to achieve this, if the trustee has been formally notified of a legitim claim relating to the property sold, the law effectively creates a resulting trust. The trustee must hold on trust a monetary sum based upon the net value of the property at the time of transfer[26] and must continue to do this until the validity of the claim is determined or it lapses.[27] If the proceeds of sale have been distributed to a beneficiary, the person with the legitimary right may claim against that beneficiary.

3. The law of obligations

Although as a part of the strategy to strengthen fiduciary obligations in general there is an expansion of the provisions dealing with matters such as the

---

[24] D J Hayton, 'Trusts and Forced Heirship Problems' (1993–4) 4 *King's College Law Journal* 9.

[25] At the time of writing the position has been amended so that the right is now viewed as a right of credit.

[26] Interest is also payable.

[27] This obligation operates for a period of five years.

'prestanome mandate',[28] in what might be termed 'pure' trust terms, it is the provisions in Articles 2095A and 2095B for matrimonial regimes which arguably merit more attention. Because the Civil Code of Malta already contained detailed provisions and reflected clear social policy decisions, addressing any problems in matrimonial property regimes was not an agenda item. Neither do we believe that the Maltese courts will use the trust to develop matrimonial property rights as has been done in England and Wales, if only because of the existence in Malta of a generally applicable community of acquests regime. Nevertheless, within these limitations and insofar as it was consistent with the provisions of the Civil Code, it was felt appropriate to insert amendments which allowed trusts to be used in a beneficial manner in the context of married couples and their families. Thus, the new law provides the holding on trust of property subject to matrimonial property regimes can be achieved only if that trust is an express written trust. No such implication will arise by operation of law. Furthermore, trusts of their community property are to be considered an act of extraordinary administration and can therefore be settled only if both spouses consent and agree on all matters pertaining to that property. Such a trust set up by spouses together can be revoked or varied only if they act together. This means, of course, that if one spouse dies, such a trust is deemed irrevocable no matter what its terms may say.

D. Aftermath: The Present, Substantive Position of the Trust under Maltese Law

Having considered and examined the way in which the new trust regime was embedded into the laws of Malta, a logical question must now be, how and in what ways has this affected the current substantive law? What is the net or combined effect of those still subsisting parts of the previous law and the amendments to it? In order to answer this, we now examine the major features of the trust under Maltese law.

1. A definition

Apart from the fact that the marginal note to section 3 of the TTA refers to the 'meaning of a trust' rather than giving an exhaustive definition, the description of

---

[28] That is, contracts whereby one person (the mandator) commissions or instructs another (the mandatory) to do something for him without reward and the mandatory accepts those instructions. The object or purpose of such a contract usually consists in general management, or the carrying out of a specific act. In the case of the 'prestanome' variety, the prestanome can be said to 'borrow' another person's name as though that person was contracting on his own behalf.

a trust and its component parts does not appear exceptional. In a description borrowing heavily (and unashamedly) from Jersey law, we are told that:

> A trust exists where a person (called a trustee) holds, or has vested in him, property under an obligation to deal with that property for the benefit of persons (called the beneficiaries) whether or not yet ascertained or in existence, or for a charitable purpose which is not for the benefit only of the trustee or for both such benefit and purpose aforesaid.

This description seems unexceptional, stressing the separate nature of the trust fund, the roles of the trustee and beneficiaries, and limiting purpose trusts to those which are charitable in nature. Closer inspection does, however, reveal a number of changes brought about by the 2004 Act. The first of these relates to the words 'holds as owner'. These reflect a response to the traditional tension between the common law which has traditionally recognized that ownership rights can exist both in relation to the equitable and the legal title and the civil law (including that of Malta) which adopts an absolutist approach under which it is not capable of being divided. Recognizing that this debate is both long running and has merit on both sides, a functional approach was adopted which clearly recognizes that the holding of trust property by a trustee is in the nature of an ownership right. Furthermore, it also addresses a limitation which existed in the earlier legislation, namely a doubt as to whether a trustee could also be a beneficiary of a purpose trust. The introduction of the word 'only' after the phrase 'which is not for the benefit' now makes it clear that a trustee may also be a beneficiary so long as he is not a sole beneficiary.

2. The discretionary trust

Maltese law recognizes all the main types of trust one would normally find in traditional common law jurisdictions. Thus, Maltese trusts can take the form of fixed-interest trusts, accumulation and maintenance trusts, protective or spendthrift trusts, charitable trusts, implied resulting or constructive trusts, and discretionary trusts. It is this last named, where the trustees normally have a choice or discretion as to how and to whom they distribute trust income and or capital, which is perhaps the most widespread. Such popularity is unsurprising given that this variety of trust offers perhaps the most flexibility to respond to changing circumstances and needs, but it was the discretionary trust which presented one of the biggest problems to the Malta legislator. This problem was the extent to which trustees of a discretionary trust could be given power to appoint new beneficiaries. Typically, such a trust set up in a common law jurisdiction would contain powers allowing the trustee if he so chose to remove and appoint beneficiaries at his absolute discretion, but these very provisions are apparently incompatible with the provisions of the Maltese Civil Code as it relates to testamentary dispositions, particularly those which prevent a testator from allowing another person to determine in due course who the heirs of that estate will be.[29]

Recognizing the potentially fatal consequences of this situation, sections 9(8) and 9(15) of the TTA specifically override the relevant Code provisions and create a legislative compromise whereby a trust deed can contain a provision allowing trustees to appoint new beneficiaries so long as either the person to be appointed is identified by name, or reference to a class of members who are 'reasonably individually identifiable' and the identification is made either in the trust instrument itself or in any other written instrument created by the settlor. Only after this discretion has been exercised in his favour does the beneficiary have any rights in relation to the trust property. In this manner, the inherent flexibility of the discretionary trust is preserved while at the same time the relevant provisions of the Civil Code are safeguarded. Moreover, since the written instrument created by the settlor need not be binding on the trustee, it will, of course, include a letter of wishes, thus in practice one may find this strategy being utilized by settlors who are not comfortable in identifying a list of potential new beneficiaries in the trust instrument.

3. Rights to information[30]

In a collection such as this, both space and an awareness of the philosophy underpinning it preclude comprehensive coverage of all the changes wrought by the Malta trusts project. At the time much of the work was being done, however, much debate – undoubtedly spurred at least in part by the decision in *Schmidt v Rosewood*[31] – centred around the extent and nature of the trustee's obligation to disclose information and the corresponding right of a beneficiary to ask for or demand it. For this reason – and because we believe the solution reached by the Maltese legislator is a sound and workable one – we now consider this area and the treatment of it by the Malta project.

[29] Inter alia Articles 688, 693 and 695.

[30] On this issue see generally, D J Hayton, 'The Irreducible Core Content of Trusteeship' (1996) 5(1) JITCP 9; G LL H Griffiths, 'Antipodean Revelation – The Beneficiary's Right to Information After *Rosewood*' [2005] *The Conveyancer and Property Lawyer* 93–8; D Steele, 'The Beneficiary's Right to Know,' A Paper presented to the Law Society of Upper Canada Fourth Annual Estates and Trusts Forum, November 2001. Available at <www.torys.com/publications/articles>; N Henry, 'Core Obligations Examined' (2004) Vol 10 No 2 *Trusts and Trustees* 9.

[31] [2003] 2 WLR 1442. The case began as a claim before the Appeal Court of the Isle of Man, was then referred to the Privy Council, and then went back to the Isle of Man Court for actual judgment to be applied.

The question may be approached as two, interrelated issues. First, in general terms, as long as a trust is being properly administered and is continuing, a beneficiary has no right to interfere in its administration but has to wait passively to receive the benefits to which he is entitled under that trust. If, however, it is not being properly administered, he will want to take steps to compel its proper running and to safeguard his position. Second, even more so, he will not be able to do anything unless he knows he is a beneficiary in the first place.

As to the first issue, not only does section 21(4) of the TTA impose upon trustees a duty to keep accurate accounts and records and to disclose these to a beneficiary who requests this information, but section 29[32] of the same statute widens the scope of this, requiring that if he receives a request in writing to this effect, the trustee must provide full and accurate information regarding the manner in which the administration of the trust has been conducted to the court, any protector of the trust, any adult beneficiaries,[33] and the settlor.

Thus, the basic principle allowing a high degree of confidentiality to trustees is now subordinated to the precept that trustees must provide full and accurate information to specified persons as to the state and amount of the trust's assets or property and any accounts relevant to those issues. Of particular note is that among those people specified as being entitled to receive this information (and so, of course, able to make the necessary request) is the settlor. By doing this, Maltese law is recognizing the fact that in practice, although trustees owe their accounting duties primarily to the beneficiaries, there will be occasions when, if he were still alive, the trustees would confer with the settlor as to whether to disclose such information.

In dealing with the second matter – what might be termed 'the potential beneficiary who wants to know if he is one' – the TTA again provides what we believe is a workable, balanced approach. Section 29(3) is specific, stipulating that:

> Unless the terms of the trust expressly determine the time when and the method how beneficiaries are to be informed of their entitlement . . . the trustee shall be obliged to inform any beneficiary of his entitlement in writing within a reasonable time of his accepting to act.

---

[32] The position differs in a trust where the property is held in relation to a commercial transaction. For a full discussion, see R Cassar Torregiani, 'The Duty of Trustees to Disclose Information to Beneficiaries Under Maltese Law' (2005) 11(6) *Trusts and Trustees* 31.

[33] If any beneficiary is a minor then this information must be supplied to his or her guardian. If the trust is charitable, then the obligation is owed to the Attorney-General or other relevant authority.

This, we submit, is an appropriate reflection of the principle that the beneficiaries, because they are beneficiaries, have an inherent right to be told of that fact in order to enforce the trust.

The position does vary slightly in the situation where a trustee is given a discretion as to who to appoint as a beneficiary. In such a situation the terms of the trust itself may suspend the duty of trustees to inform those beneficiaries until the time when such a discretion is actually exercised in their favour. However, particularly in light of the fact that the TTA operates a conservative approach to who may be included in a discretionary class,[34] it is our contention that such a prohibition does not dramatically reduce the overall position with regard to beneficiaries' rights to be informed.

E. Conclusion

The law of trusts has re-invented itself in many ways and for many reasons over its history. Among these incarnations two trends can be discerned of recent years. In some common law jurisdictions there has been what might variously be described as a wish or tendency to take concepts far beyond what would traditionally have been regarded as logical and legitimate and which have sought to challenge long-established orthodoxy.[35] A second trend is an active interest in the concept on the part of civil law countries often accompanied by attempts to introduce trusts into their legal systems by legislation. We accept and understand that these developments may be driven less by intellectual or jurisprudential motives. Only the most naive would ignore the commercial and fiscal drivers at work. If, however, the trust – with or without equity – is to find a strong footing with an essentially civil law environment, several facts must be recognized. The first of these is that it is not enough merely to introduce the trust via a single, isolated statutory measure and expect it to work. The trust can operate successfully only within a clearly defined context. In addition, while the civil law may have institutes which approximate to the trust, that is not the same as saying it has trusts.

The correct approach we believe (and the one adopted by the Malta project and carried through in subsequent legislation) was to approach the trust as another institute, not intended to replace any existing civil law devices but rather to supplement them – to offer 'another option' when that was most appropriate.

---

[34] Above, 'The discretionary trust'.
[35] The traditionalist might number among these devices such as the Cayman (S)pecial (T)rusts (A)lternative (R)egime legislation and the British Virgin Islands VISTA trust.

The third fact relates to what might be termed 'analytical underpinning'. We believe that the Malta project demonstrates that a clear legal analysis of the concepts involved is essential to success. Last, given that the motives for introducing trusts are often as much to create a vibrant financial services profile as to enhance the domestic law of the state, the legislation cannot be viewed in isolation. There must be adequate but workable regulation and also the encouragement of a judicial culture which supports not opposes. When measured against these criteria, we submit that the process by which the trust was embedded in the law of Malta is both a worthy study and a paradigm to be followed.

INDEX